Philippine National Dances

FRANCISCA REYES TOLENTINO
Supervisor of Physical Education
Department of Instruction, Republic of the Philippines

SILVER   BURDETT   COMPANY

New York   Chicago   San Francisco

INTRODUCTION

Rhythmic movements are one of the most primitive of human reactions. It should not be strange, therefore, to find these movements developing into dances characteristic of the natural reflex and response of the various ethnic groups. In the Philippines, the native dances of the Christian groups must have been basically Malay, but through intimate contact lasting for over three centuries of our song and dance-loving people with other song and dance-loving peoples like the Spanish, their form has been modified, so that the arm, hand, and body movements, most typical of the dances of the Orient, are not very dominant in Philippine folk dances of today. It has been truly said that the Philippines offers a unique field for the study of civilizations from the most primitive, as represented by the Negrito, through the various stages, to the present culture which bears the clear stamp of the West. One may observe evidences of these various stages in the dances that are characteristic of the different levels of culture found in the Philippines.

Realizing that with the further impact of Western culture many of these indigenous dances would be lost or extensively modified, Mrs. Francisca R. Tolentino, at one time Physical Director of Women Students of the University of the Philippines, with the encouragement and support of Dr. Jorge Bocobo, then President of the institution, undertook the study of folk dances as she found them in the less developed regions of the Philippines. These dances have remained unchanged, and still bear the same features that characterized them prior to the end of the Spanish occupation. Most of them are presented as square dances and show the unmistakable influence of Spain, and in some instances even of France. They represent a blend of the Orient and the Occident prior to the advent of the American regime in the Philippines. They have a charm of their own and are not too far removed from present tendencies so that they represent a rare and welcome opportunity for foreigners to look into a past that is fast receding into oblivion.

The inner urge to revive the past and thus preserve Philippine culture has become very widespread among our own people, and the presentation of these dances in all sorts of social gatherings has been very well received. It is in response to this demand that this collection is presented to the public. We only hope that this impetus to bring about a renascence of the past will gain sufficient momentum so as to stimulate the continued col-

lection of such of the most autochthonously Philippine dances as are still
extant among our peoples, thus including even the remoter regions of the
Philippines whose native culture is largely unalloyed.

B. M. GONZALEZ
President
University of the Philippines

November 16, 1945

PUBLISHER'S NOTE

The manuscript of this book, representing years of research, was sent
to the United States just prior to the Japanese invasion of the Philippines
in 1941. Publication was delayed for five years due to the impossibility of
contact with Mrs. Tolentino, whose first letter following liberation of the
Islands in 1945 reported that all her other source materials, books, records,
pictures, costumes, and musical instruments had been burned or wantonly
destroyed by the Japanese. Therefore, Philippine National Dances repre-
sents the survival of an invaluable historical, as well as entertaining, survey
of one important aspect of the culture of the Philippine people.

Table of Contents

ACKNOWLEDGMENTS

To Dr. Jorge Bocobo, former Secretary of Public Instruction, Philippine Commonwealth, who has been interested in the collection, preservation, and revival of Philippine folk songs and dances ever since he was President of the University of the Philippines when he created the University Committee on Philippine Folk Songs and Dances, and gave it financial and moral support; to the late Mr. Ramon P. Tolentino, for his help in collecting and recording the history and description of many of the dances included in the present volume, and for his constructive criticisms; to Lt. Antonino Buenaventura, Dr. Francisco Santiago and Professor Juan S. Hernandez of the Conservatory of Music, and to Mr. Telesforo Lamug of the Department of Physical Education, University of the Philippines, for the use of some of their own music and for the arrangement and harmonization of dance music collected with a number of the dances; to Miss Feliciana del Espiritu Santo of the Bureau of Education, for reading the manuscript of this volume and for her valuable suggestions; to Mrs. Maria A. Batoon for her assistance in reading proof of the text and music and for her organization and training of Philippine Dance groups in the United States, in particular in Washington and New York, pictures of whose personnel have been added to the original list of illustrations to give a wider representation of dancing details; to Pfc. Abraham Kramer, AUS, grateful thanks are expressed for pictures of the "Filipiniana" cast photographed shortly after the end of hostilities; and last but not least, to the old people who exhibited the dances and taught the collector how to perform them; to the school teachers and pupils; to the members of the U. P. Folksong-Dance Troupe who helped in testing and exhibiting the dances prior to Japanese occupation and to those of the "Filipiniana" group who performed many of them before U. S. Army and Navy personnel after our liberation under the direction of Special Services, PHIB SEC, U. S. Army; and to the many government and school officials and private citizens who most willingly gave part of their valuable time and extended their aid in many ways—to all of them, the author hereby expresses her most grateful acknowledgment and appreciation; for, without their cooperation the publication of this book would have been extremely difficult if not altogether impossible.

F. R. TOLENTINO

PREFACE

Folk dancing is a wholesome form of entertainment, enjoyed by children and adults whether participants or spectators. It is simple, inexpensive recreation.

For centuries, singing and dancing have been the principal pastimes of our people. At social gatherings, our forefathers danced and sang spontaneously—often for several days, as in wedding celebrations, "velacion" or "parasal," and "pabasa."

Our country is rich in materials in this phase of the arts. We have dances and songs for all occasions—weddings, christenings, "fiestas" in town or "barrio" (village), religious ceremonies and celebrations, war and victory dances of the non-Christian tribes, occupational songs and dances (pounding, harvesting, planting, fishing, digging, rowing, and tubâ gathering, etc.), torture dances of the Negritos, funerals, and courtships. Many of these may still be seen in remote sections of the Islands where modern civilization has not yet penetrated.

In 1924 the author started the collection of folk dances, songs, and games. A part of the material gathered from 1924 to 1926 was used in a Master's thesis which was later revised and published in book form as *Philippine Folk Dances and Games*. For several years further research was officially conducted by Lt. Antonino Buenaventura, the late Ramon P. Tolentino, Jr., and the author under the auspices of the President's Committee on Folk Songs and Dances, University of the Philippines. Costumes, music, and musical instruments were collected as well as songs and dances.

People used to say that there was nothing unique in Philippine dances. To them, all the dances were alike—long, monotonous, and boring rather than entertaining. Uninformed people thought that we had no dances other than the much overdanced "Cariñosa," "Surtido," "Pandango," "Curacha," and "Planting Rice." However, that misinformation toward our folk dances has been noticeably corrected since the University of the Philippines and the Bureau of Education took up the task of reviving our varied and almost unknown dances and songs.

These were collected directly from the old people in out-of-the-way regions who had performed them in their younger days, and from the students or trainees who came from remote places where such dances are still kept alive and practiced.

Folk dances are no longer a mere fad in our country. In fact they are now considered an invaluable addition to physical education work in our schools. Philippine folk dance exhibitions and competitions are held as part of the school activities. When visiting foreigners are entertained, folk songs and dances form a major part of the program. There has been an eager and appreciative response as is shown by the requests of organizations for exhibitions of and lectures on Philippine folk dances. Folk dancing awakens in us a sense of national pride.

Many of our so-called native dances are of Spanish origin. Others show French, English, and Malayan influences. Nevertheless, our forefathers have performed them for so long, giving them their own interpretation, execution, and expression, that they have become traditionally Filipino.

The dances included in this book have been tested by the students of the University of the Philippines and by public school children. They were transcribed as authentically as possible without loss of distinctive qualities, local color, or native form. Oftentimes, however, it has been desirable to rearrange, cut, or add to some of the dances so that they could be presented more interestingly and effectively. Their peculiar formations, individual qualities, and distinctive movements have been preserved as they were found.

There are fifty-four folk dances and corresponding music in the present collection. Illustrations, diagrams, and photographs are included to make descriptions and instructions clearer. Classified and graded lists of these dances have been added to the alphabetical index for the guidance of teachers. The fundamental positions performed with music, dancing terms, and dance steps used in Philippine folk dances are also included.

Illustrations

In Memory of
My Husband

Tagalog Costumes

Girl in "balintawak" style
Boy in "barong tagalog" and red
trousers

Girl in "Maria Clara" style
Boy in "barong tagalog" and black
trousers

Visayan Costumes

Girl in "patadiong"
Boy in "barong tagalog" with white
trousers

Ilocano Peasant Costumes

Abaruray

"Abaruray" is a contraction of the words "Aba" and "Ruray." "Aba!" is an exclamation which is equivalent to "Hey!", "Hi!" or "Hail!" in English. "Ruray" is the nickname for Aurora.

This dance is known in the Philippines by several names, such as "Hapayan," "Tagayan," "Pandango sa Baso," and "Abaroray."

In any social gathering in the remote "barrios" of the Philippines, it is customary to offer wine to the visitors. The offering is usually made by a young lady. She goes around with a glass and a bottle of native wine offering a drink to the visitors. This wine offering is a signal for the beginning of folk dancing and singing.

The musicians play the introduction of the "Abaruray" music. The girl who is offering the wine picks out a young man from among the guests and offers him a drink. This is her way of hinting at her desire to dance with him. The young man has to accept it or he commits a breach of etiquette and the girl is offended. His acceptance of the drink signifies that he will dance with the girl. He then stands and they begin dancing, with the girl leading him on. The girl dances with the glass of wine on her head from which the young man drinks. Her dancing skill is shown in her ability to keep the glass on her head and in not spilling a drop of the wine. The audience sing and clap their hands in time with the music.

The description given below is the "Abaruray" from Tayabas.

COSTUME. The girl is dressed in "balintawak" and the boy in "barong tagalog" and long, red trousers. Both dancers are barefooted.

MUSIC is divided into three parts: Introduction, A, and B.

COUNT *one, two, three* to a measure.

FORMATION. Partners stand opposite each other about eight feet apart. The girl stands at her partner's right side when facing the audience. A few boys and girls may take part in this dance to represent the townsfolk attending a social gathering. The girls are dressed like the dancer. The boys are dressed in "barong tagalog" or "camisa de chino" and long trousers. They clap hands in time with the music.

INTRODUCTION

Music Introduction and A.

The girl goes around with the glass of wine in her right hand looking for a partner. She moves freely around using walking steps, close, and waltz steps alternately. She pauses once in a while as she looks for a suitable partner. She offers a drink to the chosen one. He accepts the wine, stands up after drinking, and follows the girl to the middle of the room. (The boy stands at the left side of the girl.) .... 25 M.

1

Music A.

(a) The girl waltzes around in any direction, holding the glass with her right hand. Places the left hand on the waist.

The boy follows the girl closely and he executes the same steps. Places hands on waist. . . . . 16 M.

II

Music B.

Girl's Part:

(a) The girl faces the audience. She takes four waltz steps sideward R and L alternately. Holding the glass with the right hand she moves it to sideward R and L alternately. . . . . 4 M.

(b) Takes waltz steps forward right and backward left (2 M). One waltz-turn right in place (two waltz steps) (2 M). Transfers the glass to the left hand. Bends the right arm forward and holds the elbow in front at shoulder-level. Places the glass on the crook of the right elbow. . . . . 4 M.

(c) Repeats the same steps as in (a) starting with the L foot. Holds the glass with the left hand and moves it sideward L and R alternately. . . . . 4 M.

(d) Repeats (b) starting with the L foot. Transfers the glass to the right hand and places it on the crook of the left elbow. . . . . 4 M.

Boy's Part:

As the girl is doing the above steps, the boy simultaneously executes the following steps around the girl.

(a) Two waltz steps forward (R, L). . . . . 2 M.

(b) One waltz-turn right (two waltz steps). Arms in lateral position moving sideward R and L alternately. . . . . 2 M.

(c) Repeats (a) and (b) three times more going counterclockwise around the girl. . . . . 12 M.

III

Music B.

Girl's Part:

She stands in place while doing the following hand movements:

(a) The girl takes the glass from her left elbow and holds it in the palm of her right hand. Starting with the R hand down in front, she turns her hand counterclockwise, raising it slowly and gradually upward to the top of the head. The glass is still in the palm of the hand. (See illustration.) . . . . 4 M.

ABARURAY, Figure III

(b) She takes the glass from her head and turns the hand clockwise bringing it slowly and gradually down to the starting position. . . . . 4 M.

(c) Repeat (a). . . . . 4 M.

(d) Places the glass of wine firmly on the head. . . . . 4 M.

Boy's Part:

Boy stands about six feet from the girl, in front of her, with his left shoulder towards the audience. He taps with the R foot and at the same time claps hands on the second and third beats of every measure. . . . . 16 M.

IV

Music A.

Girl's Part:

(a) With the glass of wine on her head, she executes a pivot turn with a point to the right and left alternately four times. Takes four measures for every complete turn. R arm in fifth position and L hand holding the skirt when pivoting to the right. Reverses the hand positions when turning to the left. "Kumintang" the raised hand clockwise every measure. . . . . 16 M.

Boy's Part:

Repeats the steps in figure II. . . . . 16 M.

3

Music A.

Girl's Part:

(a) Places the R foot in fifth position in front and bends the knees slightly. Holds this position for sixteen measures. Bends the L forearm in front of chest, horizontally, and R forearm upward, vertically. The right elbow rests on the back of the L hand (palm down). (See illustration.) "Kumintang" R hand clockwise (cts. 1, 2, 3). Reverses the position of the hands and "kumintang" counterclockwise with the L hand (cts. 1, 2, 3). . . . .   2 M.

ABARURAY, Figure V

(b) Repeats (a) once more. . . . .   2 M.

(c) Arms in lateral position (waist-level) moving sideward from right to left alternately four times. "Kumintang" hands as above. . . . .   4 M.

(d) Repeats all (a, b, c). . . . .   8 M.

Boy's Part:

Repeats the steps of figure II, starting with the L foot and turning clockwise. Finishes at the left side of the girl. . . . .   16 M.

VI

Music B.

(a) Partners stand about eight feet apart facing each other. Take six sway balance steps with a point, R and L alternately. Arms in fourth position, R and L arms high alternately. . . . .   12 M.

(b) Starting with the R foot, take four waltz steps forward to exchange places. Pass by each other's right shoulder. Arms in

4

lateral position moving sideward R and L alternately. . . . .   4 M.

   (c) Repeat all (a and b) finishing in proper places. . . . . 16 M.

VII

Music B.

Girl's Part:

Starting with the R foot, executes waltz steps forward going in any direction. Hands holding the "tapis" (apron) or skirt, wiggling it forward and backward in time with the music. . . . . 14 M.

Boy's Part:

Starting with the R foot, executes two waltz steps and a waltz-turn (R or L) following the girl closely. Turns around her clockwise or counterclockwise.

In doing the waltz-turn he swoops down like a hawk near the girl. Swing the arm (L or R) downward-upward. Arms are in lateral position moving sideward R and L (or L and R) when doing the waltz step. . . . . 14 M.

Saludo: The girl takes the glass from her head. Partners stand side by side with the girl at the right side. Join inside hands and girl turns counterclockwise under the arch of their joined hands (cts. 1, 2, 3). Both bow to the audience (cts. 1, 2, 3). . . . .   2 M.

ABARURAY

1. Abaruray, abarinding, isauli mo ang singsing
   At kung di mo isasauli, magagalit ang may ari.

   Chorus:

   Ringinding, ginding ang sinta ko'y wala rito ringinding,
   Ringinding, ginding nasa kabilang ibayo, ringinding,
   Ringinding, ginding kaya di makaparito, ringinding,
   Ringinding, ginding walang masakiyang kabayo.

2. Abaruray, abarinding, isauli mo ang suklay,
   At kung di mo isasauli, magagalit ang may ari.

3. Abaruray, abarinding, isauli mo ang tubiak,
   At kung di mo isasauli, magagalit ang may ari.

4. Abaruray, abarinding, isauli mo ang tigad,
   At kung di mo isasauli, magagalit ang may ari.

5. Abaruray, abarinding, isauli mo ang tukil,
   At kung di mo isasauli, magagalit ang may ari.

Abaruray

TAYABAS

Notation by
F. E. ALVISO

Harmonized by
FRANCISCO SANTIAGO

B II-III-VI-VII

Aetana

This dance is from Santa Cruz, Marinduque. It is snappy, short, and always delights the audience as well as the performers. The "jaleo" and "la mano" (shaking hands) are the two interesting figures of this dance.

COSTUME. Girls wear "balintawak" and boys, "barong tagalog" and white trousers.

FORMATION. Dancers stand in two parallel lines facing the audience about six feet apart. Girls stand at partner's right side. From one to any number of pairs may take part.

Audience

X   O

X   O

X   O

MUSIC is divided into two parts: A and B.

COUNT *one, two, three* to a measure.

INTRODUCTION

Music Introduction.

Take three steps forward (R, L, R), arms hanging loosely at the sides (cts. 1, 2, 3). Point L foot in front. Raise R arm high in fifth and L bent forward at shoulder level with elbow in front (cts. 1, 2, 3). . . . . 2 M.

I

Music A.

Partners face each other.

Dancers do the following steps going the same direction toward the audience.

(a) *Girls*—Step R foot sideward in second position (ct. 1), brush L forward (ct. 2), step L close to R foot in 1st position (ct. 3). R arm in reverse "T" position and L bent in front at shoulder level. . . . . 1 M.

Boys—Do the same, starting with the L foot. Reverse the arm positions. . . . . 1 M.

(b) Repeat (a) two times more. . . . . 2 M.

(c) *Girls*—Step R foot sideward (ct. 1), brush L forward and tap close to R foot (ct. 3). *Boys* do the same starting with the L foot. 1 M.

8

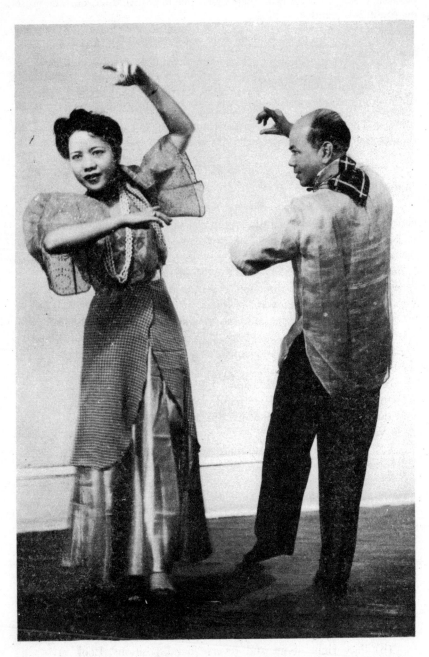

AETANA, FIGURE I (a)

Note: For small children do (c) in this manner: Step sideward (ct. 1), tap close (cts. 2, 3). This gives them more time to change direction. The brush on count 2 is omitted.

(d) Repeat (a, b, c), starting with the other foot. Reverse the arm positions. . . . . 4 M.

(e) Repeat all (a, b, c, d). . . . . 8 M.

(f) Starting with the R foot, repeat the above movements four times, going to sideward R and L alternately. Arms as above . . . . . 16 M.

Note: The boys put weight on the L foot at the last closing of the foot on the sixteenth measure in order to be able to start with the R foot in (f).

II

Music B.

(a) *Girl* turns back to partner. Starting with the R foot, take eight waltz steps backward moving in a clockwise direction. Arms in lateral position at shoulder level, moving sideward R and L alternately. Finish facing partner. . . . . 8 M.

Boy faces partner. Starting with the R foot, take eight waltz steps forward in a clockwise direction. Arm positions the same as the girls. Finish with backs toward partners. . . . . 8 M.

(b) *Girls*—Repeat the same movement as boys in (a) moving counterclockwise. . . . . 8 M.

Boys—Repeat the same movement as girls in (a) moving counterclockwise. . . . . 8 M.

(c) Partners join right hands, keeping elbows relaxed and straight at shoulder-level. Free hand of the girl holding the skirt and the boy's free hand on waist. Starting with the R foot, take eight waltz steps clockwise. . . . . 8 M.

(d) Drop right hands and join left hands.

Repeat (a) going counterclockwise, starting with the R foot. . . . . 8 M.

III

Music A.

(a) "Jaleo"

Partners face left. Place right hands on waists (free hand of girl holding skirt, boy's free hand on waist). Go near each other so that the right elbows are almost touching each other. Look at partner over the right shoulder.

Take eight steps (as in figure I (a)) going clockwise, starting with the R foot. . . . . 8 M.

(b) Face right about and reverse hand positions. Look at partner over the left shoulder. Starting with the L foot, repeat (a) moving counterclockwise. . . . . 8 M.

10

(c) Repeat all (a and b). . . . . 16 M.
Partners finish facing each other about four feet apart.

IV

Music B.

(a) Shaking hands.

Step R foot forward (cts. 1, 2), hop on the same foot and raise
the L in rear with the knee bent (ct. 3). Shake hands (right
hands) with the partner and nod to each other on count 3. . . . . 1 M.

Release hands. Step L foot backward (cts. 1, 2), turn right about
pivoting on the L foot, at the same time raising the R knee in
front with toes pointed downward and swiftly describe a circle
clockwise with the R foot while in this position (ct. 3). Do this
simultaneously with the turning right about. . . . . 1 M.

(b) Repeat (a) facing away from partner. Omit the shaking
of hands. Girl holding skirt and boy's hands on waist. . . . . 2 M.

(c) Repeat all (a and b) three times more, facing to and away
from partner alternately. Finish facing away from partner. . . . . . . 12 M.

(d) Face right. In sets of three or four pairs, take eight waltz
steps clockwise forming a big circle, starting with the R foot. Arms
in lateral position at shoulder level moving sideward R and L al-
ternately. . . . . 8 M.

(e) Turn right about and repeat (d) counterclockwise. Finish
in proper places and bow to partner on the last measure. . . . . 8 M.

Aetana

MARINDUQUE

Notation by
A. BUENAVENTURA

12

Alcamfor

The name of the dance was perhaps derived from the plant called camphor or from its perfume. It was originally known as "Alcanfor" but possibly "Alcamfor" is more appropriate. Camphor or "Camfor" is a plant having a peculiar hot, aromatic taste and a pleasant smell. The girl's handkerchief is supposed to be scented with the perfume taken from this plant.

The first and third figures of this dance have slow and dignified movements like the French minuet. The other figures are fast and lively, like the Spanish dances.

COSTUME. The girl is dressed in Maria Clara style. A large embroidered handkerchief hangs at the right side of the waist. The boy is dressed in "barong tagalog" and black trousers. He wears a hat ("buri" or "buntal").

MUSIC is divided into two parts: A and B.

COUNT *one, two, three* to a measure.

FORMATION. Partners stand side by side facing the audience. The girl stands at the boy's right side. From one to any number of pairs may take part in this dance:

Audience

X O   X O

X O   X O

X O X O

X O X O

I

Music A.

Partners join right hands. The boy holds his hat at the crown with his left hand. The hat is held upside down under the right elbow of the girl. The left hand of the girl is placed on the waist or is holding the skirt.

(a) Starting with the outside foot raised in fifth in front, slide forward (ct. 1), close the inside foot in third in rear (ct. 2) raise heels up (ct. 3). . . . . 1 M.

(b) Lower heels down (cts. 1, 2), step the inside foot backward (ct. 3). . . . . 1 M.

13

(c) Close the outside foot (with the toe pointed) to the instep of the inside foot (cts. 1, 2), raise the outside foot in fifth in front and step with the same foot forward (ct. 3). . . . . 1 M.

(d) Step inside foot forward (ct. 1), step outside foot forward (ct. 2), turn about inward (left about for girl and right about for boy), and point with the outside foot in front (ct. 3). . . . . 1 M.

(e) Repeat (a, b, c), starting with the outside foot. . . . . 3 M.

(f) Boy turns left about and girl turns under the arch of right arms by taking a two-step turn counterclockwise. Partners finish facing the audience. . . . . 1 M.

(g) Repeat (a, b, c, d, e). . . . . 7 M.

(h) Partners execute a two-step turn to separate from each other. They are now about four feet apart. Girl turns left and boy turns right. Finish facing each other. The boy puts on the hat. . . . . 1 M.

II

Music B and C

Start counting on the second measure.

Girl's Part:

(a) Girl stands in place. "Kumintang" the right hand. Left hand is placed at the back slightly pushing the skirt up. Bend the knees slightly (cts. 1, 2) and straighten (ct. 3). The body is bent slightly to the right side following the movement of the right hand. 1 M.

(b) Repeat (a) twenty-one times more with left and right hands changing positions every measure. . . . . 21 M.

(c) Turn right about to face partner. . . . . 2 M.

Boy's Part:

(a) Starting with the R foot, take two waltz steps obliquely forward right. Hands on waist. . . . . 2 M.

(b) Execute a waltz-turn right (use one waltz step) (cts. 1, 2, 3) and tap the L foot in rear of R (cts. 1, 2, 3). Finish the turn at left side of the girl facing her. Hands as in (a). . . . . 2 M.

(c) Starting with the L foot, take two waltz steps obliquely forward right. Hands as in (a). . . . . 2 M.

(d) Take a waltz-turn right and tap the R foot in rear of L. Finish the turn at the back of the girl facing her. Hands as in (a). 2 M.

(e) Repeat (a) and (b), finishing at the right side of the girl. 4 M.

(f) Repeat (c) and (d), finishing in proper place, facing the girl. . . . . 4 M.

(g) Repeat (a, b, c, and d). Partners finish facing each other. The girl is now at the left side of the boy when facing the audience. 8 M.

Note: The boy's and girl's parts are done at the same time.

14

ALCAMFOR, Figure I (a)

ALCAMFOR, Figure III (a)

III

Music A.

The boy takes off the hat and holds the top with the right hand. The girl takes the handkerchief hanging at her waist and holds it at one corner with the right hand.

Starting Position—The boy holds the hat close to his chest with his left hand on his waist. The girl holds the handkerchief close to her chest with left hand holding skirt.

(a) Waltz balance forward right. The girl moves her handkerchief toward partner about the level of his nose. The boy extends his hand forward holding the hat right under the handkerchief of the girl. The hat is held with the top down (See illustration). .... 1 M.

(b) Step L foot backward (ct. 1), and close the R foot to L with the toe of the R foot pointing close to the instep of the L (cts. 2, 3). Partners bring their right hands close to the chest as in the starting position. .... 1 M.

(c) Starting with the R foot, take three-step turn obliquely forward right. Partners finish in one line facing each other about three feet apart (see diagram a). Bring the right hand to second position. .... 2 M.

(d) Repeat all (a, b, c) three times more, finishing always facing each other. The first time the boy finishes at the girl's place and the girl at the boy's place (see diagram b). The second time they are in one line again with the boy facing and the girl's back toward the audience (see diagram c). The last time they finish in their starting place (see diagram d). .... 12 M.

| Start | (a) | (b) | (c) | (d) |

IV

Music B and C.

The boy puts on the hat and the girl puts the handkerchief back in its place.

(a) Hop on the L foot six times. Raise the right knee in front swinging the R foot forward and backward across the other leg six times. The swinging is done at the same time as the hopping. Girl holds her skirt and boy places hands on waist. .... 2 M.

16

(b) Take a three-step turn right obliquely forward right and finish in one line as in figure III(a). . . . . 2 M.

(c) Repeat (a) and (b) five times more, following the same direction as in figure III. This time they finish in their proper places, with the girl at the right side of the boy, by repeating the movements six times. . . . . 20 M.

V

Music B.

Partners face each other.

(a) Take one sway balance with a point to the right. Arms are bent forward in front at shoulder level swinging the R and L forearms away and near the chest alternately. . . . . 2 M.

(b) Execute a waltz-turn left (two waltz steps). Hands as above. . . . . 2 M.

(c) Repeat (a) and (b), starting with the left foot and turning to the right. . . . . 4 M.

(d) Repeat all (a, b, and c) twice more. Finish with partners near each other and facing the audience. . . . . 16 M.

VI

Music B and C. (Do not repeat C.)

(a) Partners join inside hands. Free hand of the girl holding her skirt and free hand of the boy placed on waist. Take two step-swings forward (R, L). . . . . 2 M.

(b) Starting with the R foot, take two mazurka steps obliquely forward. . . . . 2 M.

(c) Repeat (a) and (b). . . . . 4 M.

(d) Repeat (a), moving obliquely left backward. . . . . 2 M.

(e) Repeat (b). . . . . 2 M.

(f) Repeat (d). . . . . 2 M.

(g) Girl turns around counterclockwise under the arch of the joined hands. The boy takes off the hat and partners bow to the audience. . . . . 2 M.

Alcamfor

NATIVE COSTUMES (left to right)

(1) Patadiong, (2) Barong Tagalog and red trousers, (3) Balintawak,
(4) Barong Tagalog and white trousers, (5) Ilocano

19

Anuncio

This is a wedding dance popular in the provinces of Mindoro and Marinduque. It is usually danced during a marriage celebration, although it may be performed in any social gathering.

A young man starts dancing, looking for a partner who is seated somewhere in the place where the social gathering is being held. (If it is a wedding party, it is danced by the bride and groom.) He makes known his intention by means of "hapay," an act in which he flourishes his handkerchief before the lady with whom he wishes to dance.

To tease the dancers the onlookers may sing the following words of the song, adding more fun and gaiety to the dance.

Music C.

> Anong pagka rikit, anong pagka ganda,
> Anong pagka rikit, lagay ninyong dalawa
> Isang "eme a ma" isang "eme o mo"
> Ang kahulugan nito'y, pakasal na kayo.

NOTE: The above words may be sung as many times as desired while the partners are dancing. There are also other words sung for this dance but the version given above is the most popular.

COSTUME. Girl wears an old style costume or any native costume which is appropriate for a wedding dress, the boy wears "barong tagalog" and black trousers.

MUSIC is divided into four parts: A, B, C, and D.

COUNT *one, two, three* to a measure.

FORMATION. The girl is seated. The boy stands on one side, facing the girl.

I

Music A.

Boy—Executes eight sway-balance steps with a point, R and L alternately. Arms in fourth position, R and L arms high alternately.   16 M.

II

Music B. Play three times.

(a) Boy—Takes two big waltz steps forward (R, L) toward the girl, arms hanging loosely at the sides. ....   2 M.

(b) Boy—Takes a handkerchief from his pocket and flourishes it at the girl (with a bow). This is known as "hapay." ......   1 M.

20

(c) Girl—Shakes her head refusing the invitation. . . . . 1 M.

(d) Boy—Starting with the R foot, turns right about and executes four small waltz steps forward to starting place. Replaces handkerchief. Finishes facing the girl. . . . . 4 M.

(e) Repeat all (a, b, c, d). This time the boy shows signs of disgust because the girl has refused him for the second time. . . . . . . 8 M.

(f) Repeat (a) and (b). . . . . 3 M.

Repeat (c). This time the girl nods her head showing acceptance of the invitation. . . . . 1 M.

(g) Boy takes the girl's right hand with his right hand and leads her to the middle of the room or stage. Both execute four waltz steps. The girl stands at partner's right side at the end of the fourth waltz step. . . . . 4 M.

III

Music C.

(a) Boy gives one end of his handkerchief (triangular fold) to the girl. They hold it with their right hands. The left hand of the boy is placed on his waist. The girl's hand holds her skirt.

Execute fourteen waltz steps, alternately forward right and backward left, moving ahead little by little. They look at each other. . . . 14 M.

(b) With two big waltz steps backward (R, L), separate about six feet. Boy puts the handkerchief in his pocket. . . . . 2 M.

IV

Music D.

Partners face each other.

(a) Execute three sway-balance steps with a point, R and L alternately. Right arm in reverse "T" position and left bent in front at shoulder-level when doing the sway balance to the right. Reverse the arm positions when going to the left. . . . . 6 M.

(b) Partners take two waltz steps forward to exchange places, passing by each other's right shoulder. Arms in lateral position at shoulder level moving sideward right and left. . . . . 2 M.

(c) Repeat all (a, b), finishing in proper places. . . . . 8 M.

V

Music C.

(a) Jump in place with the R foot across the L in front (ct. 1), step R foot sideward right (ct. 2), step L across the R in front (ct. 3). Step R foot obliquely backward (ct. 4), point L foot in front (cts. 5, 6). Cross hands down in front with right over left and body slightly forward in "sarok" on count 1, and arms in

21

fourth position R arm high on counts 5–6. Trunk erect when arms are in fourth position. .... 2 M.

(b) Repeat (a) with the L foot across the R in front. Reverse the arm positions. .... 2 M.

(c) Repeat all (a, b) three times more. .... 12 M.

NOTE: See to it that the jump puts the dancers back into their places.

VI

Music D.

(a) Starting with the R foot, partners take three steps forward to meet at the center (cts. 1, 2, 3). Step L close to R foot (cts. 4, 5, 6). Girl holding skirt, boy's hands on waist. .... 2 M.

(b) Point R foot in intermediate in front (cts. 1, 2), point R close to L foot (ct. 3). Arms in fourth position, L arm high. ...... 1 M.

(c) Repeat (b) (cts. 1, 2), step R close to L (ct. 3). .... 1 M.

(d) Starting with the L foot, take three steps sideward left (cts. 1, 2, 3). Step R close to L foot (cts. 1, 2, 3). Hands as in (a). .. 2 M.

(e) Repeat (b and c) with the L foot. Reverse arm positions... 2 M.

(f) Repeat (d) going sideward right, starting with the R foot. 2 M.

(g) Repeat (b and c). .... 2 M.

(h) Repeat (d and e). .... 4 M.

VII

Music C.

(a) Partners hold as in ordinary ballroom dance position. Waltz around. .... 14 M.

(b) With two waltz steps backward, separate about six feet. 2 M.

VIII

Music D.

(a) Girl—Claps hands in this manner. Claps on count 1, silent on count 2, claps on count 3. Does this for six measures. Looks at partner.

Boy—Executes three sway-balance steps with a point, R and L alternately. Arms in fourth position, R and L arm high alternately. 6 M.

(b) Partners execute a waltz-turn right going to partner's place. The boy starts with the L foot and the girl with the R. Finish facing each other. .... 2 M.

(c) Repeat (a). .... 6 M.

(d) With two waltz steps, meet at center and hold as in ordinary ballroom dance position. Boy and girl start with the same foot as in (b). .... 2 M.

22

Music C.

Repeat figure VII. . . . . 16 м.

Music D.

Repeat figure VIII, this time the girl dancing and the boy clap-
ping hands. . . . . 16 м.

Music C.

(a) Repeat figure VII. . . . . 14 м.

(b) Join right hands. Girl turns counterclockwise under the
arch of arm, then both bow to the audience. . . . . 2 м.

Anuncio

MINDORO

Notation by
A. BUENAVENTURA

23

Areuana

This is a Visayan dance from Janiuay, Iloilo. It is known in other places as Lariajuana or Jota Rojana.

Areuana may have been derived from the Visayan phrase "Aré," and "Juana," meaning "Here, Juana."

It is a lively dance and has a great deal of Spanish influence as seen in the different figures.

COSTUME. The dancers are dressed in Visayan costume. (See illustration.)

MUSIC is divided into five parts: A, B, C, D, E.

COUNT *one, two, three* to a measure.

FORMATION. Partners stand opposite each other about eight feet apart. Girls stand at partners' right when facing the audience. From one to any number of pairs may take part in this dance.

INTRODUCTION

Music Introduction.

Partners face each other. Make a three-step turn right in place and bow to each other. Girls hold skirts and boys place hands on waist. .... 2 M.

Face the audience. Point R foot in front. Arms in fourth position; L arm high. .... 1 M.

I

Music A.

Girls face the audience, boys face away from the audience.

(a) Take one "bacui" step to the left going to partner's place. Partners pass each other front to front. .... 4 M.

(b) Repeat (a) going to the right to proper places. Reverse the arm positions. .... 4 M.

(c) Repeat (a). .... 4 M.

(d) Partners face away from each other (back to back).

Starting with the R foot, take three step-hops backward, going to proper places. Pass by each other's right shoulder. Start with the right forearm in front of the body at waist-level and the left forearm behind the body. Reverse the position of the arms at every measure. .... 3 M.

(e) Step L foot close to R (cts. 1, 2, 3), arms hanging loosely at the sides. .... 1 M.

(f) Boys face the audience and girls face away from the audience.

(g) Repeat all (a, b, c, d, e). .... 16 M.

AREUANA, Figure I (b)

II

Music B.

Partners face each other.

(a) *Girls* take one waltz step sideward right and left alternately four times. Arms in lateral position at shoulder-level moving sideward right and left alternately. .... 4 M.

Boys (at the same time) starting with the R foot, take four waltz steps forward to front of partner. Take the same arm movements as the girls. .... 4 M.

(b) Boys turn right about. Starting with the R foot, partners take four waltz steps forward, going to the boys' place. The girls follow closely behind their partners. Take the same arm movements as in (a). .... 4 M.

(c) Partners turn right about. Repeat (b) going to the girls' place. The boys follow closely behind their partners. Take the same arm movements. .... 4 M.

(d) Partners turn right about. Boys starting with the R foot, take four waltz steps forward to proper places. Take the same arm movements. Girls repeat (a). .... 4 M.

(e) Repeat all, this time the girls repeat the boys' movements and vice-versa. .... 16 M.

III

Music C.

(a) Step R foot forward (cts. 1, 2), hop on the same foot and raise L foot in front (ct. 3). Cross hands down in front for three counts. .... 1 M.

(b) Step L forward and bend both knees slightly. Swiftly bring the hands to fifth position. Partners are standing side by side, right shoulder to right shoulder, when in this position (bent knees). They look at each other over their right shoulders (cts. 1, 2, 3). .... 1 M.

(c) Take one waltz-turn right using two waltz steps to partner's place. Arms in fifth position or lateral at shoulder-level, moving sideward right and left. Partners finish the turn facing each other. .... 2 M.

(d) Repeat (a) and (b) three times more. Always pass by right shoulders. .... 12 M.

IV

Music D.

(a) Dos-a-dos (Do-si-do). Starting with the R foot, partners take four waltz steps forward passing by right shoulders and four waltz steps backward passing by left shoulders. Start with the right forearm in front of the body at waist-level and the left forearm behind the body. Reverse the arm positions every three counts. ..... 8 M.

(b) Repeat (a), passing by left shoulders forward and by right shoulders backward. .... 8 M.

Pause. .... 2 M.

V

Music A.

Boys face away from the audience. Girls face toward the audience.

(a) Take one "bacui" step to the left, going to partner's place. Pass each other front to front. .... 4 M.

(b) Repeat (a) to the right, going to proper places. Pass each other back to back. .... 4 M.

(c) Repeat (a) and (b). .... 8 M.

(d) Turn right about and repeat all (a, b, c). .... 16 M.

VI

Music B.

Partners face each other.

(a) Take two waltz steps forward (R, L) to meet at the center, arms in lateral position at shoulder-level moving sideward right and left. .... 2 M.

(b) Face left. Take one waltz step sideward right (partners go inward near each other) and one waltz step sideward left (partners go outward away from each other). Arms as in (a). ... 2 M.

(c) Turn right about and take one waltz step sideward right and left as in (b). Arms as in (a). .... 2 M.

(d) Repeat (c) four times more. .... 8 M.

(e) Take two waltz steps backward (R, L) to proper places. Arms as in (a). .... 2 M.

(f) Repeat all, facing right in (b). Always make a right about turn. .... 16 M.

VII

Music C.

(a) Execute a "sarok" with a jump, R foot across the L in front (ct. 1), take a three-step turn obliquely right forward (cts. 2, 3, 4) and pause (cts. 5, 6). Cross hands in front, R over L, on count 1. Girls hold their skirts and boys place their hands on waists on counts 2, 3, 4, 5, 6. Partners finish the turn facing each other in one line. .... 2 M.

(b) Repeat (a) three times more moving counterclockwise. Finish in proper places.

For every turn take one side of an imaginary diamond. (See diagram A)

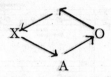
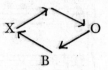

A   B

(c) Repeat all, starting the "sarok" with the L foot across the R in front. The three-step turn is done to the left always. (See diagram B.)

VIII

Music E.

(a) Starting with the R foot, partners take two waltz steps forward to meet at center. Arms in lateral position at shoulder-level moving sideward right and left. .... 2 M.

(b) Partners join both hands. Point R foot in front (cts. 1, 2), step forward on the same foot (ct. 3). .... 1 M.

(c) Repeat (b) five times more, L and R alternately, moving clockwise. .... 5 M.

(d) Turn right about and repeat (b) and (c) moving counterclockwise. .... 6 M.

(e) Drop hands and take two waltz steps backward (R, L) to proper places. Arms as in (a). .... 2 M.

FINALE

Music Finale:

Take three steps forward to meet at center (R, L, R—cts. 1, 2, 3). Cross and join hands, R with R of partner over L with L of partner. In crossed hands position raise hands up to waist-level (ct. 1) and swiftly lower them (cts. 2, 3). .... 2 M.

Raise the right hands upward. The girl turns right under the arch of the right arms. .... 1 M.

The girls then stand, backs to their partners, hands still joined. Raising the left hands up and lowering the right hands, point R foot sideward and bend body slightly to the right. Partners are now looking at each other over the right shoulder of the girl. Pause in this position. .... 3 M.

Areuana

31

Aringginding—Ginding

This is a simple, delightful, courtship dance from Mindoro. The participants sing as they perform easy dance steps. The words of the songs, alternately sung by the boy and the girl, speak mostly of love in a tender but humorous way.

COSTUME. The girl wears "balintawak." The boy wears "barong tagalog" and white trousers.

MUSIC is only one part, played eight times.

COUNT *one, two, three* to a measure.

FORMATION. This dance may be performed by one couple. They stand opposite each other about eight feet apart, the girl standing at the boy's right when facing the audience.

INTRODUCTION

Music Introduction

Waltz forward R (cts. 1, 2, 3) and backward L (cts. 1, 2, 3). L hand on waist, R hand in front at waist level (palm up) (cts. 1, 2, 3), bring R hand close to chest (cts. 1, 2, 3). .... 2 M.

Waltz-turn right in place (two waltz steps). Place both hands on waist. .... 2 M.

I

(a) *Girl* sings the first verse.

Partners execute eight sway-balance steps with a point, R and L alternately. Arms in fourth position, R and L arm high alternately. .... 16 M.

(b) *Boy* sings the second verse.

Partners repeat (a). .... 16 M.

II

(a) *Girl* sings the third verse.

Starting with the R foot, partners take two waltz steps forward to meet at center. Arms in lateral position at shoulder level, moving sideward R and L. .... 2 M.

One sway balance with a point to R. Arms in fourth position, R arm high. .... 2 M.

One waltz-turn right (2 waltz steps L, R) moving forward to exchange place with partner. Pass by each other's left shoulder. Arms in lateral position at shoulder level moving sideward L and R. Finish facing partner. .... 2 M.

Take one sway-balance step with a point to L. Arms in fourth position, L arm high. . . . . 2 M.

    (b) Repeat (a). Girl singing the last eight measures. . . . . 8 M.

    (c) *Boy* sings the fourth verse.

Repeat all (a) and (b). . . . . 16 M.

III

    (a) *Girl* sings the fifth verse.

Point R foot in fourth in front (cts. 1, 2), point R close to L foot in first position (ct. 3), L hand on waist, R hand in front at waist level (palm up) on cts. 1, 2 and bring it close to chest on ct. 3 (1 M.). Repeat the same movements once more (1 M.). . . . . . . 2 M.

Repeat all, starting with the L foot. Reverse the hand positions. 2 M.

Take four waltz steps forward R and backward L alternately. Girl holding skirt, boy's hands on waist. . . . . 4 M.

    (b) Repeat all. . . . . 8 M.

    (c) *Boy* sings the sixth verse.

Repeat all (a) and (b). . . . . 16 M.

IV

    (a) *Girl* sings the seventh verse.

  Starting with the R foot, partners take four small close steps forward to meet at center. Girl holding skirt, boy's hands on waist. 4 M.

    (b) *Girl*—"Kumintang" R and L hand alternately four times. If the R hand is doing the "kumintang" the L is placed on the waist and vice-versa.

Boy—executes four waltz steps sideward R and L alternately. Hands on waist. . . . . 4 M.

    (c) Partners take four close steps backward. Hands as in (a). 4 M.

    (d) *Girl*—executes one waltz-turn right in place (two waltz steps) and to left in place (two waltz steps). Hands as in (a).

Boy. "Kumintang" hands as the girl in (b). . . . . 4 M.

    (e) *Boy* sings the eighth verse.

Partners repeat all (a, b, c, d). . . . . 16 M.

These words are sung while doing the above dance steps.

ARINGGINDING–GINDING

Girl—   I. Aringginding-ginding, ang sinta ko'y limang bagay, aring-ginding

        Aringginding-ginding, may sa puso at sa atay, aringginding

        Aringginding-ginding, may sa noo at sa kilay, aringginding

        Aringginding-ginding, may sa dulo nang galamay.

Aringginding—Ginding

MINDORO

Notation by
A. BUENAVENTURA

Repeat as many times as desired

Boy— II. Aringginding-ginding, ang sinta ko'y tunay mandin, aring-
ginding
Aringginding-ginding, malinaw pa sa salamin, aringginding
Aringginding-ginding, kung sana sa iilawin, aringginding
Aringginding-ginding, di ko pahipan sa hañgin.

Girl— III. Aringginding-ginding, ang sinta nang bagong kasal, aring-
ginding
Aringginding-ginding, matamis pa sa asukal, aringginding
Aringginding-ginding, pag lumaon at tumagal, aringginding
Aringginding-ginding, parang sukang binantuan.

Boy— IV. Aringginding-ginding, ang sinta nang matatanda, aring-
ginding
Aringginding-ginding, parang bigas na pinawa, aringginding
Aringginding-ginding, pag nalagpak na sa lupa, aringginding
Aringginding-ginding, manok man ay di tumuka.

Girl— V. Aringginding-ginding, ang huni nang ibong pipit, aring-
ginding
Aringginding-ginding, na sa dulo nang kalumpit, aring-
ginding
Aringginding-ginding pag ang dalaga ay pañgit, aringginding
Aringginding-ginding biruin mo't nagagalit.

Boy— VI. Aringginding-ginding, ang huni nang ibong maya, aring-
ginding
Aringginding-ginding, na sa dulo nang papaya, aringginding
Aringginding-ginding, pag ang dalaga'y maganda aring-
ginding
Aringginding-ginding, biruin mo't tumatawa.

Girl— VII. Aringginding-ginding, ang sinta ko'y wala rito, aringginding
Aringginding-ginding, nasa kabilang ibayo, aringginding
Aringginding-ginding, kaya ayaw pumarito, aringginding
Aringginding-ginding, nahihiya raw sa iyo.

Boy—VIII. Aringginding-ginding, ang huni nang kulo kulo, aring-
ginding
Aringginding-ginding, nasa dulong antipolo, aringginding
Aringginding-ginding, pag ang dalaga'y mabango, aring-
ginding
Aringginding-ginding, ang binata'y naloloko.

NOTE: There are many more verses which may be included in this song if
the dancers desire to prolong the dance.

36

Bahay Kubo

Among the Tagalog folk songs this is perhaps the easiest and best known by the children.

"Bahay Kubo" means nipa hut. The story of the song is this: the dancer talks about his or her nipa hut which is very small. It has a vegetable garden full of "sinkamas," egg-plant, "sigarillas," peanuts, tomatoes, squash, onions, mustard, and other vegetables.

This dance was arranged for small children. The dancers sing the words of the song as they dance.

COSTUME. The girls are dressed like farmerettes and the boys as workers in the fields. The sleeves of the "camisa" of the girls and boys and the trousers of the boys are rolled up. The girls may cover their heads with a neckerchief or any piece of cloth. The girls carry baskets of vegetables mentioned in the song and the boys carry any small farm implement which they can easily handle with their small hands.

MUSIC * has only one part of sixteen measures.

COUNT *one, two, three* to a measure.

FORMATION. Partners stand opposite each other about six feet apart. Girl stands at partner's right side when facing the audience. From one to any number may take part, the more the better.

Audience

X	O
X	O
X	O

INTRODUCTION

Music Introduction.

Three-step turn right in place and bow to audience or partner. . . . 2 M.

I

Sing the first verse.

Girls carry the baskets with both hands and boys their farm implements. Partners face each other.

(a) Take fourteen step-swings sideward R and L alternately. Swing their baskets and implements to sideward right and left alternately. . . . . 14 M.

* Words and music will be found in *The Progressive Music Series*, Philippine Edition, Book Two, page VII.

37

BAHAY KUBO, Figure II (b)

(b) Put the baskets and implements down on the floor out of the way of the dancing. .... 2 м.

II

No Singing.

(a) Starting with the right foot, partners take three steps forward to meet at the center (cts. 1, 2, 3). Point L foot in front (cts. 1, 2, 3). Girls holding their skirts and boys' hands on waist... 2 м.

(b) Bend the trunk slightly to sideward right and "kumintang" right hand, left hand on waist (cts. 1, 2, 3). .... 1 м.

(c) Repeat (b) to the left. Reverse the position of the hands. 1 м.

(d) Repeat (a) going backward, starting with the L foot. .... 2 м.

(e) Repeat (b) and (c), starting with the left hand. .... 2 м.

(f) Repeat all. .... 8 м.

III

Sing the second verse.

(a) Take one waltz step sideward right (cts. 1, 2, 3) and one sideward left (cts. 1, 2, 3). Arms in lateral position moving sideward right and left. .... 2 м.

(b) Point R foot in front (cts. 1, 2), close the same foot to the L (ct. 3). Place left hand on waist, bring right hand forward with palm up on counts 1, 2, and bring it close to chest on count 3. .... 1 м.

(c) Point R foot again in front (cts. 1, 2). Step the same foot close to L (ct. 3). Repeat the same hand movements in (b). ...... 1 м.

(d) Repeat (a, b, c), starting with the L foot. Reverse the hand positions. .... 4 м.

(e) Repeat all (a, b, c, d). .... 8 м.

IV

No singing.

(a) Take two sway-balance steps with a point (R, L), arms in fourth position, R and L arm high alternately. .... 4 м.

(b) Starting with the R foot, take four waltz steps forward going to partner's place. Turn about on the fourth waltz step. Partners pass by each other's right shoulder. Arms are in lateral position moving sideward R and L alternately. .... 4 м.

(c) Repeat all, finishing in proper place. Bow to partner or to the audience on the last measure. .... 8 м.

Exit. Take baskets and tools from the floor. Starting with R foot, execute waltz steps forward to exit. Use any native music in 3/4 time.

Los Bailes de Ayer

"Los Bailes de Ayer" means dances of yesteryear. It is a quadrille, combining old ballroom dance steps and figures, such as the "polka," "schottische," "mazurka," "paso doble," etc.

According to Mrs. Elvira Bocobo Castro, who made the report on this dance, the original music and dance steps came from Tarlac. In fact, this was known as "Pre-Revolutionary-War Dance" or "Maharlika" in Tarlac and neighboring provinces.

The above name was chosen because it fitted the dance very well. The original dance was re-arranged and some figures were changed to make the dance interesting and typically native.

COSTUME. Girls wear any old-style costume (Maria Clara, Serpentina, etc.) and boys, "barong tagalog" and black trousers.

MUSIC is divided into twelve parts: Introduction, A, B, C, D, E, F, G, H, I, J, and K.

COUNT *one, two, three* to a measure in 3/4 time, *one and, two and* in 2/4 polka time, *one, two* in 2/4 time, and *one, two, three, four* in 4/4 time.

FORMATION. Partners stand near each other, ladies at partner's right side. Dancers stand in a quadrille formation all facing in a hollow square. From four to any number of even pairs may take part. (See diagram A.)

```
                      III
            O X        O X
        X                    O
        O                    X
    I                            II
        X                    O
        O                    X
            X O        X O
                      IV
```

Diagram A

I and II are "cabeceras" or head pairs, III and IV are "costados" or side pairs.

ENTRANCE

Music Introduction.

Boys lead their partners to their respective places, taking plain walking steps. Girl takes the right arm of her partner when going to their places. .... 11 M.

I
CROSS FORMATION

Music A.

Head Pairs: Face inside the square.

(a) Partners hold as in ballroom dance position. Starting with the L for the boys and with the R for the girls, brush or slide sideward (cts. 1, 2), raise the same foot in rear of the other foot (ct. 3). . . . . 1 M.

(b) Starting with the same foot take three steps sideward (cts. 1, 2, 3). . . . . 1 M.

(c) Face the opposite direction and repeat (a) and (b), starting with the opposite foot (girls with the L and boys with the R foot). Finish in place. . . . . 2 M.

(d) Partners execute a quarter-turn right (girls turning backward, boys forward). Repeat (a, b, c). . . . . 4 M.

(e) Repeat (d) two times more. Finish in proper places. (See Diagram B.) . . . . 8 M.

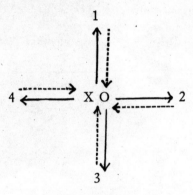

Diagram B

Side Pairs:

(f) Repeat all (a, b, c, d, and e). . . . . 16 M.

NOTE: Bend the body toward the sliding foot and look at it.

II
IN AND OUT

Music B.

Head Pairs:

Partners face each other and join both hands. Extend both arms to the sides.

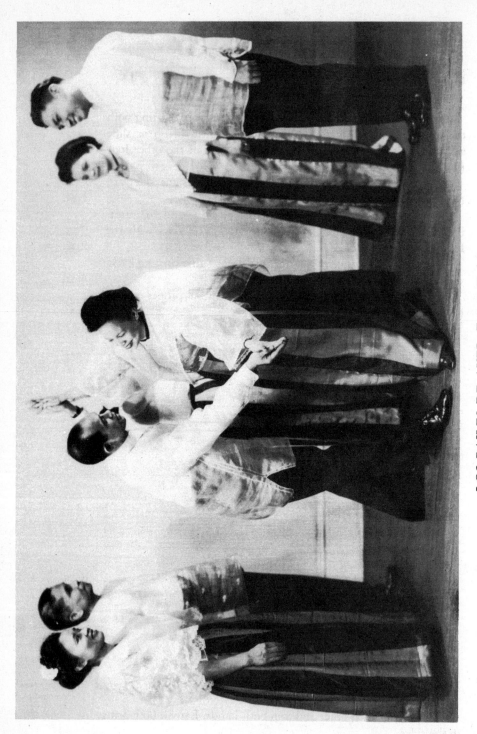

LOS BAILES DE AYER, FIGURE II (a)

(a) Repeat figure I (a, b, c), going toward the center of the square. .... 2 M.

(b) Face the opposite direction and repeat (a) going to proper places. .... 2 M.

(c) Repeat all (a and b). .... 4 M.

Side Pairs:

(d) Repeat all (a, b, and c). .... 8 M.

III

MAZURKA

Music C.

Head Pairs:

Partners hold as in ballroom dance position, facing in.

(a) Take three mazurka steps forward, going inside the square. Girls start with the R and boys with the L foot. .... 3 M.

(b) Take three-step-half-turn right so that partners are facing away from the center. (Do not put weight on the foot at the third step, it is just a tap.) .... 1 M.

(c) With partners going away from the center of the square, repeat (a) and (b), starting with the same foot (R for girls and L for boys). .... 4 M.

(d) Repeat all (a, b, and c). .... 8 M.

Side Pairs:

(e) Repeat all (a, b, c, and d). .... 16 M.

IV

CROSS STEPS

Music D.

Head and side pairs dance at the same time. Partners face each other about one or two feet apart. Girls hold their skirts, boys keep hands on waists throughout this figure.

(a) Starting with the R foot, take three cross steps sideward right. .... 3 M.

(b) Step R foot sideward (ct. 1), brush L forward (ct. 2), hop on R (ct. 3). .... 1 M.

(c) Repeat (a) and (b), starting with the L foot, going to sideward left. .... 4 M.

(d) Repeat all (a, b, and c). .... 8 M.

Partners finish where figure was started.

43

V

"PASO ESPAÑOL"

Music E.

Head Pairs:

Partners face the center of the square, girls holding skirts, boys' hands placed on waists throughout this figure.

(a) Starting with the R foot, take three "paso español" steps forward. At the end of the third step the opposites are at the center of the square. .... 12 M.

(b) Starting with the R foot, take seven steps backward to proper places, partners then face each other and bow. The feet are together when bowing. The hands remain in the same place. .. 4 M.

Side Pairs:

(a) Repeat all (a and b). .... 16 M.

VI

SWAY–BALANCE STEPS

Music F.

All face the center of the square and all dance.

(a) Take eight sway-balance steps with a point, R and L alternately. Arms in fourth position, R and L arm high alternately. 16 M.

(b) Turn right about (face out) and pause. .... 2 M.

(c) Repeat (a). .... 16 M.

(d) Turn right about (face in) and pause. .... 2 M.

NOTE: Any one of the sway-balance step series may be executed if desired (hop, brush, or raise).

VII

HEEL AND TOE POLKA

Music G.

Head Pairs:

Partners join inside hands. Free hands of the girls holding skirts, boys' on waists.

(a) Starting with the R foot, take four heel and toe polka steps forward. At the end of the fourth step the opposites are standing about a foot from each other. .... 8 M.

(b) Partners release hands. The opposites (girls of one side and boys of the other side) join both hands. Starting with the R foot, take four polka steps clockwise. .... 4 M.

(c) Release hands of the opposites. Partners face toward their proper places and join inside hands. Free hands are placed as in (a). Starting with the R foot, take four polka steps forward going to proper places. Finish facing the center. . . . .   4 M.

Side Pairs:

(d) Repeat all (a, b, and c). . . . .   16 M.

VIII
"PASO DOBLE"
(Two-Step)

Music H. Play four times.

Head Pairs:

Girls of side I and boys of side II dance first.

(a) Starting with the R foot, take four change steps forward to meet at the center, girls holding skirts, boys' hands on waist. . .   4 M.

NOTE: Take bigger steps to reach the center.

(b) Join right hands, left remains in place. Starting with the R foot, take four change steps clockwise. . . . .   4 M.

(c) Release hands. Starting with the R foot, take four change steps forward to proper places. Hands as in (a). . . . .   4 M.

(d) Partners join both hands. Take four change steps clockwise, starting with the R foot. . . . .   4 M.

Girls of side II and boys of side I dance.

(e) Repeat all (a, b, c, and d). . . . .   16 M.

Side Pairs:

Girls of side III and boys of side IV dance.

(f) Repeat all (a, b, c, and d). . . . .   16 M.

Girls of side IV and boys of side III dance.

(g) Repeat all (a, b, c, and d). . . . .   16 M.

IX
"CHOTIS"
(Native Schottische)

Music I.

Head Pairs:

Partners hold as in ballroom dance position facing the center (extended arms toward the center). Always look at the brushing or sliding foot.

(a) Girls start with the R and boys with the L foot. Take one native schottische ("chotis") making a half-turn right (clockwise) only. Finish the turn with the extended arm outside (away from the center). . . . .   2 M.

45

(b) Repeat (a) starting with the other foot. Finish the turn facing the center. .... 2 M.

(c) Repeat all (a and b). .... 4 M.

Side Pairs:

(d) Repeat all (a, b, and c). .... 8 M.

X
GALOP

Music J.

All dance at the same time. Partners face each other, standing about a foot apart.

(a) Starting with the R foot, take three galop steps sideward right (cts. 1, 2, 3), pause (ct. 4). Girls hold skirts, boys place hands on waist. .... 1 M.

(b) Repeat (a), starting with the L foot, to former position. ... 1 M.

(c) Partners hold as in ballroom dance position with the girls a little to the right of their partners.

(d) Starting with the R foot, take three step-hops turning clockwise in place (cts. 1–6). Pause and release hold (cts. 7–8). .... 2 M.

(e) Repeat all (a, b, c, d) three times more. .... 12 M.

XI
"DOBLE CADENA"
(Double Grand Right and Left)

Music K. Play as many times as necessary.

Partners face each other and join right hands. Boys move counterclockwise, girls clockwise. The movement is similar to the "Grand Chain" or "Grand Right and Left" of the Rigodon described in this book. The only difference is that dancers turn around clockwise once when right hands are joined, once counterclockwise when left hands are joined. Before advancing to meet the next dancer, the turn must be completed. Continue turning around until all are in their proper places and with their own partners.

XII
"ESTRELLA"
(Star)

Music K. Play as many times as necessary.

All face the center of the square.

(a) All girls take the left arm of their partners. Dancers of

46

LOS BAILES DE AYER, FIGURE XI DOBLE CADENA

sides I, II, III and IV advance to meet at center. All girls join right hands to form a star. All march around clockwise once.

(b) Turn right about and reverse positions.

All boys stay inside and join left hands. All march around counterclockwise once.

(c) As soon as one turn is complete all march forward to proper places and finish facing the center of the square.

NOTE: If there are four or more pairs in one side of the square, each side may do their own "star" formation.

XII
"SALUDO"
(Bow)

Music K. Play as many times as necessary.

Head Pairs:

(a) Girls take the left arm of their partners. The opposites walk forward to center and bow to each other.

(b) Walk backward to proper places.

Side Pairs:

(c) Repeat (a) and (b).

NOTE: If desired the dance may be followed by an old time waltz.

RIGODON, "Casamiento" FIGURE III (b)
(see page 263)

Los Bailes de Ayer

REPORTED BY
MRS. ELVIRA DE CASTRO

Arranged by
F. R. TOLENTINO

H VIII

K XI-XII

Repeat the last part as
many times as necessary

Bakya Dance

(Philippine Wooden Shoe Dance)

"Bakya" means wooden shoes. They are the common footwear of the poor in the "barrios." During the rainy season almost all people wear them. They are made in different materials, colors, and shapes.

This dance is very interesting and lively. In a playful mood, young boys and girls are supposed to be teasing each other rhythmically with their "bakya."

COSTUME. Girls wear "balintawak" and boys "barong tagalog" with red trousers. All have on "bakya."

MUSIC is divided into four parts: A, B, C and D.

COUNT *one, two, three* to a measure of 3/4 time and *one, two* to a measure in 2/4 time.

FORMATION. Partners stand opposite each other about six feet apart. The girl stands at partner's right when facing the audience. From two to any number of even pairs may take part.

INTRODUCTION

Music Introduction.

With the weight of the body on the L foot, tap R in fourth in front (ct. 1), tap in second (ct. 2), stamp on the same foot close to the L in first position (ct. 3), stamp L in place (ct. 1), pause (cts. 2, 3). .... 2 M.

I

Music A.

(a) Take one waltz step forward R (cts. 1, 2, 3), and one waltz step backward L (cts. 1, 2, 3). Girls holding skirts, boys' hand on waist. .... 2 M.

(b) Take one sway-balance with a point, starting with the R foot. Arms in fourth position, R arm high. .... 2 M.

(c) Repeat (a) and (b), starting with the L foot. Reverse the arm positions in (b). .... 4 M.

(d) Repeat all (a, b, c), three times. .... 24 M.

II

Music B.

(a) Partners take two waltz steps forward (R, L) to meet at center. Arms are in lateral position moving sideward right and left. .... 2 M.

(b) Turn right about to a back-to-back position with partner. Take one waltz step sideward right (cts. 1, 2, 3), and one waltz sideward left (cts. 1, 2, 3). Girls holding their skirts and boys' hands on waist. Turn head to right and left to look at partner. .... 2 M.

(c) Turn right about to face each other. Execute one waltz step sideward right (cts. 1, 2, 3) and sideward left (cts. 1, 2, 3). Hands as in (b). .... 2 M.

(d) Step R foot backward (cts. 1, 2), step L backward (ct. 3). Close R foot with the L without putting weight on the R foot (ct. 1), pause (cts. 2, 3). The steps are heavy, like stamping. ...... 2 M.

(e) Repeat all (a, b, c, and d) three times more. .... 24 M.

NOTE: On the fourth time do the heavy steps in place (d) so that partners are near each other at the end of this figure.

III

Music A.

Partners take off their wooden shoes and sit down in a semi-squat or full-knee bend position facing each other. Hold one wooden shoe in each hand by the heel.

(a) Girls: Strike own "bakya" together once (ct. 1), strike left "bakya" on the floor followed immediately by the right in the same manner (ct. 2 or *and* 2), strike left "bakya" once again on the floor (ct. 3). .... 1 M.

(b) Girls repeat (a) three times more. .... 3 M.

NOTE: Boys rest and watch the girls as they do this movement. (4 M.)

(c) Boys: Repeat (a, b). .... 4 M.

NOTE: Girls rest and watch the boys. (4 M.)

(d) Boys and girls together:
Strike own "bakya" together once (ct. 1), strike left "bakya" once on the floor (ct. 3), right "bakya" once on the floor (ct. 3). ... 1 M.

(e) Repeat (d) five times more. .... 5 M.

(f) Partners: Strike own "bakya" together once (ct. 1), strike both "bakya" with partner's twice (ct. 2, 3), strike own (both) "bakya" on the floor (ct. 1), pause (cts. 2, 3). .... 2 M.

(g) Repeat all (a, b, c, d, e and f). .... 16 M.

NOTE: At the last measure partners stand and quickly go to proper places. (Last two counts.)

IV

Music B.

Partners still hold their own "bakya."

(a) Starting with the R foot, take two waltz steps forward to meet at center. Hands hanging loosely at the sides. .... 2 M.

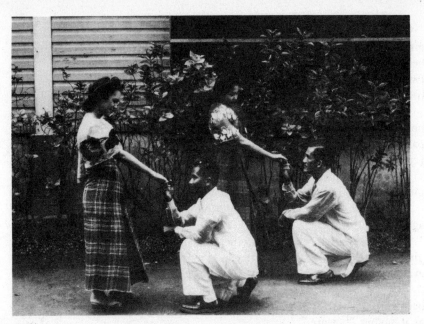

MARAMION, FIGURE VI (b)
(see page 185)

BAKYA, FIGURE IV (b)

(b) Strike own "bakya" together once (ct. 1), pause (ct. 2), girl feigns striking partner's head with her right "bakya" while boy bends knees and evades being hit by covering his head with his two "bakya" so that the girl strikes his "bakya" instead of his head (ct. 3). . . . . 1 M.

(c) Partners turn right about so that they are in a back-to-back position. Immediately strike own "bakya" together once (ct. 1), pause (ct. 2), girl strikes left "bakya" of the boy with her right once (ct. 3). . . . . 1 M.

(d) Strike own "bakya" together once (ct. 1), pause (ct. 2), girl strikes the right "bakya" of the boy with her left once (ct. 3). 1 M.

(e) Turn right about so that partners are facing each other again.

(f) Strike own "bakya" together once (ct. 1), pause (ct. 2), girl strikes the boy again, this time as if aiming at the face but he evades it by covering the face and bending the body down (ct. 3). 1 M.

(g) Starting with the R foot, partners take two waltz steps backward to places, boy shaking the right "bakya" to the girl as if saying "beware." . . . . 2 M.

(h) Repeat all (a, b, c, d, e and f), this time the boys doing the hitting movements and the girls evading the blows. . . . . 8 M.

(i) Repeat all (a, b, c, d, e, f and g). . . . . 16 M.

NOTE: The hitting movements should be vigorous and natural.

V

Music C. Play four times.

Dancers put on the "bakya" as quickly as possible. The music is not played until they are ready.

Girls holding skirts, boys' hands on waist throughout this figure.

(a) Starting with the R foot, take two change steps forward to meet at the center. . . . . 2 M.

(b) Tap R foot in second position (ct. 1), tap in fourth in front (ct. 2), tap in second (ct. 1), tap in fourth in front (ct. 2). 2 M.

(c) Starting with the R foot, take two change steps backward. 2 M.

(d) Tap R foot in second (ct. 1), tap in fourth in front (ct. 2). . . . . 1 M.

Take two stamps in place (R, L) (cts. 1, 2). . . . . 1 M.

(e) Repeat (a) and (b). . . . . 4 M.

(f) Starting with the R foot, take two change steps forward to opposite place, partners passing by right shoulders. . . . . 2 M.

(g) Starting with the R foot, take four stamps in place turning right about to face partner. . . . . 2 M.

(h) Repeat all (a, b, c, d, e, f and g). Finish in proper places. 16 M.

Music D.

Dancers group in sets of two couples.

(a) Starting with the R foot, partners take two change steps forward to meet at center. Arms in fifth position swaying sideward right and left. . . . . 2 м.

(b) Turn to face the center of the set. Take two change steps forward (R, L) to meet at the center (see diagram A). Arms as in (a). . . . . 2 м.

(c) All face outward. Take two change steps obliquely forward (R, L) to proper places. (See diagram B.) Arms as in (a).　2 м.

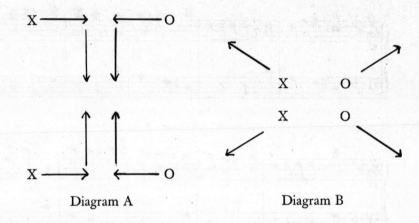

Diagram A　　　　　　　　　　　Diagram B

(d) Starting with the R foot, dancers of each set take twelve change steps forward moving clockwise. Arms as in (a). Finish in proper places facing the audience. . . . . 12 м.

FINALE

Music Introduction.

Take a three-step turn right in place and bow to the audience.　2 м.

Bakya Dance

Tagalog

Repeat as many times as desired

KANDINGAN, Figure II (a)

(see page 147)

Ba-o

(Coconut Shell Dance)

"Ba-o," in Tagalog, means coconut shell. It has many purposes such as fuel, water dippers, food containers, individual savings banks, musical instruments, etc. Each dancer holds two half-coconut shells, one in each hand. The backs are struck together to produce sounds in different rhythms.

This Tagalog dance was created for the U. P. Participation in the Varsity Night during the 1933 Philippine Exposition. The dance steps are based on Tagalog and Visayan dances.

COSTUME. Girls are dressed in "balintawak" and boys in "barong tagalog" with white trousers.

MUSIC is divided into four parts: A, B, C, and D.

COUNT *one, two, three* to a measure of 3/4 time and *one, two* or *one, and, two* to a measure of 2/4 time.

FORMATION. Partners stand opposite each other about six feet apart. When facing the audience, the girls are at their partners' right. Each set is composed of three couples. From one to any number of sets may take part in this dance.

Audience

X   O

X   O

X   O

ENTRANCE

Music. Any part of the music in 3/4 time.

Boys are in one line at the left side and girls at the right side.

Starting with the R foot, take waltz steps forward to proper places. Click own shells together in front and behind alternately the first beat of every measure. .... 16 M.

I

Music A.

(a) Waltz forward R and backward L alternately, four times. Click own shells together in front and behind alternately the first beat of every measure, four times. .... 4 M.

65

(b) Waltz sideward R and L alternately, four times. Click own shells together the first beat of every measure, four times. .... 4 M.

(c) Repeat (a) and (b). .... 8 M.

II

Music B.

(a) Take three steps sideward right (R, L, R—cts. 1, 2, 3), point L foot in front (cts. 1, 2, 3). Hold shells overhead and click them together at the first beat of the second measure, that is, when the L foot is pointing. .... 2 M.

(b) Repeat (a) to the left and point R in front. Click the shells as above. .... 2 M.

(c) Repeat (a) and (b) alternately, three times more. .... 12 M.

III

Music C. Play three times.

Steps Used:

(a) Take two steps forward to the center (R, L) (cts. 1, 2). M. 1

(b) Hop on L and raise R foot in front and swing R inward (to the left) at the same time (ct. 1), hop on L again and swing R foot outward (to the right) (ct. 2). .... M. 2

(c) Three-step turn right in place (cts. 1, and, 2). .... M. 3

(d) Hop on R and raise L in front and swing L inward (to the right) at the same time (ct. 1), hop on R again and L foot outward (to the left) (ct. 2). .... M. 4

(e) Three-step turn left in place (cts. 1, and, 2). .... M. 5

(f) Repeat (b). .... M. 6

(g) Take two steps backward to places (R, L, cts. 1, 2). ...... M. 7

(h) Close R to L foot and pause (cts. 1, 2). .... M. 8

Click Shells in This Manner:

(a) Hands on waists (cts. 1, 2). .... M. 1

(b) Click own shells together twice (cts. 1, 2). .... M. 2

(c) Click own shells together three times (cts. 1, and, 2). .... M. 3

(d) Click own shells together twice (cts. 1, 2). .... M. 4

(e) Click own shells together three times (cts. 1, and, 2). .... M. 5

(f) Click own shells together twice (cts. 1, 2). .... M. 6

(g) Hands on waists. .... MS. 7 & 8

Always click shells in front.

Dance in This Order:

(a) Partners execute steps and clicking of shells together. .... 8 M.

(b) *Boys* dance steps, hands on waists.

Girls click shells, standing in their places. .... 8 M.

66

(c) *Girls* repeat the same steps, hands on waists.
Boys click shells standing in their places. .... 8 M.

IV

Music A.

(a) Take three steps forward to meet partner at center
(R, L, R—cts. 1, 2, 3), brush L foot forward (cts. 1, 2, 3). Hands
on waists on counts 1, 2, 3, strike R shell against partner's R shell
at the first beat of the second measure, that is, after the brush. .... 2 M.

(b) Take three steps backward to places (L, R, L—cts. 1, 2, 3),
brush R foot forward (cts. 1, 2, 3). Hands on waist on counts
1, 2, 3, click own shells together overhead, after the brush. .... 2 M.

(c) Repeat (a) and (b) three times more. .... 12 M.

V

Music B.

(a) Starting with the R foot, partners take three steps to the
center (cts. 1, 2, 3), and pause (cts. 1, 2, 3). For hand movements
see the description below. .... MS. 1–2

(b) Partners stand in front of each other while doing the following shell rhythms .... MS. 3–7

Shell Rhythms

(1) Hands on waists (cts. 1, 2, 3, 1), then click own shells
together twice (cts. 2, 3). .... MS. 1 & 2

(2) Strike R shell with R of partner (ct. 1), own shells together twice (cts. 2, 3). .... M. 3

(3) Strike L shell with L of partner (ct. 1), own shells together twice (cts. 2, 3). .... M. 4

(4) Strike both shells with partner's (ct. 1), own shells together twice (cts. 2, 3). .... M. 5

(5) Repeat (2) and (3). .... MS. 6 & 7

(c) Partners change places by taking three steps forward to
partner's place (L, R, L). Pass by right shoulders. Finish facing
partner. Hands on waists. .... M. 8

(d) Repeat all, finishing at proper places. .... 8 M.

VI

Music D.

(a) Take two step-hop steps forward (R, L). Click own shells
together in front at the third beat of measures 1 and 2. .... 2 M.

(b) Take two waltz steps forward (R, L) to partner's place
passing by right shoulders. Click own shells in front on the last
two beats of measures 3 and 4. .... 2 M.

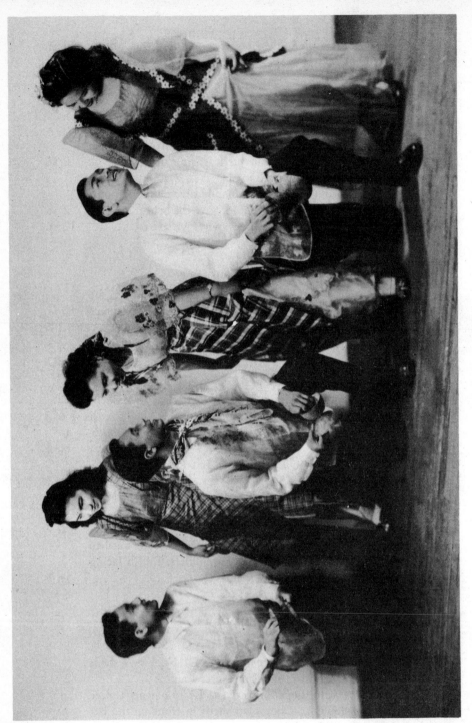

BA-O, Figure VIII

(c) Face right and take three slide steps sideward to proper places, passing in front of each other. Click own shells overhead at the third beat of measures 5, 6, and 7. .... 3 м.

(d) Step R sideward and point L foot in front (cts. 1–6). Arms in fourth position, R arm high. Bend the body to the left and look at the partner for six counts. .... 2 м.

(e) Repeat all (a, b, c, and d) starting with the L foot, passing by left shoulders. Face left while doing the slide steps. .... 9 ꜰ.

VII

Music A.

(a) In sets of three pairs, dancers take eight waltz steps forward, clockwise, starting with the R foot. Click own shells together the first beat of every measure in front and behind alternately. Diagram A. .... 8 м.

(b) Turn right about and repeat (a) going counterclockwise. Click own shells together every first beat of every measure, sideward R and L alternately. Diagram B. .... 8 м.

VIII

Music B. Play twice.

(a) *Boys.* Kneel on R knee in place for fifteen measures and stand up on the sixteenth measure. Click own shells together R and L sideward alternately each beat. .... 16 м.

Girls. (1) Take two waltz steps obliquely forward right (R, L).   2 м.

(2) Waltz-turn right in place (use two waltz steps). Finish at partner's left side facing him. .... 2 м.

(3) Repeat (1) and (2), finishing at partner's back. .... 4 м.

(4) Repeat (1) and (2), finishing at partner's right side. .... 4 м.

(5) Repeat (1) and (2), finishing in proper places. .... 4 м.

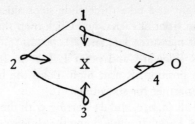

(b) *Girls* kneel and click shells as the boys did in (a).
Boys repeat 1, 2, 3, 4, 5. .... 16 M.

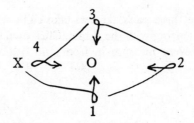

EXIT

Music C. Play as many times as necessary.

With the girls in one line and boys in another, execute change steps forward, starting with the R foot. Click the shells three times to a measure (cts. 1, and, 2), sideward R and L alternately.

Ba-o

TAGALOG

70

B II-V-VIII 2x

C III- Exit *Lively*

Play 3 times

71

Barangay

"Barangay" is derived from the Tagalog word "balangay," a large and swift kind of native boat, which the early Malay immigrants from the Malay Peninsula and the Malay Archipelago used in coming to the Philippines. "Barangay" also refers to the unit of government of the Filipinos in early times.

This "barangay" dance was especially created by the author for the "Barangay" club of Manila. It was first danced by some of the prominent members of the club, on September 9, 1938, when a "harana" party was given by them in the beautiful garden of President Osmeña's home on the occasion of his birthday.

It is of square formation consisting of six figures based on ancient Filipino traditional dance steps. It is an easy, stately, graceful dance and it will be enjoyed by both young and old people.

COSTUME. The girls are dressed in Maria Clara style and boys in "barong tagalog" and black trousers.

MUSIC is divided into two parts: A and B.

COUNT *one, two, three* to a measure.

FORMATION. Partners stand side by side with the girl at the right of the partner. Participants stand in square formation. Eight or sixteen pairs may take part in the dance. (See diagram.)

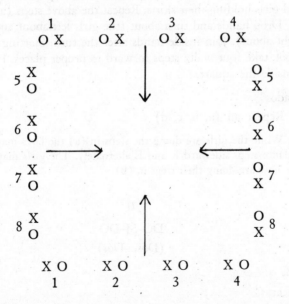

Pairs 1, 2, 3, 4 are "cabeceras" or head pairs standing opposite each other. Pairs 5, 6, 7, 8 are "costados" or side pairs standing opposite each other.

73

INTRODUCTION

Music Introduction.

(a) Partners bow to each other. . . . . 2 M.

(b) Partners bow to opposites. . . . . 2 M.

Girls hold and spread out their skirts sideward, boys bring their right hands to the chest when bowing. The left is hanging loosely at the side.

I

STEP, POINT

Music A.

"Cabeceras"

(a) *Girls*—Step R foot sideward (cts. 1, 2), point L foot in front (ct. 3). Hands holding skirts. . . . . 1 M.

Starting with the R foot, take two waltz steps forward. Hands as above. . . . . 2 M.

(b) *Boys*—Repeat the same movements of the girls in (a) R hand at the back of the waist and L hand hanging loosely at the side. Finish in line with the partner. . . . . 4 M.

(c) Partners join inside hands. Free hands of the boys are placed at the back of the waist (knuckles in, and palm facing out) and girls holding their skirts. Repeat the above steps (a). 4 M.

(d) Drop hands and turn about (the girls left about and the boys right about). Join inside hands after the turn. Starting with the R foot, take four waltz steps forward to proper places. Finish facing inside the square. . . . . 4 M.

"Costados"

(e) Repeat all (a, b, c, d). . . . . 16 M.

NOTE: While the girls are doing the steps in (a) the boys may execute four waltz balance steps sideward R and L alternately. The girls may do the same while the boys are doing their steps in (b).

II

DO–SI–DO

(Dos-a-Dos)

Music B.

"Cabeceras"

(a) Partners join inside hands, free hands as in figure I (c). Starting with the R foot, take four big waltz steps forward to meet the opposites at center (about two feet apart). . . . . 4 M.

(b) Take two close steps sideward right. Hands as above. . . . .   2 M.

(c) Repeat (b) to the left. . . . .   2 M.

(d) Partners drop inside hands. Perform the Do-Si-Do with the opposites (girl of one side with the boy of the opposite side) by taking two waltz steps forward (R, L), and two waltz steps backward (R, L). Girls holding skirts, boys' hands on waist . . . . . .   4 M.

(e) Starting with the R foot, take four waltz steps backward to proper places. Hands as in (a). . . . .   4 M.

"Costados"

(f) Repeat all (a, b, c, d, e). . . . .   16 M.

III

SQUARE

Music A.

All dance together at the same time. Pairs 1 and 2, 3 and 4, 5 and 6, 7 and 8 face each other. Girls stand at the right side of the partners. (See diagram of one set.)

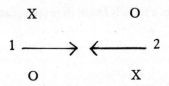

(a) Step R foot forward (ct. 1), step L close to the R (ct. 2), step R foot backward (ct. 3). Point L foot in front (cts. 1, 2, 3). Girls holding skirts, boys' hands on waist. It may be done also with arms in fourth position R arm high. . . . .   2 M.

(b) Repeat (a) starting with the L foot. Hands as in (a) or reverse the arm positions in fourth position. . . . .   2 M.

(c) Starting with the R foot, take four waltz steps forward to exchange places with the opposites, passing by right side. Hands as in (a). Turn right about on the fourth waltz step and finish facing the opposites. . . . .   4 M.

(d) Partners face each other and join right hands. Free hands as in figure I (c). Starting with the R foot, take four waltz steps around clockwise. . . . .   4 M.

(e) Drop right hands and join the left hands. Repeat (d) going counterclockwise. . . . .   4 M.

(f) Repeat all (a, b, c, d, e). Finish in proper places facing inside the square. . . . .   16 M.

IV

GIRLS CHANGE PLACES

Music B. Play twice.

"Cabeceras"

(a) Partners join inside hands, free hands as in figure I (c). Starting with the R foot, take four small waltz steps forward (to cover about one-fourth of the way). .... 4 M.

(b) Partners drop hands. *Girls* take eight waltz steps forward to exchange places with the opposite girls, starting with the R foot. Pass each other by the right shoulder, hands holding skirts. Finish facing the center of the square at the right side of the new partner. 8 M.

Boys in the meantime take eight waltz steps sideward R and L alternately. Hands on waists. .... 8 M.

(c) The new partners hold as in the ordinary ballroom dance position. Boys waltz around the new partner, back to their proper places. .... 4 M.

"Costados"

(d) Repeat all (a, b, c). .... 16 M.

"Cabeceras"

(e) Repeat all (a, b, c). Girls finish in proper places with their partners. .... 16 M.

"Costados"

(f) Repeat (e). .... 16 M.

V

FOUR POINTS

Music A.

All dance together at the same time. Girls stand in front of their partners inside the square. They face each other about two feet apart.

(a) Partners point R foot in front (cts. 1, 2) point R close to L foot (ct. 3). Repeat the same three times more. Girls holding skirts, boys' hands on waist. .... 4 M.

(b) Repeat (a) starting with the L foot. .... 4 M.

(c) "Jaleo"—Girls place R hand on waist and L holds skirt, boys place hands on waist.

Face left so that the right elbows are near each other. Starting with the R foot, partners take four waltz steps around clockwise. Look at each other over the right shoulders. .... 4 M.

(d) Turn right about and girls reverse the hand positions. Repeat (c) going counterclockwise. Partners finish in proper places facing the center of the square. .... 4 M.

HANDKERCHIEF

Music B.

All dance together at the same time.

(a) Partners each hold a corner of a handkerchief which is folded in a triangular form. Hold the handkerchief with the right hand, free hands as in figure I (c).

Take sixteen waltz steps forward R and backward L alternately. Move forward little by little to the center. At the end of the sixteenth waltz step the original square becomes smaller. .... 16 M.

(b) Partners drop hands, girl still holding the handkerchief with the right hand, and face each other. Starting with the R foot, take three steps sideward right (cts. 1, 2, 3). Point L foot in front (cts. 1, 2, 3). R arm in fifth position, L hand on waist. Girl waves the handkerchief as the L foot points in front. .... 2 M.

(c) Repeat (b), starting with the L foot. Reverse the arm positions. .... 2 M.

(d) Repeat (b and c) once more. .... 4 M.

(e) All turn to face outside the square. Partners hold the handkerchief again as in (a). Starting with the R foot, take waltz steps forward R and backward L alternately. Move forward little by little going to proper places. .... 8 M.

Saludo:

Repeat the introduction. .... 4 M.

The following is suggested for entrance and exit.

ENTRANCE

Music B. Play twice.

Formation before the entrance.

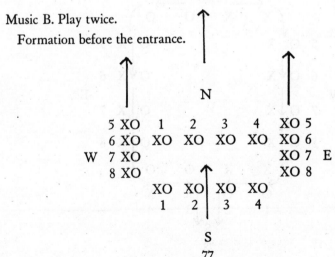

(a) Pairs 1, 2, 3, 4 of the North side enter first. Partners join inside hands, free hand as in figure I (c). Starting with the R foot, take sixteen waltz steps forward to proper places. As they reach their places (on the fourteenth waltz step) boys swing around their partners so that they stand at right side when facing the center of the square. . . . . 16 M.

(b) Pairs 5, 6, 7, 8 of the West and East sides enter at the same time. They hold hands as in (a). Starting with the R foot, take as many waltz steps forward as necessary to proper places. Upon reaching their places the boys swing their partners as in (a) and take proper distances by waltzing sideward R and L. . . . . 16 M.

(c) Pairs 1, 2, 3, 4 of the South side enter on the ninth measure of the music on the repetition (last eight measures) while the West and East sides are going to their places. Join hands as above. Starting with the R foot, take eight waltz steps forward to proper places.

EXIT

Music A. Play as many times as necessary.

Boys place their partners at their right sides. With Pairs 2 and 3 of the South Side leading, all execute waltz steps forward to exit, starting with the R foot, and joining inside hands as above. The square is divided into two halves. See diagram.

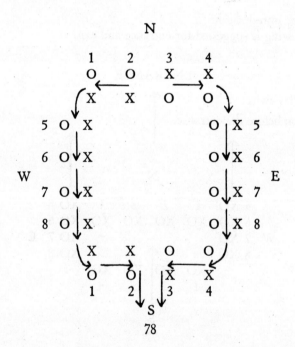

Barangay

F. SANTIAGO

TINIKLING, Figure VII

(see page 346)

81

Baruray

This is a simple and interesting dance from the province of Mindoro. It is made up of two movements. The first is in a lively 2/4 time. The second is a moderate 3/4 rhythm.

COSTUME. Girls are dressed in "balintawak"; boys in "barong tagalog" and long trousers, white or colored.

MUSIC is divided into four parts: A, B, C, and D.

COUNT *one, two* to a measure of 2/4 time and *one, two, three* to a measure of 3/4 time.

FORMATION. Partners stand opposite each other about eight feet apart. Girls stand at boys' right when facing audience. From one to any number of pairs may take part.

AUDIENCE

X	O
X	O
X	O

I

Music A.

(a) Starting with the right foot, take four steps forward, arms swinging loosely at the sides (cts. 1, 2, 3, 4). Partners stand side by side at the end of the fourth step. . . . . 2 M.

(b) Point R foot in front (ct. 1) close to L (ct. 2). Arms in fourth position, L arm up. "Kumintang" R hand clockwise and L counterclockwise (2 cts.). . . . . 1 M.

(c) Repeat (b) once more. . . . . 1 M.

(d) Put the weight on the R foot and take four steps backward, starting with the L foot. Arms as in (a). . . . . 2 M.

(e) Repeat (b) and (c) pointing with the L foot. Reverse the position of the arms. . . . . 2 M.

(f) Repeat all (a, b, c, d). . . . . 6 M.

Music Saludo.

Three step-turns right in place and bow to the partner, girls holding skirts, boys' hands on waists. 2 M.

II

Music B.

Dancers face left.

(a) Step R foot sideward (ct. 1), slide the left foot across the R in rear (ct. 2), bend the knees slightly (ct. 3). Girls holding skirts, boys' hands on waist. . . . . 1 M.

(b) Repeat (a) seven times more moving counterclockwise. Finish in proper places facing partners. . . . . 7 M.

Dancers face right.

(c) Repeat (a) and (b), starting with the L foot, moving clockwise. . . . . 8 M.

(d) Repeat all (a, b, c) finishing at proper places. . . . . 16 M.

Music Saludo.

Three step-turn right in place and bow to partners. . . . . 2 M.

III

Music C.

Partners face each other.

(a) Step R foot sideward (ct. 1), brush L forward (ct. 2), step L close to R (ct. 3). R arm up, L arm bent forward in front with the elbow at shoulder level. . . . . 1 M.

(b) Repeat (a) six times more going to the right, arm positions as above. . . . . 6 M.

(c) Step R foot sideward (cts. 1, 2) close L to R (ct. 3). . . . . . . 1 M.

(d) Repeat the same, starting with the L foot, going back to places. The arms are in the reverse positions. . . . . 8 M.

IV

Music D.

(a) Starting with the R foot, partners take eight waltz steps clockwise. Arms in lateral position at shoulder level moving sideward R and L. . . . . 8 M.

(b) Repeat the same movements moving counterclockwise. . . 8 M.

V

Music C.

Dancers face left.

(a) Repeat figure III going to the opposite place (to partner's place). Partners pass each other front to front. . . . . 8 M.

(b) Repeat (a) going to proper places, starting with the L foot. The arms are in the reverse positions. . . . . 8 M.

VI

Music D.

(a) Leap with R to sideward right and cross L in front of R foot at the same time (ct. 1), raise R foot in rear (ct. 2), step R in rear of L (ct. 3). Girls holding skirts, boys' hands on waist. ...... 1 M.

(b) Leap with L to sideward left and cross R in front of L foot at the same time (ct. 1), raise L in rear (ct. 2), step L in rear of R (ct. 3). Hands as above. .... 1 M.

(c) Repeat six times (a) and (b) alternately. .... 6 M.

(d) Starting with the R foot, take eight waltz steps clockwise. Boys follow closely behind their partners. Arms in lateral position at shoulder level moving sideward R and L. .... 8 M.

Finish with a bow, partners holding inside hands.

Baruray

Mindoro

Notation by
A. Buenaventura

84

85

Bayuhan

(Pounding Rice)

"Bayuhan" (pounding rice) comes after the harvest. This occupational dance is still performed in places where there are no rice mills. "Bayuhan" is usually celebrated with a social gathering. Young men and women are invited to participate on this occasion. The young men do the pounding of the rice and the young women the winnowing. The dance is performed to the accompaniment of guitars, songs, or rhythmical sounds produced by striking two sticks together.

COSTUME. The participants are dressed as workers in the fields with colored trousers and "barong tagalog" of cheap materials. The sleeves and the trouser legs are rolled up.

MUSIC is divided into two parts: A and B.

COUNT *one, two* to a measure.

FORMATION. The mortar is centrally placed. Four boys stand around it, numbering from one to four consecutively. Any number of mortars may be used. If more mortars than one are used, they may be arranged in a line or in a semicircle. Each boy is provided with a wooden pestle. "Palay" grains are placed in the mortar.

Equipment used:

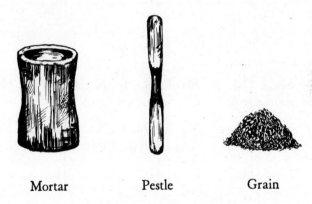

Mortar   Pestle   Grain

INTRODUCTION

Music Introduction.

The pestle is held at the lower end with the right hand, and carried over the R shoulder.

(a) Starting with the R foot, dancers walk gaily once around the mortar clockwise. . . . . 4 M.

Music A.

All face the mortar and hold the pestle at the smallest part (middle part) with the right hand. They pound one after the other as indicated below:

(a) No. 1 pounds with the pestle on ct. 1, and lifts it on ct. 2...   1 м.

     No. 2 repeats the movements of No. 1. ....   1 м.

     No. 3 repeats the same. ....   1 м.

     No. 4 repeats the same. ....   1 м.

(b) Nos. 1, 2, 3 and 4 repeat (a). ....   4 м.

(c) No. 1 pounds on ct. 1, lifts up on ct. 2 and simultaneously No. 2 pounds on the same count (ct. 2). ....   1 м.

No. 2 lifts up and simultaneously No. 3 pounds on ct. 1. No. 3 lifts up and simultaneously No. 4 pounds on ct. 2. ....   1 м.

(d) No. 4 lifts up. Repeat (c) three times more. ....   6 м.

(a) 8 м. 2/4 RHYTHM.

No. 1	No. 1	No. 2	No. 2	No. 3	No. 3	No. 4	No. 4
POUNDS	LIFTS	POUNDS	LIFTS	POUNDS	LIFTS	POUNDS	LIFTS
1	2	1	2	1	2	1	2

(c) 8 м. 2/4 RHYTHM.

No. 1	No. 2	No. 3	No. 4	No. 1	No. 2	No. 3	No. 4
POUNDS	POUNDS	POUNDS	POUNDS	POUNDS	POUNDS	POUNDS	POUNDS
	No. 1	No. 2	No. 3	No. 4	No. 1	No. 2	No. 3
	LIFTS	LIFTS	LIFTS	LIFTS	LIFTS	LIFTS	LIFTS
1	2	1	2	1	2	1	2

Music A.

(a) No. 1 pounds on ct. 1, lifts up and simultaneously No. 2 stirs the pounded "palay" on cts. 2, 1, 2. ....   2 м.

(b) No. 3 pounds and No. 4 stirs the "palay" as in (a). ......   2 м.

(c) Repeat (a) and (b) three times more. ....   12 м.

4 M. OF 2/4 RHYTHM.

(a)   (b)

No. 1   No. 3
POUNDS   POUNDS
LIFTS   LIFTS

        No. 2   No. 4
        STIRS   . . . .   STIRS   . . . .

1   2   1   2   1   2   1   2

III

Music B.

(a) No. 1 pounds with the R hand (ct. 1), transfers the pestle
to the L hand and pounds it (ct. 2). . . . .   1 M.
    No. 2 repeats the same movements in (a). . . . .   1 M.
    No. 3 repeats the same movements in (a). . . . .   1 M.
    No. 4 repeats the same movements in (a). . . . .   1 M.
(b) Repeat (a) three times more. . . . .   12 M.

4 M. OF 2/4 RHYTHM.

No. 1   No. 2   No. 3   No. 4
POUNDS   (SAME)   (SAME)   (SAME)

R—,   L—   R—,   L—   R—,   L—   R—,   L—

1   2   1   2   1   2   1   2

IV

Music B.

Hold the pestle with the R hand.

(a) No. 1 pounds on ct. 1, lifts the pestle up on ct. 2. . . . .   1 M.
    No. 2 pounds on ct. 1, and pounds again on ct. 2. . . . .   1 M.
(b) No. 3 repeats the movements of No. 1. . . . .   1 M.
    No. 4 repeats the movements of No. 2. . . . .   1 M.
(c) Repeat (a) and (b) three times more. . . . .   12 M.

4 M. OF 2/4 RHYTHM.

No. 1   No. 2   No. 3   No. 4
POUNDS   LIFTS   POUNDS   POUNDS   POUNDS   LIFTS   POUNDS   POUNDS

1   2   1   2   1   2   1   2

Music A.

(a) No. 1 pounds on ct. 1 and throws the pestle up into the air. Turns right about, catching it with the left hand (ct. 2). Transfers it to right hand while waiting for his turn to pound again..... 1 M.

No. 2 repeats the same movements. .... 1 M.

No. 3 repeats the same movements. .... 1 M.

No. 4 repeats the same movements. .... 1 M.

(b) All repeat the same movements three times more....... 12 M.

4 M. OF 2/4 RHYTHM.

No. 1		No. 2		No. 3		No. 4	
POUND	THROW	(SAME)		(SAME)		(SAME)	
•	TURN						•
•	CATCH						•
1	2	1	2	1	2	1	2

VI

Music A.

Repeat the same movements as in I (c) and (d)............ 16 M.

EXIT

Music B.

Carry the pestles over right shoulders and walk out gaily.

NOTE: If the Winnowing dance (PAGTATAHIP), is to be performed by the girls after this, the boys sit on the sidelines.

Bayuhan

NATIONAL
FOLK DANCE

Notation by
A. BUENAVENTURA

Bulakenya

This is a marital dance from Camarines Norte. The following wifely duties are rhythmically portrayed: placing the hat of the husband on his head before he goes out, wiping his forehead, combing and smoothing his hair, etc.

COSTUME. Girls may wear "patadiong" or "balintawak" and boys "barong tagalog" with white trousers. The pocket of his camisa must contain a comb and a handkerchief.

MUSIC is divided into two parts: A and B.

COUNT *one, two, three* to a measure.

FORMATION. One couple.

I

Music A.

Boy is seated on a chair in the middle of the room or stage, profile to audience.

Girl holds a "buri" hat in her right hand, left hand on waist. She starts from the right or left corner up stage going toward the boy by executing the following steps:

(a) Starting with the R foot, takes two close steps forward. Moves the hat sideward right and left. . . . . 2 M.

(b) Starting with the R foot, takes two waltz steps forward. Moves the hat as in (a). . . . . 2 M.

(c) Repeats (a) and (b) three times more and finishes about four feet in front of the boy. . . . . 12 M.

II

Music B.

The boy is still seated watching the movements of the girl.

Girl puts the hat on her head.

(a) Executes eight sway balance steps with a point, R and L alternately, starting with R arm in fifth position, L arm bent in front at shoulder level. Reverses the position of the arm every two measures. . . . . 16 M.

III

Music A.

The boy is still seated.

Girl takes off hat and holds it in her right hand.

(a) Takes one waltz step sideward R and one waltz step sideward L, arms in lateral position shoulder level moving sideward right and left. . . . . 2 M.

(b) Takes one waltz-turn right moving forward. Arms as in (a)... 2 M.

(c) Repeats (a) and (b) three times more moving around the chair counterclockwise. Finishes in front near chair and on the last measure puts hat on boy's head............................. 12 M.

IV

Music B.

The boy is still seated.

Girl goes through the motion of:

(a) Fixing the hat and fitting it nicely on the head of the boy. 4 M.

(b) Going away from and toward the boy to see if it is well placed... 4 M.

(c) Repeat (a) and (b)................................... 8 M.

Use waltz, close, or plain walking steps in (b).

V

Music A.

Boy takes off the hat and holds it in the right hand. Uses it for fanning as if feeling warm.

Girl takes the handkerchief from boy's pocket and dries his forehead and neck, going from right to left side of the chair........ 16 M.

All these motions should be done rhythmically.

VI

Music B.

(a) *Girl* takes a comb from the boy's pocket and goes through the motion of combing and parting his hair. She waltzes right to left of the chair. Once in a while she dances away to better view her work... 14 M.

Boy shows expression of satisfaction. He holds his head still while the girl combs his hair............................... 14 M.

(b) Boy stands up (last 2 M.) and puts on the hat. Girl sits down on the chair....................................... 2 M.

VII

Music A.

(a) *Girl* looks at the boy while he is dancing.

Boy repeats the steps of the girl in figure III, omitting the last waltz-turn.. 14 M.

(b) Girl stands up at the last two measures. Boy takes two waltz steps forward (R, L), finishing about four feet in front of the girl.. 2 M.

94

VIII

Music B.

Partners take eight sway-balance steps with a point, R and L alternately, moving little by little counterclockwise. Arms in fourth position, R and L arm high alternately.......................... 16 м.

IX

Music B. Play once more at a faster tempo.

Execute waltz, chasing each other, girl leading. Finish bowing to audience. Boy takes off hat while bowing.................... 8 м.

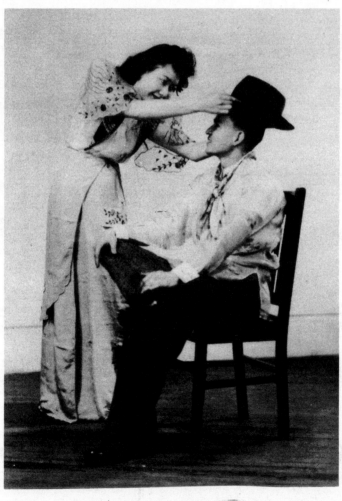

BULAKENYA, Figure IV (a)

95

Bulakenya

CAMARINES
NORTE

Notation by
A. BUENAVENTURA

Play 4 times

Bulaklakan

During the month of May it is the custom in many parts of the Philippines to celebrate the "Santa Cruz de Mayo," a procession, usually followed by a social gathering in the house of the "Hermana Mayor."

In some places, the celebration takes the form of folk dances held in front of a provisional altar built by the "Hermana Mayor." "Bulaklakan," a lovely and attractive dance, is appropriate for this occasion.

The girls in this dance each hold a garland of leaves and flowers attached to a wire, bamboo, or rattan so that the garlands will arch when held overhead.

MUSIC is divided into four parts: A, B, C, and D.

COUNT *one, two, three* to a measure.

FORMATION: Girls of Group A stand at the right side and those of Group B at the left side of their partners. From eight to twenty-four pairs may take part. They are divided into two groups (A, B). (See diagram 1.)

AUDIENCE

1	X	O		O	X	1
2	X	O		O	X	2
1	X	O	← 8-10 →	O	X	1
2	X	O	ft.	O	X	2
1	X	O		O	X	1
2	X	O	□	O	X	2
1	X	O	Center	O	X	1
2	X	O		O	X	2

A   Diagram 1   B

ENTRANCE

Music—Any part.

Starting with the R foot, waltz forward to proper places. Girls hold the garlands with two hands overhead swaying them sideward R and L. Boys place hands on the waists................. 16 M.

INTRODUCTION

Music Introduction.

All face the audience.

Girls hold the garlands overhead, boys stand still in place...... 4 M.

97

Music A.

Boys of Group A face right and those of Group B face left (face partners).

(a) *Girls* all face the audience holding their garlands over-head. One waltz step sideward R and L. Sway the garland side-ward right (cts. 1, 2, 3) and left (cts. 1, 2, 3)................. 2 м.

(b) Turn right about and repeat (a)...................... 2 м.

(c) Turn right about and repeat (a) and (b) three times more.. 12 м.

Boys

(a) Waltz forward R and backward L sixteen times. Hands on waist... 16 м.

Music A.

Girls face each other.

(a) *No. 1's*—Waltz backward L and forward R. Sway the garlands downward (cts. 1, 2, 3) and upward (cts. 1, 2, 3)...... 2 м.

(b) Repeat (a) seven times more......................... 14 м.

No. 2's

(a) Waltz forward R and backward L. Sway the garlands upward (cts. 1, 2, 3), and downward (cts. 1, 2, 3)............... 2 м.

(b) Repeat (a) seven times more......................... 14 м.

Boys

Waltz sideward R and L. Clap hands on the second and third beats of each measure....................................... 16 м.

Music B.

Girls

(a) *No. 1's*—Stand in place, point R foot in front for four measures. Sway the garlands sideward R and L overhead four times... 4 м.

(b) Four waltz steps forward R and backward L alternately. Sway the garlands four times upward and downward............ 4 м.

No. 2's

(a) Starting with the R foot, take eight waltz steps for-ward to opposite places. On the eighth waltz step, turn right about. Hold the garland overhead and sway it sideward R and L....... 8 м.

(b) *No. 1's.* Repeat the movements of No. 2's in (a)........ 8 м.

No. 2's. Repeat the movements of No. 1's in (a)........ 8 м.

(c) Repeat all (a and b) finishing in proper places.......... 16 м.

Boys

Take sixteen sway-balance steps with a point, R and L. Arms
in fourth position, R and L arms high alternately.............. 32 M.

IV

Music C.

Girls

(a) *No. 1's.* Starting with the R foot, take eight waltz steps
forward to the center, forming a circle. Hold the garlands overhead and sway them sideward R and L. Regulate the steps so
that at the eighth waltz step all are at the center. (See diagram 2.) 8 M.

No. 2's—Take eight waltz steps sideward R and L. Sway
garlands like No. 1's... 8 M.

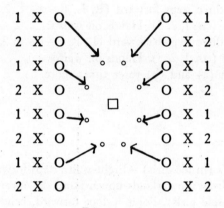

Diagram 2

(b) *No. 1's*—Eight waltz steps forward R and backward L
alternately. Sway the garlands upward and downward.......... 8 M.

No. 2's—Starting with the R foot, take eight waltz steps forward to the center. On the eighth step, turn right about and
stand back to back with No. 1's. Sway the garlands as in (a).
(See diagram 3.)... 8 M.

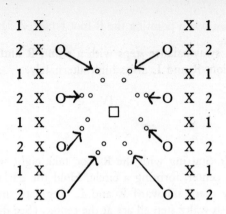

Diagram 3

Boys

(a) Take three steps forward (R, L, R—cts. 1, 2, 3), point L foot in front (cts. 1, 2, 3). Hands on waists.................... 2 M.

(b) Take three steps backward (L, R, L—cts. 1, 2, 3), point R foot in front (cts. 1, 2, 3). Hands on waists................... 2 M.

(c) Repeat (a) and (b) three times more.................. 12 M.

V

Music D.

Girls

(a) *No. 1's* (inside girls).—Eight waltz steps forward R and backward L. Sway the garlands upward and downward......... 8 M.

No. 2's (outside girls). Point R foot forward, bend the body forward. Hold the garlands down in front and sway them sideward R and L eight times........................... 8 M.

(b) No. 1's and 2's turn right about so that No. 1's face outside and No. 2's face inside the circle (girls face each other).

No. 1's. (1) Hold the garlands overhead. Take three steps forward (R, L, R, cts. 1, 2, 3), point L foot in front (cts. 1, 2, 3). Put garlands down when pointing the L foot.................... 2 M.

(2) Hold the garlands down. Take three steps backward (L, R, L—cts. 1, 2, 3), point R foot in front (cts. 1, 2, 3). Raise the garlands overhead when pointing the R foot.............. 2 M.

No. 2's. (1) Hold the garlands down. Take three steps forward, passing by right shoulder of No. 1 girl (R, L, R—cts. 1, 2, 3), point L in front (cts. 1, 2, 3). Raise the garlands overhead when pointing the L foot............................. 2 M.

(2) Hold the garlands overhead. Take three steps backward (L, R, L—cts. 1, 2, 3), point R foot in front (cts. 1, 2, 3). Bring

the garlands down when pointing the R foot (cts. 1, 2, 3). Pass by each other's right shoulder. . . . .   2 M.

(c) No. 1's and 2's repeat (b). . . . .   4 M.

Boys. Starting with the R foot, waltz forward to the center forming a big circle around the girls. On reaching places, clap hands in time to the music (Figure II) and execute waltz steps sideward R and L. . . . .   16 M.

VI

Music A.

Girls

(a) *No. 2's* (outside circle). Face left. Starting with the right foot, take eight waltz steps forward, going clockwise. Hold the garlands overhead swaying them sideward R and L. . . . .   8 M.

(b) Turn right about. Repeat (a) counterclockwise. . . . .   8 M.

No. 1's (inside circle). Turn right about to face inward. Waltz forward R and backward L. Sway the garlands upward and downward. . . . .   16 M.

Boys

Continue clapping hands and waltzing sideward R and L. . . . .   16 M.

(c) *Girls* exchange places.

No. 1's go outside and No. 2's go inside the circle passing by right shoulders.

No. 1's repeat the same movements as No. 2's (a and b) and vice-versa. . . . .   16 M.

Boys—Starting with the right foot, take waltz steps backward, hands on waists. On reaching proper places waltz sideward R and L. . . . .   16 M.

FINALE

Music Finale.

No. 2's (inside circle). Stand side by side forming a circle. Hold the garlands overhead in such a way that each girl touches the hands of her neighbor (L and R).

No. 1's (outside circle). Bend body forward and point R foot in front. Hold the garlands down.

Boys—Bow to each other on the last two measures. . . . .   5 M.

NOTE: The dance may end in this position or the dancers may go out. With the front couples as leaders, cast off (turn around outward) and waltz to exit. Hold the garlands as in the entrance. Use any part of the music.

Bulaklakan

TAGALOG

Music by
T. LAMUG

KAKAWATI, Figure I (b)

(see page 139)

Chotis

This ballroom dance was as popular as the "waltz," ballroom polka, polka-mazurka, or mazurka during the Spanish regime. It could be danced as an ordinary ballroom dance. It may be used in demonstrations using different formations, i.e., quadrille, long formation, or sets of four pairs.

COSTUME. Dancers are dressed in any old-style costume.

MUSIC is divided into three parts: A, B, and C.

COUNT one, two, three, four to a measure.

FORMATION. Partners hold as in ordinary ballroom dancing position. Any number may take part in this dance.

I

Music A.

(a) Partners execute sixteen native chotis steps in any direction. The girl starts with the R and the boy with the L foot. ...... 16 M.

II

Music B.

Partners release hold. Girl holds her skirt and boy places hands on waist.

(a) Take three galop steps sideward right (cts. 1, 2, 3), pause (ct. 4). .... 1 M.

(b) Repeat (a) to the left to former places. .... 1 M.

(c) Hold as in ballroom dancing position. Starting with the R foot, take three step-hop steps turning around clockwise in place (cts. 1–6), pause and release hold (cts. 7–8). .... 2 M.

(d) Repeat all (a, b, and c) three times more. .... 12 M.

III

Music A.

Repeat figure I. .... 16 M.

IV

Music C.

(a) Starting with the R foot, execute sixteen step-hop steps turning clockwise, going in any direction. .... 16 M.

NOTE: Repeat the dance as many times as desired.

Chotis

CAMARINES SUR

CIV

Finale

108

Esperanza

This is a lively dance from Camarines Sur. It was supposedly named after a lovely maiden called Esperanza. The steps of this dance are simple but interesting.

COSTUME. The girl wears "balintawak" or "patadiong" and the boy "barong tagalog" with white trousers.

MUSIC is divided into two parts: A and B.

COUNT *one, two* or *one, and two* to a measure.

FORMATION. Partners stand side by side about three feet from each other, facing the audience. The girl stands at partner's right. Any number of couples may take part.

INTRODUCTION

Music: Finale.

Take a three-step turn right in place and bow to the audience. Girl holds her skirt and boy opens his hands in second position when bowing. .... 2 M.

.I

Music A.

(a) Starting with the R foot, take three steps forward (cts. 1, 2, 1), tap L close to R in first position (ct. 2) arms hanging loosely at the sides, swinging gracefully forward and back. .... 2 M.

(b) Starting with the L foot, take three steps backward to proper places (cts. 1, 2, 1), tap R close to L in first position (ct. 2). Arms as in (a). .... 2 M.

(c) Repeat (a) and (b) three times more. .... 12 M.

II

Music B.

(a) Dancers face right. With the L foot leading, execute mincing step sideward left (toward the audience). Take four tiny steps for each measure. Left arm is in reverse "T" position doing the "kumintang" at every measure, right hand on waist. .... 12 M.

(b) With the R foot leading, take seven galop steps sideward right going to proper places. Pause on the last count. Girl holds her skirt and boy places hands on waist. (Take two galops for every measure.) .... 4 M.

(c) Turn right about and repeat all. This time with the R foot leading in (a) and the L in (b). Reverse the arm positions in (a). Finish facing the audience. .... 16 M.

Music A.

    Repeat figure I. .... 16 м.

IV

Music B.

    (a) Starting with the R foot, take twelve small change steps forward. Arms in lateral position moving sideward right and left. 12 м.

    (b) Face right and galop to places as in Figure II(b). Finish facing the audience. .... 4 м.

    (c) Repeat (a). .... 12 м.

    (d) Face left and repeat (b). .... 4 м.

V

Music A.

    Repeat Figure I. .... 16 м.

VI

Music B.

    Partners face each other.

    (a) Girl hops on L and boy on R foot twenty-four times, going little by little toward the audience. The knee of the other leg is raised in front and the foot swings sideward right and left for the girl and left and right for the boy. Girl holds her skirt and the boy places hands on waist. *Take one hop* for every count. .... 12 м.

    (b) Galop sideward to places as in Figure II(b). .... 4 м.

    (c) Partners turn right about to face away from each other. Repeat all, hopping on the other foot in (a). .... 16 м.

VII

Music A.

    Repeat Figure I. .... 16 м.

VIII

Music B.

    Partners join hands in crossed position with the right hands over the left.

    (b) Repeat (a) and (b) twice with hands always joined and using only one foot for hopping. .... 32 м.

IX

Music A.

Repeat Figure I. .... 16 M.

FINALE

Music Finale.

Take a three-step turn right in place and bow to audience. Girl holds her skirt. Boy's hands in second position. .... 2 M.

MARIA CLARA COSTUME AND BARONG TAGALOG

Esperanza

CAMARINES SUR

112

Garambal

The name of this dance came from two Spanish words, "gran" and "valse" (which means "grand waltz"), corrupted into one word, "garambal." This dance came from Camiling, Tarlac. It is performed by two girls and one boy.

COSTUME. The girls are dressed in Ilocano costume, the boy in "barong tagalog" and black trousers. The girls have "buri" hats on.

MUSIC is divided into two parts: A and B.

COUNT *one, two, three* to a measure.

FORMATION. The boy stands between the two girls who are about six feet from each other. All face the audience. (See diagram A.)

O   X   O

Diagram A

INTRODUCTION

Music Introduction.

(a) Take a three-step turn right in place. .... 2 M.

(b) Point the R foot across the L in rear and bend the knees slightly. "Kumintang" counterclockwise with the right hand, the boy places his left hand on waist, the girls hold their skirts with the left. Look at the right hand. .... 1 M.

(c) Step R foot sideward and point the L across the R in rear. Reverse the position of the hands and "kumintang" clockwise with the left hand. Look at the left hand. .... 1 M.

I

Music A. Play slowly.

(a) Starting with the R foot, take three close steps forward. Girls holding their skirts and boy's hands on waist. .... 3 M.
Pause. Girls look at the boy; the boy looks at both girls. .... 1 M.

(b) Take a three-step turn right in place. Girls hold their skirts and boy places hands on waist (cts. 1, 2, 3). Point the R across the L foot in rear, bend knees slightly and "kumintang" with the right hand counterclockwise. The left hand of the boy is on waist and the girls' left hands are holding skirts (cts. 1, 2, 3)... 2 M.

(c) Repeat (b) turning to the left. Reverse the hand positions. 2 M.

(d) Repeat (a). .... 4 M.

(e) Girls take off hats with the right hand. Starting with the

113

GARAMBAL, Figure II (b)

R foot, all take six steps backward to proper places. Take one step
for every count. . . . . 2 M.

(f) Close the R foot together with the L in first position and
bow to audience. . . . . 1 M.

(g) Girls put on hats again. . . . . 1 M.

(h) Repeat all (a, b, c, d, e, f). . . . . 15 M.

(i) The boy steps forward in front of the girls with his back
toward the audience. The girls face each other holding their hats.
(See diagram B.) . . . . 1 M.

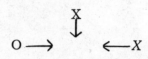

Diagram B

II

Music B.

Boy's Part:

(a) Take three sway-balance steps, R and L, arms in. fourth
position, R arm high. . . . . 6 M.

(b) Pause with the L foot pointing in front and arms in
fourth position, R arm high. . . . . 2 M.

(c) Repeat (a), starting with the L foot. Reverse the arm
positions. . . . . 6 M.

(d) Take three steps forward to proper place. . . . . 2 M.

Girls' Part:

(a) Point the R across the L foot in rear and bend the knees
slightly. Holding the hats with both hands (the right hand holding the top, the left the brim of the hat), sway the hat gracefully
to sideward R and L (taking two measures for each side). . . . . 8 M.

(b) Face the audience and repeat (a). (See illustration.) . . . . 8 M.

III

Music C. Play a little faster.

The boy faces the girl on his right side. Girls put on hats and
face each other.

Girls' Part:

(a) Girls execute sixteen sway-balance steps with a point,
R and L. Arms in fourth position, R and L arm high alternately. 32 M.

GARAMBAL, FIGURE III

116

Boy's Part:

(a) Two sway-balance steps with a point (R and L). Arms in fourth position, as in (a). . . . . 4 M.

(b) Turn right about pivoting on the R foot to face the girl at his right. Repeat (a). . . . . 4 M.

(c) Repeat (b) six times more facing the girl on his left and right side alternately. He dances in an opposite direction to the girl he faces. (See illustration.) . . . . 24 M.

Note: He smiles at the girls. The girls smile when he is facing them and frown when his back is turned.

Saludo: The girls take off hats and all bow to the audience. . . . . 2 M.

MORO COSTUMES

117

Garambal

Habanera

This is a beautiful Ilocano dance from Magsingal, Ilocos Sur, having hand movements ("kumintang"), which are especially characteristic. The dance depicts the modest and retiring traits of the Ilocano women.

COSTUME. Dancers are dressed in Ilocano peasant costume. (See illustration, p. x.)

MUSIC is divided into four parts: A, B, C and D.

COUNT *one, and, two* or *one, two* to a measure.

FORMATION. Partners stand opposite each other about six feet apart. Girl stands at partner's right when facing the audience. From one to any number of pairs may take part in this dance.

I

Music A.

   (a) Starting with the R foot, take four change steps forward to opposite place passing by right shoulders. Right hand in reverse "T" position doing a "kumintang," left hand on waist when executing the change step with the right foot, reversing the position of the hands on the left foot. . . . .   4 M.

   (b) Face left and take two change steps forward (R, L), hands as in (a). . . . . : . . . .   2 M.

   (c) Face right about and take one change step forward with the right foot. Hands as in (a). . . . .   1 M.

   (d) Face partner and step L foot sideward (ct. 1), point R in rear of L foot and bend knees slightly. "Kumintang" with the right hand and place the left hand on waist (ct. 2). . . . .   1 M.

   (e) Repeat all (a, b, c, and d), finishing in proper places. . . . .   8 M.

II

Music B.

  Exchange place with partner by executing the following steps and passing by right shoulders.

   (a) Starting with the R foot, execute a change-step turn right moving forward. . . . .   2 M.

   (b) Take two change steps forward (R, L). . . . .   2 M.

   (c) Repeat (a). . . . .   2 M.

   (d) Take one change step forward right. . . . .   1 M.

   (e) Face right about to face partner and repeat (d) of Figure I. . . . .   1 M.

   (f) Repeat all (a, b, c, d, and e), finishing in proper places. . .   8 M.

  Throughout this figure execute the same hand movements as in Figure I(a).

120

Music C.

(a) Face right. Take one change step forward right (cts. 1, 2). Point L foot in fourth in front (cts. 1, 2). Girl holding skirt, boy's hands on waist. . . . . 2 M.

(b) Face left about and repeat (a) starting with the L foot. Hands as in (a). . . . . 2 M.

(c) Repeat all (a and b) three times more. Move forward little by little and finish about three feet away from and facing partner. Hands as in (a). . . . . 12 M.

IV

Music D.

(a) Take one change step obliquely forward right to center (cts. 1, 2). Girl holding skirt and boy's hands on waist. . . . . 1 M.

(b) Stamp L foot and clap hands (ct. 1), pause (ct. 2). By this time the partners are in one line standing by each other's left shoulder. . . . . 1 M.

(c) Take one change sideward left passing in front of each other. Hands as in (a). Partners are in one line standing by right shoulders. . . . . 1 M.

(d) Stamp with the R foot and clap hands as in (b). . . . . 1 M.

(e) Change places by taking one change step forward right passing by right shoulders. . . . . 1 M.

(f) Face partner, stamp L foot, and clap hands. Put weight on the L foot. Partners are close to each other. . . . . 1 M.

(g) Turn right about and take one change step forward right to partner's place. . . . . 1 M.

(h) Turn right about to face partner and repeat Figure I(d). 1 M.

(i) Repeat all (a, b, c, d, e, f, g and h), finishing in proper places. . . . . 8 M.

V

Music C.

(a) Starting with the R foot, take seven change steps forward to partner's place passing by right shoulders. "Kumintang" right and left hands alternately as in Figure I(a). . . . . 7 M.

(b) Repeat Figure I(d). . . . . 1 M.

(c) Repeat all, finishing in proper places. . . . . 8 M.

VI

Music D.

(a) Starting with the R foot, take three running steps forward (cts. 1, and 2), girl holding skirt, boy's hands on waist. . . . . 2 M.

121

(b) Partners join right hands at eye level. The boy supports the right elbow of the girl with his left hand. They look at each other through the arch of the joined hands and the boy swings the right forearm of the girl sideward three times (left, right, left of the boy) (cts. 1, 2, 1), pause (ct. 2). The left arm of the girl is hanging loosely at her side. . . . .   2 M.

(c) Starting with the right foot, take three change steps forward to partner's place passing by right shoulders. Girl holding her skirt, boy's hands on waist. . . . .   3 M.

(d) Repeat Figure I(d). . . . .   1 M.

(e) Repeat all (a, b, c, and d), finishing in proper places. . . . .   8 M.

VII

Music C.

(a) Starting with the R foot, take three running steps forward to center (cts. 1, *and* 2), close L to R foot and pause (cts. 1, *and* 2). Girl holding skirt, boy's hands on waist. . . . .   2 M.

(b) Point R and L foot alternately in fourth in front four times; hands as in (a). . . . .   4 M.

(c) Repeat (a), moving backward to proper places. . . . .   2 M.

(d) Repeat all (a, b and c). . . . .   8 M.

VIII

Music D.

(a) Starting with the R foot, partners take three running steps forward to meet at center. Girl holding skirt, boy's hands on waist (cts. 1, *and* 2). Point L foot in fourth in front (cts. 1, *and* 2).

(b) Join right hands. Repeat (a) starting with the L foot going clockwise. . . . .   2 M.

(c) Drop right hands and join left hands. Repeat (b) in reverse direction, starting with the R foot. . . . .   2 M.

(d) Starting with the L foot, take two steps forward going to proper places. . . . .   1 M.

(e) Repeat Figure I(d). . . . .   1 M.

(f) Repeat all (a, b, c, d, and e) and finish with a deep curtsy. . . . .   8 M.

Habanera

Notation by
A. Buenaventura

Ilocos Sur

123

KANDINGAN, entrance (a)
(see page 146)
125

Inahaw

This is a dance from Malaybalay, Bukidnon. "Inahaw" or "anahaw" is a palm tree commonly used for decoration throughout the Philippines. The dancer holds one "anahaw" leaf in each hand. The leaves produce sounds in rhythm with the foot movements. This solo dance may be performed by either a boy or a girl. The dancer wears "singuel" (metal anklets) or bells tied at the ankles or below the knees. No instrument other than one of these, is needed.

COSTUME. Bukidnon costume. (See illustration.)

FORMATION. The dancer stands at the center and back part of the room facing the audience. Holds arms in reverse "T" position. (See illustration.)

I

Rhythm:

(a) Step L foot forward (ct. 1), tap R close to L foot (ct. and), heavy step on R forward (ct. 2).

Arm Movements:

Bend arms upward. Shake leaves once to the left side (ct. 1), and twice to the right side (cts. and, 2). .... 1 M.

  (b) Repeat (a) six times more. Hands as above. .... 6 M.

  (c) Step L forward (ct. 1), pause (ct. 2). .... 1 M.

  (d) Repeat all, starting with the R foot. .... 8 M.

II

Rhythm:

Going half-around clockwise, execute the following steps:

  (a) Step R forward (ct. 1), step L forward (ct. 2) one change step forward R (cts. 1, 2). .... 2 M.

  (b) Repeat (a) starting with the L foot, seven times more moving clockwise. .... 14 M.

Hand Movements:

  (a) Shake R leaf once forward (ct. 1), shake L leaf once forward (ct. 2). .... 1 M.

(b) Shake R leaf forward and immediately shake L leaf once forward (cts. 1, and), shake R leaf forward (ct. 2). .... 1 M.

(c) Repeat (a) and (b), starting with the L hand. .... 2 M.

(d) Repeat all (a, b, and c), three times more. .... 12 M.

III

Rhythm:

$$\frac{2}{4}$$ ♪‖:♫♩ | ♫♩ | ♫♩ | ♫♩ | ♫♩ | ♫♩ | ♫♩ | ♫♩:‖

Going sideward to the right, execute the following steps:

Step R sideward (one beat of broken measure).

(a) Raise L in front and cut R foot backward and immediately tap R close to L foot (cts. 1, and), step R sideward (ct. 2). .... 1 M.

(b) Repeat (a) seven times more. .... 7 M.

Step L sideward (one beat of broken measure). Going sideward left.

(c) Repeat all (a and b), starting with R foot. .... 8 M.

Arm Movements:

Hold arms in reverse "T" position and shake leaves three times to a measure (♫♩) following rhythm of the feet. .... 16 M.

IV

Rhythm:

$$\frac{2}{4}$$ ‖:♫♩ | ♫♩ | ♩♩ | ♫♩ | ♫♩ | ♩♩:‖ *Repeat 4 times*

Going around clockwise, execute the following steps:

(a) Take two change steps forward (R, L—cts. 1, and, 2, 1, and, 2). .... 2 M.

(b) Step R forward (ct. 1), step L forward (ct. 2). .... 1 M.

(c) Repeat all (a and b) seven times more. .... 21 M.

Arm Movements:

(a) Bend arms upward. Shake the leaves three times to a measure (R, L, R hands— ♫♩) .... 1 M.

(b) Repeat (a) with L, R, L hands. .... 1 M.

127

(c) Shake R leaf once (ct. 1) and L leaf once (ct. 2). .... 1 M.
(d) Repeat all (a, b, and c), seven times more. .... 21 M.

V

Rhythm:

$$\frac{2}{4} \ \|: \quad \text{♩.♫ ♫♩ | ♩.♫ ♫♩ | ♩.♫ ♫♩ | ♩.♫ ♫♩ :\|} \quad \textit{Repeat 4 times}$$

Going to sideward right execute the following steps:
(a) Place the feet with R foot in fifth position in front.
Execute mincing steps with R foot leading, following the
rhythm. .... 8 M.
(b) Reverse the feet positions. Execute mincing steps going to
sideward left. .... 8 M.

Arm Movements:
(a) With arms down at the sides, move them gradually side-
ward-upward, shaking the leaves jerkily in the same rhythm with
the feet movements. .... 8 M.
(b) Move the arms gradually to sideward-downward and
shake the leaves in the same manner. .... 8 M.

VI

Rhythm:

$$\frac{2}{4} \ \|: \quad \text{♫♩̄ | ♫♩̄ | ♫♩̄ | ♫♩̄ :\|} \quad \textit{Repeat 4 times}$$

(a) Step L forward (ct. 1) and immediately tap R close to
L twice (cts. and, 2). .... 1 M.
(b) Repeat (a) starting with the R. .... 1 M.
(c) Repeat all (a and b) seven times more. .... 14 M.

Arm Movements:
Arms bent upward as in Figure I.
(a) Shake the leaves once to the left side (ct. 1), shake them
twice to the left side (cts. and, 2). .... 1 M.
(b) Shake the leaves once to the right side (ct. 1), shake them
twice to the right side (cts. and, 2). .... 1 M.
(c) Repeat all (a and b) seven times more. .... 14 M.

128

Rhythm:

$\frac{2}{4}$ ‖: ♩ ♫ | ♩ ♫ | ♩ ♫ | ♩ ♫ :‖ *Repeat 4 times*

(a) Step R forward (ct. 1), step L backward close to R foot and immediately slide on the L foot backward (like a "buck" step in tap dancing) (ct. and, 2). . . . . 1 M.

(b) Repeat (a) seven times more going around clockwise in place. . . . . 7 M.

(c) Repeat all, going counterclockwise. 8 M.

Arm Movements:

Place the leaves behind the neck and shake them in the same rhythm as the feet. . . . . 16 M.

Finale:

Swiftly bend the body forward flinging the hands downward—backward.

INAHAW

Inkoy-Inkoy

This dance is popular in the Visayan and Bicol regions. "Inkoy," in the Visayan Islands, is the pet name for Francisco. Adults often start the dance with a ballroom waltz, using music A. The dance is easy and can be performed by unskilled groups. The dance described below comes from Albay.

COSTUME. Girls wear "patadiong," camisa, and a soft neckerchief hanging over one shoulder. Boys wear "barong tagalog" with white or colored trousers.

MUSIC *one, two, three* to a measure.

FORMATION. Younger partners stand in front of each other, with both hands joined, arms stretched sideward. (Adults hold as in ordinary ballroom dance position.) From one to any number of pairs may take part in this dance.

I

Music A.

    (a) The girl takes two close steps sideward right and two sideward left. The boy follows, starting with the L foot, two left and two right. . . . . 4 M.

    (b) Partners waltz in place or in any direction. The girl starts with the R and the boy with the L foot. . . . . 4 M.

    (c) Repeat (a) and (b), two times. . . . . 16 M.

    (d) Repeat (a). . . . . 4 M.

    (e) Take two waltz steps in place (or around). . . . . 2 M.

    (f) Partners separate about four feet by executing a three-step turn or a waltz-turn (right for the girl and left for the boy). 2 M.

II

Music B.

    Partners face each other.

    (a) Take three "engaño" steps with a close, R and L alternately. Right arm in reverse "T" position and L bent in front at shoulder level when doing the step to the right. Reverse the arm positions to the left. . . . . 6 M.

    (b) Take a three-step turn left. Girl holds her skirt, boy places hands on waist. . . . . 2 M.

    (c) Repeat (a) and (b) starting with the L foot and L arm in reverse "T." Make the turn to the right in (b). . . . . 8 M.

    (d) Repeat all (a, b, c). . . . . 16 M.

Music C.

Partners face left.

(a) Starting with the R foot, take eight waltz steps forward, moving clockwise. Arms in lateral position moving sideward right and left alternately. .... 8 M.

(b) Turn right about and repeat (a) moving counterclockwise. .... 8 M.

(c) Repeat (a). .... 8 M.

(d) Starting with the R foot, take four waltz steps moving in a small circle, clockwise. .... 4 M.

(e) Take two waltz steps forward (R, L), to meet at center. 2 M.

(f) Join inside hands and bow to the audience (if ending dance). Place the free hand on waist. .... 2 M.

NOTE: The whole dance may be repeated as many times as desired. If it is repeated, figure III (f) is not performed. Instead partners meet at center and assume the starting position of the dance.

KAKAWATI, Introduction (a)

(see page 139)

Inkoy-Inkoy

ALBAY

Jota Batangueña

The "Jota" dances are the Philippine's most popular national folk dances. We have Jota Zapatilla, Jota Aragonesa, La Jota Purpuri, La Jota, A la Jota, Jota Batangueña, Jota Rojana, and La Jota Surtido.

Like all the native Jotas, this dance has a Spanish influence. It comes from Batangas, the province of the "Sublis."

Costume. The girls are dressed in "balintawak" and the boys in "barong tagalog" with white trousers.

Music is divided into five parts: A, B, C, D and E.

Count *one, two, three* to a measure.

Formation: Partners stand opposite each other about eight feet apart. Girls and boys stand in sets of two pairs. (See diagram.) From one to any number of sets may take part in this dance.

```
     X              O

     O              X


     X              O

     O              X
```

INTRODUCTION

Music Introduction.

Partners execute a three-step turn right in place and bow to each other, girls holding skirts and boys' hands on waists. .... 2 M.

Repeat the same to the left. .... 2 M.

I

Music A.

(a) Raising the R foot in front, cut the L foot backward (ct. 1) and execute eight mincing steps sideward right (cts. 2-9). The feet are in the fifth position with the R foot in front, while doing the mincing steps. Stamp L close to R foot (ct. 10), pause (cts. 11, 12), girls holding skirts and boys' hands on waists. ...... 4 M.

(b) Repeat the same with L foot cutting R backward and going sideward left. .... 4 M.

(c) Repeat all (a and b). .... 8 M.

Repeat the same to the left. .... 2 M.

134

II

Music B.

   (a) Take eight sway-balance steps with a point, R and L. Arms in fourth position, R and L arms high alternately. . . . . 16 м.

III

Music C.

   (a) Partners take three running steps forward to meet at the center (R, L, R—cts. 1, 2, 3). (See diagram below.) Close L to R foot (ct. 1), pause (cts. 2, 3). Girls hold skirts and boys place hands on waists. . . . . 2 м.

   (b) Point R foot in intermediate in front (cts. 1, 2), point the same foot close to L (ct. 3). Arms in fourth position, L arm high, "kumintang" the hands clockwise. . . . . 1 м.
   (c) Repeat (b) three times more. . . . . 3 м.
   (d) Repeat (a) going backward to places. . . . . 2 м.

IV

Music D.

   (a) With R foot in front, cut L backward (ct. 1). Execute a four-step turn left in place (cts. 2–5), pause (ct. 6). . . . . 2 м.
   (b) Repeat the same three times more turning to right, left, right. Cut R foot when turning right. . . . . 2 м.
   (c) Repeat all (a and b). . . . . ∴. 8 м.

V

Music E.

   (a) In sets of two pairs, repeat figure III going obliquely forward to the center in (a) and obliquely backward in (d). (See diagram below.) . . . . 8 м.

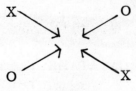

(b) Turn right about, facing outside the square. Repeat figure III going outward in (a). (See diagram below.)

FINALE

Music Finale.

All face the audience.

Starting with the inside foot, execute a three-step turn inward. Dancers finish in a single line formation, the boys standing behind their partners (2 м.). Join R hands down and L hands up in fifth position. Point R foot in intermediate in front. Girls look at their partners over right shoulders (1 м.). .... 3 м.

Note: If the dance is to be performed twice, the finale is omitted the first time through.

PAGATATAHIP, Figure II (a)
(see page 193)

Jota Batangueña

Kakawati

"Kakawati," "marikakao," or "madre de cacao" is a tree growing in the Philippines. Its flowers are a mixture of lavender, purple, pale pink, and yellow colors. When the tree is in blossom the leaves fall off leaving only the beautiful and graceful clusters of flowers clinging to the branches.

To glorify the beauty of the "kakawati" in bloom, the University of the Philippines celebrated the first "Kakawati Festival" on February 25, 1939, at the University Campus, under the sponsorship of Secretary Jorge Bocobo, then the University's President.

The following dance was first shown at the "Kakawati Festival."

COSTUME. Dancers are dressed in "balintawak" style. Only girls perform this dance. They hold a twig of "kakawati" blossoms in each hand. The twig, about a foot in length, is held at the middle.

MUSIC is divided into three parts: A, B, and C.

COUNT *one, two, three* to a measure.

FORMATION. Partners stand opposite each other about eight feet apart. They are grouped in sets of three pairs. Any number of sets may take part in this dance.

INTRODUCTION

Music: Introduction.

Partners face the audience.

(a) Take one waltz step forward R and swing the arms upward (cts. 1, 2, 3), one waltz backward L and swing the arms downward (cts. 1, 2, 3). .... 2 M.

(b) Cross-step turn right, hands on waists (cts. 1, 2, 3). Pause (cts. 1, 2, 3). .... 2 M.

I

Music A.

Partners face the audience.

(a) Starting with the R foot, partners take three running steps sideward right (cts. 1, 2, 3), point L in front (cts. 1, 2, 3). Arms in fourth position, R arm high. .... 2 M.

(b) Sway the left hand from first to second position making a horizontal figure eight. Look at the left hand while doing the figure eight. .... 2 M.

(c) Repeat (a) and (b) three times more, L, R, L alternately. Reverse the arm positions with each change of direction. .... 12 M.

Partners face each other.

(d) Repeat all. .... 16 M.

139

Music B.

Partners face each other.

(a) Step R foot forward (ct. 1), brush L forward (ct. 2), hop on R forward (ct. 3). Right arm in fifth position and left hand on waist. Look at the right hand. .... 1 M.

(b) Waltz forward with the L foot (cts. 1, 2, 3). Partners are standing by each other's left shoulder in one line at the end of the waltz step. Arms as in (a). .... 1 M.

(c) Partners turn right so that one girl faces the audience and the other girl away from the audience. Take two slide steps to the right (to proper places). Arms as in (a), right hand doing a "kumintang" for every three counts. Finish facing partner. .... 2 M.

(d) Repeat (a, b, and c) starting with the L foot. Stand by each other's right shoulder in (b) and face left in (c). Reverse the arm positions. .... 4 M.

(e) Repeat all (a, b, c, and d) three times more. .... 24 M.

Music C.

Partners face each other.

Pointing from front to side.

(a) Point R foot in front (cts. 1, 2), point R close to L (ct. 3). Arms in fourth position left arm high, right hand doing a figure eight as in I (b). .... 1 M.

(b) Repeat pointing with the R foot three times at different angles as in the diagram below. Repeat the same hand movements as in (a). .... 3 M.

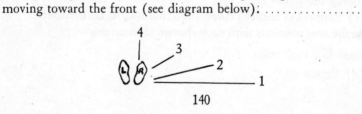

(c) Repeat (a) and (b) with the L foot. Reverse the arm positions. .... 4 M.

(d) Repeat all (a, b, and c). .... 8 M.

Pointing from side to front.

(e) Repeat all (a, b, c, d), this time pointing from R side moving toward the front (see diagram below): .... 16 M.

IV

Music A.

Partners face the audience.

(a) Take eight sway-balance steps with a hop, R and L alternately. Arms in fourth position, right and left arm high alternately. Look at the high hand always. . . . .   16 M.

(b) Face right.

Take four sway balance steps with a hop, R and L alternately. Arms as in (a). . . . .   8 M.

(c) Turn right about.

Repeat (b). . . . .   8 M.

V

Music B.

Partners face each other.

(a) Point R foot across the L in front. Cross hands down in front with the right hand over the left. Bend the trunk forward (cts. 1, 2, 3). . . . .   1 M.

(b) Trunk erect. Point R foot in second position, open the arms to second position (cts. 1, 2, 3). . . . .   1 M.

(c) Repeat (a) and (b). . . . .   2 M.

(d) Repeat (a, b, and c), starting with the L foot. Left hand over the right. . . . .   4 M.

(e) Take eight waltz steps forward right and backward left. Swing the arms upward and downward. . . . .   8 M.

(f) Repeat all (a, b, c, d). . . . .   16 M.

VI

Music C.

In sets of three or four pairs.

(a) Starting with the R foot, take sixteen waltz steps forward moving clockwise. Arms in fifth position, sideward right and left for four measures, bringing down the arms in lateral position to waist level moving sideward right and left for four measures. Do the same arm movements alternately (from fifth position to waist level). . . . .   16 M.

(b) Repeat (a) counterclockwise.

Arms as above. Finish bowing to the audience or to the partner.   16 M.

Kakawati

Music by
A. BUENAVENTURA

TAGALOG

144

Kandiñgan

This is a Moro wedding dance from Jolo, Sulu. Its figures are based on the old, traditional Moro dances.

Some of the old people say that the name of this dance is derived from the word "gandang" or "gandañgan." "Gandang" is an instrument similar to the drum, cylindrical in form and covered with goat's skin at both ends. It is played by tapping the two ends with the hands. "Gandañgan" is the act of playing on the "gandang."

When the natives from Sulu perform this dance, no definite number of steps, no sequence of figures, no lines of direction, no particular feet and arm movements are incorporated. The dance may be prolonged or shortened, depending upon the ability and mood of the individual dancer.

For purposes of teaching, a figure sequence and a definite number of steps are given here. These figures and steps, as danced by four Moro dancers, were arranged in the order described below.

The music was written by Lt. A. Buenaventura and is based on Moro folk melodies.

COSTUME. The dancers are dressed in typical Joloano costume and are barefoot. (See illustration.)

MUSIC is divided into two parts: A and B. It is played continuously until the dancers finish. The tempo increases on the last figure or when the performers are about to end the dance.

COUNT *one, two* to a measure.

FORMATION. Partners stand side by side facing the audience. They are about eight feet apart. The girl stands at the right side of the boy.

Audience

X   O

Steps Used.

I. Throughout the figure the knees are slightly bent and turned a little outward. Slide R foot forward with toes turned outward (ct. 1), step on the same foot (ct. 2). Do this step L and R alternately. It should be a smooth and easy movement, with no bobbing.

II. Shuffling steps with toes creeping forward little by little. Put as many steps as possible in one beat or measure.

III. Slide R toe in a semicircle across the L foot in front (ct. 1), lower the heel of the same foot and step on it (ct. 2). Continue this step with the L and R crossing each other. The dancer is moving forward with each step. (See diagram below.)

145

IV. With knees together and straight execute very fine parallel tortillier steps to sideward right. (See diagram.)

Start with toes pointed in front, feet flat on the floor. Turn toes to sideward right, pivoting on the heels; raise heels and turn them sideward right pivoting on the balls of the feet, and so on.

Execute this step either to sideward left or right. Put as many steps as possible in one count or measure.

ENTRANCE

Music Introduction.

(a) Starting with the R foot, execute running steps to place. Hands are held obliquely, backward-downward with palms outward, fingers together and stiff. The girl enters from the right and the boy from the left.

Place R foot across the L in front and bend the knees slightly. The right hand is held in front with the finger tips pointing towards the left and the palm facing front in level with the eyes. The elbow is flexed. The left hand is held obliquely backward-downward, elbow slightly flexed, fingers close together, held stiffly with the palm down. The finger tips point inward. This position is held at the last, long chord of the fourth measure of the introduction. (See illustration.) .... 4 M.

I

Music A.

(a) Do step I eight times, R and L alternately, clockwise. (See diagram (a).) With arms sideward at shoulder-level in a relaxed position, move the wrists up and down, hands waving up and down at every movement, the fingers curling in and stretching out. . . . . 8 м.

     (b) Turn right about and repeat (a) moving counterclockwise. . . . . 8 м.

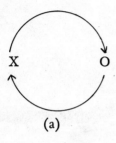

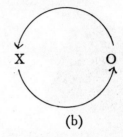

              (a)   (b)

II

Music B.

     Dancers face the audience.

     (a) Starting with the R foot, execute step I eight times moving forward.

Arm Movements.

Hold the right hand in front at the level of the eyes, the left hand down and back, fingers stiff and close together (except the thumb). Turn the right hand counterclockwise (from the wrist only) and the left clockwise.

Take two counts for each turn of the hand.

Reverse the arm positions on every two counts. There must be a flowing movement of the arms as they change from one position to the other. . . . . 8 м.

     (b) Turn right about and repeat (a) going back to proper places. . . . . 8 м.

III

Music A.

Girl's Part.

     (a) Stand with R foot in third position in front. With knees slightly bent turn around right, taking tiny steps in place, both feet flat on floor, always in third position. The body is inclined a little to the right side.

Arm Movements.

The right hand is held in front at the level of the eyes, palm facing front, elbow flexed. The left is held down at the back, palm

KANDÍNGAN, Figure V

148

facing out. The fingers are close together (except the thumb). Curl the fingers in and out, imitating the tail of a fish. . . . . 2 M.

(b) Repeat (a) turning to the left. Reverse the position of the feet and arms. Incline the body to the left side. . . . . 2 M.

(c) Repeat (a) and (b). . . . . 4 M.

(d) Repeat all (a, b, c). . . . . 8 M.

Note: Letter (d) may be omitted if desired.

Boy's Part.

(a) Starting with the R foot, execute step I eight times, moving clockwise. . . . . 8 M.

(b) Repeat (a) counterclockwise. . . . . 8 M.

Arm Movements.

As one arm is raised the other one is lowered. Raise the forearm forward keeping the elbows close to the body. Flex the wrist of the right hand downward, the palm facing front, fingers close together. The left wrist is flexed upward, finger tips pointing up, palm: facing front, fingers close together. (See illustration.)

(a) Gradually raise the right forearm upward and lower the left downward without changing the position of the hands (cts. 1, 2, 3, 4). . . . . 2 M.

(b) Quickly change the position of the fingers (left pointing downward, right upward). Gradually raise the left forearm up and lower the right. Palms always face front (cts. 1, 2, 3, 4). . . . . . . 2 M.

(c) Repeat (a) and (b). . . . . 4 M.

(d) Repeat all (a, b, c). . . . . 8 M.

The hands may be brought closer together as they are raised and lowered. The shoulders follow the movements of the arms.

IV

Music B.

Partners face each other.

(a) Starting with the R foot, execute step I eight times moving diagonally forward right. . . . . 4 M.

(b) Turn right about and repeat (a) going back to places. 4 M.

Arm Movements.

Repeat the arm movements of figure II. The forefinger and thumb are almost touching each other, the other three fingers are hyperextended and separated. The right and left arms are raised and lowered alternately as in figure II. . . . . 16 M.

149

Music A.

(a) Starting with the R foot, execute step II clockwise. ..... 8 M.

(b) Turn right about and repeat (a) counterclockwise. .... 8 M.

Arm Movements.

(a) The arms are bent upward, hands level with the eyes, palms facing front, fingers close together, the tips of the third fingers of each hand almost touching each other. Rotate the hands gradually turning the fingers outward (away from each other), bringing the wrists closer (4 cts.). (See illustration.) .... 2 M.

(b) Continue rotating the hands in and out, palms facing front. .... 14 M.

VI

Music B.

Partners face the audience.

(a) Starting with the R foot, execute step III eight times moving forward.

(b) Starting with the L foot, repeat (a) moving backward to places. .... 8 M.

(c) Repeat (a) with faster movement, one count for each step, taking two steps per measure. .... 4 M.

(d) Repeat (c) going backward. .... 4 M.

Arm Movements.

Hold arms down at the back, palms of the hands facing out, third fingers of each hand almost touching each other, fingers close together and stiff.

(a) Open the arms gradually outward bringing them to the front parallel to each other, the right hand above the left, palms facing front. (See illustration.) .... 8 M.

(b) Gradually bring the hands back to the starting position. 8 M.

Music A (First 8 M.).

(c) Repeat (a) with a faster movement. .... 4 M.

(d) Back to starting position. .... 4 M.

VII

Music A (Last 8 M.).

Girl faces the audience.

(a) Place R foot across the L in front. In this position gradually bend the knees until almost kneeling on the left. .... 4 M.

(b) Slowly rise to standing position. .... 4 M.

150

Music B (First 8 м.).

(c) Turn left about and repeat (a) until almost kneeling on the right. .... 4 м.

(d) Repeat (b). .... 4 м.

Arm Movements.

Arms sideward at shoulder level, elbows and hands relaxed. Pull inward and push outward the right and left shoulders alternately with the fingers curling in and stretching out as in figure I. (8 м. of Music A, and 8 м. of B.) .... 16 м.

VIII

Music B (Last 8 м.).

Partners face each other.

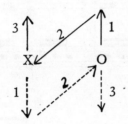

Partners execute step IV, the girl following the heavy lines and the boy the dotted lines as indicated in the diagram.

Put in as many steps in a measure as possible. Take four counts for each line of direction. Turn left at every change of direction. 6 м.

Arm Movements.

The arms are bent upward, hands in front of the face, palms facing front, fingers pointed upward and close together, hands parallel to each other. Gradually lower the finger tips to sideward right and left alternately every four counts. .... 6 м.

FINALE

Music B (Last two measures).

Partners run to the center to their proper places as in the Formation. Hold the position as in Entrance (b). (See illustration.) .... 2 м.

NOTE: If an exit is desired, run around once and then off, taking the same arm position as in Entrance (b) while running (2 м.).

Kandiñgan

Moro Wedding Dance
from Jolo, Sulu

Music by
A. Buenaventura

La Jota

This is a delightful, lively dance from Iriga, Camarines Sur. Its air and figures are very much like the "Jotas" of Spain. The "Jota" dances have many variations and are as popular as the "Fandangos."

During the Spanish regime La Jota was danced by the Spaniards at social affairs. Whenever there were not enough Spaniards at those gatherings, the Filipinos who were present were called upon to take part. Thus, the latter learned the dance and taught it to other Filipinos. It was so easy to learn that it spread throughout the Philippines. It is now found everywhere, but known by other names and in different versions.

COSTUME. Girls are dressed in Maria Clara style and boys in "barong tagalog" with black trousers.

MUSIC is divided into four parts: A, B, C and D.

COUNT *one, two, three* to a measure.

FORMATION. Partners stand opposite each other six feet apart. Girls stand at partners' right when facing the audience.

Audience

X	1	O
X	2	O
X	3	O
X	4	O

Diagram A

Couples are given numbers. (See Diagram A.)
From four to any number of pairs may take part.

INTRODUCTION

Music Introduction.

Three-step turn right in place and bow to the partner. .... 2 M.

I

Music A.

Partners face each other.

(a) Take eight sway-balance steps with a brush, R and L, arms in fourth position, R and L arm high alternately. .... 16 M.

154

(b) Turn right about (facing away from partner) and repeat (a). Finish facing each other. .... 16 M.

II

Music B.

(a) Waltz balance forward R (cts. 1, 2, 3) and backward L (cts. 4, 5, 6). R hand forward with the palm up, L hand on the waist on cts. 1, 2, 3, bringing the R hand close to the chest on cts. 4, 5, 6. .... 2 M.

(b) Sway balance R with a point (heavy steps), arms in fourth, R arm high. .... 2 M.

(c) Repeat (a) and (b) starting with the L foot. Reverse the arm positions. .... 4 M.

(d) Repeat all (a, b, and c). .... 24 M.

NOTE: If too long, dance twice only. (Use 16 measures.)

III

Music C. Play four times.

(a) *Even Numbers.*

Step R foot forward (ct. 1), brush L forward (ct. 2), hop on R raising the L knee in front at the same time (ct. 3). Raise R hand up and place L on the waist. .... 1 M.

Waltz balance forward L. Hands as in the first measure. Partners are in one line standing side by side (L to L shoulder). Partners look at each other over the left shoulder. .... 1 M.

Starting with the R foot, take three heavy running steps backward (cts. 1, 2, 3). Girls holding skirts, boys' hands on waist. ..... 1 M.

Close L to R foot with a stamp (cts. 1, 2, 3). Hands as in measure 3. .... 1 M.

Odd Numbers.

While the even numbers are dancing clap hands on the first and third beats of measures 1 and 2. .... 2 M.

Clap at every beat of measure 3. .... 1 M.

Clap the first beat of measure 4. .... 1 M.

(b) *Even and Odd Numbers.*

Repeat (a) three times. .... 12 M.

(c) Repeat all. This time the odd numbers dance and the even numbers clap. .... 16 M.

IV

Music D.

Girls face the audience, boys face away.

155

(a) Take two slide (or Spanish draw) steps sideward left. Girls holding skirts, boys' hands on waist. .... 2 M.

(b) Three-step turn left to partner's place (cts. 1, 2, 3). Partners pass in front of each other. Hands as in (a). .... 1 M.

(c) Close R to L foot (cts. 1, 2, 3). Hands as in (a). .... 1 M.

(d) Repeat all (a, b, c), three times, starting with the R, L and R foot, turning R, L, R respectively. .... 12 M.

NOTE: Finish the turn with girls always facing toward and boys away from the audience. If the slide-step-close is started with the L foot, the three-step turn is to the left, but if started with the R foot, turn to the right.

V

Music A. Play three times.

A. Partners face each other.

(a) Stamp R foot across the L in front (cts. 1, 2, 3). Stamp the same foot sideward in second position (cts. 4, 5, 6). Girls hold skirts, folding them in on counts 1, 2, 3 and spreading them out to the sides on counts 4, 5, 6. Boys snap their fingers in front on counts 1, 2, 3 and sideward in second position on counts 4, 5, 6..... 2 M.

(b) Three-step turn right in place. Girls holding their skirts, boys' hands on waist. .... 2 M.

(c) Repeat (a) and (b) three times starting with the L, R and R foot. .... 12 M.

B. *Even Numbers.*

(a) Girls take four waltz steps forward, boys waltz backward, starting with the R foot. Arms in lateral position moving sideward R and L. .... 4 M.

Odd Numbers.

(a) Girls take four waltz steps backward, boys forward, starting with the R foot. Arms as above. .... 4 M.

Even and Odd Numbers.

(b) Repeat (a) in the reverse direction, going to original places. .... 4 M.

(c) Repeat same movements as above (a and b). This time even numbers repeat the movements of the odd numbers in (a) and vice versa. .... 8 M.

C. (a) Starting with the R foot, partners take eight waltz steps clockwise. Arms as in B (a). Finish in proper places. .... 8 M.

(b) Turn right about and repeat (a) going counterclockwise. 8 M.

156

"SALUDO"

Music Finale.

Partners join R hands. Girls turn under the arch of their partners arms counterclockwise (2 м.), and clockwise (2 м.). (Use three-step turn in place.) .... 4 м.

Partners bow to the audience. .... 2 м.

La Jota

CAMARINES SUR

157

B II

158

159

Lawiswis Kawayan

"Lawiswis kawayan" means the hissing sound of the wind in the bamboo. The dance which bears this name is popular in Leyte and Samar. The version described below was discovered in Davao when performed by the Visayan settlers there. The accompaniment for the dance is sung by the spectators.

COSTUME. The dancers are dressed in Visayan peasant costume. (See illustration.)

MUSIC is divided into two parts: A and B.

COUNT *one, two, three* to a measure.

FORMATION. Partners stand opposite each other eight feet apart. When facing the audience, the girls stand at their partners' right. It is danced in sets of four pairs. Any number of sets may take part.

INTRODUCTION

Music Introduction.

Partners take a three-step turn right in place and bow to each other, boys' hands on waist, girls holding skirts. .... 2 M.

I

Music A.

(a) Partners execute three double sway balance steps (R, L, R). Arms in fourth position, R and L arm high alternately. The low arm is raised to shoulder-level for the first two measures. For the last two measures, boys place hands on waist, girls hold skirts. .... 12 M.

(b) Take one sway balance step with a point to the left. Arms in fourth position, L arm high. .... 2 M.

(c) Make a three-step turn right in place, boys' hands on waist, girls holding skirts. .... 2 M.

(d) Repeat all (a, b, c), starting with the L foot. Reverse the arm positions and the turn. .... 16 M.

II

Music B.

(a) Take one sway balance step with a point to the right. Arms in fourth position, R arm high. .... 2 M.

(b) Take one waltz step obliquely forward left with the L foot, girls holding skirts, boys' hands on waist. .... 1 M.

(c) Step R foot obliquely forward right (ct. 1), turn left about to face partner and point L foot in front (cts. 2, 3). Partners pass each other by right shoulders. Hands as in (b). .... 1 M.

(d) Repeat (a), starting with the L foot. Reverse the arm positions. .... 2 M.

(e) Take one waltz step obliquely forward right with the R foot. Hands as in (b). .... 1 M.

(f) Step L foot obliquely forward right (ct. 1), turn right about and point R foot in front (cts. 2, 3). Hands as in (b). ...... 1 M.

(g) Repeat (a, b, c). .... 4 M.

(h) Starting with the L foot, take four waltz steps forward to proper places, passing by right shoulders. Turn on the fourth waltz step. When waltzing with the L foot, left hand is forward, palm up and right hand on waist. Reverse hand positions when waltzing with the R foot. Change hand positions every measure.   4 M.

(i) Repeat all (a, b, c, d, e, f, g). .... 16 M.

III

Music A.

(a) Take seven sway balance steps with a raise, R and L, arms in fourth position, R and L arm high alternately (lower arm at shoulder-level). .... 14 M.

(b) Make a three-step turn left in place, girls holding skirts, boys' hands on waist. .... 2 M

(c) Repeat (a), starting with the L foot. Reverse the arm positions. .... 14 M.

(d) Repeat (b) to the right. .... 2 M.

IV

Music B.

Partners face right (girls facing and boys away from the audience).

(a) Execute "espunti" steps to the left (going inward), four times (4 M.). At the end of the fourth "espunti" step, partners are in one line facing each other, girls holding skirts, boys' hands on waist. .... 4 M.

(b) Take one waltz-turn left in place (use two waltz steps L, R). Hands as in (a). .... 2 M.

(c) Take two waltz steps forward to proper places (R, L). Finish facing right again. .... 2 M.

(d) Repeat all (a, b, c) three times, finishing in proper places. 24 M.

V

Music A.

Face right as in figure IV.

(a) Starting with the L foot, take two cross steps sideward left (going inward), girls hold skirts, boys' hands on waist. Part-

ners finish in one line as in IV (a). .... 2 M.
    (b) One waltz step sideward left. Hands as above (a). ...... 1 M.
    (c) Three-step turn right going to proper places. Finish
facing right. .... 1 M.
    (d) Repeat all (a, b, c), seven times more. .... 28 M.

VI

Music B. Play once.

Partners take two waltz steps forward, meet at center, and hold
as in ordinary ballroom dance position. .... 2 M.
    (a) Boys point L foot twice and girls the R foot twice on
the first beats of measures 3 and 4 of Music B. .... 2 M.
    (b) Each set of four pairs waltz around moving counterclock-
wise in a big circle formation. .... 4 M.
    (c) Repeat (a). .... 2 M.
    (d) Repeat (b), continuing the counterclockwise movement. 4 M.
    (e) All four pairs finish in a single line at center facing the
audience. Partners join inside hands and bow to audience on the
last measure. .... 2 M.

AN DAHON HAN LAWISWIS KAWAYAN

I. An ini ñga hogpo, Lawis-wis kawayan
  Di-in an higugma, waray rayan dayan.
  Binorogto, gayud, mga guin a-ñgayan.
  Mag lipay ñga tanan, mag ca sangcayan.

CHORUS

An ini ñga picoy, pag lupad pag lupad morayao.
Pag hapon han sañga, dagos paparayao.
Binoklad an paco an paco, dao hilaw ñga dahon.
An iya pag rayhak guin kikinantahon.

II. Ay, dida hinin lindong, hini ñga kawayan
  Di-in an cago-ol sa dang pahowayan,
  Bisan adton Picoy ñga firme guina-pos
  Nag yayawit guihapon, hulat han caraptos.

CHORUS

Diri pa gad domog, diri pa lawis-wis kawayan
Na gamit pag pingot, badad ñga molayan,
An ini ñga bucad ñga bucad amo an casakit
Ñgan amo man liwat, an at calipayan.

162

Lawiswis Kawayan

LEYTE

Lubi-Lubi

"Lubi-lubi" is a Bikol dance, a combination of simple folk and social steps. (Literally, "lubi" means coconut. A game called "lubi-lubi" is played with coconut shells.)

According to the Bikols, this dance originated in Leyte and Samar where it is still danced like the balitaw. In the Bikol regions, whenever there is ballroom dancing the "lubi-lubi" is often introduced to break the monotony. It is also popular in Albay and Sorsogon.

MUSIC is divided into two parts: A, B. (The original music used for the folk dance has four parts.)

COUNT *one, two, three* to a measure.

FORMATION. Partners hold as in the ordinary ballroom dance position. From one to any number of couples may take part, the more the merrier. Partners start to dance at any time and may go in any direction.

Music Introduction:

Partners face each other about three feet apart. Make a three-step turn right in place and bow to each other. . . . .   2 M.

NOTE: This may be omitted.

I

Music A.

Partners hold in the ordinary ballroom dance position, and waltz going in any direction. . . . .   22 M.

Partners separate from each other. . . . .   2 M.

II

Music B.

Girl's Part.

(a) Clap hands in time on the second and third beats of each measure. . . . .   32 M.

Boy's Part.

(a) Take sixteen "engaño" steps with a waltz, R and L, arms in third position, R and L arm high alternately. . . . .   32 M.

III

Music A.

Partners hold as in the ordinary ballroom dancing position.
Repeat figure I. . . . .   24 M.

Music B.

Girl's Part.

(a) Take sixteen "engaño" steps with a waltz, R and L, arms in third position, R and L arm high alternately. .... 32 M.

Boy's Part.

(a) Clap hands as in II (a). .... 32 M.

V

Music A.

Partners hold as in the ordinary ballroom dancing position.
Repeat I. .... 24 M.

VI

Music B.

Both partners take sixteen "engaño" steps with close or waltz, R and L, arms in third position, R and L arm high alternately. .... 32 M.

NOTE: The dance may be repeated as many times as desired. It is more enjoyable to the dancers if the ones clapping hands shout "ey," "echa," "hala," "uy," or any word of the kind to animate their partners doing the "engaño" steps. Those who are dancing respond with more life and spirit to the cheering. After figure VI, dancers may change partners to make the dance more interesting.

If dancers find Part B music too long, it may be played once, dancers taking eight "engaño" steps, R and L alternately.

The following words may be sung by the performers or by the onlookers during the dance.

LUBI-LUBI LINCORANAY

Music A.

Enero, Febrero, Marzo, Abril, Mayo
Junio, Julio, Agosto
Septiembre, Octubre
Noviembre, Diciembre, Lubi-Lubi

Music B.

Con waray sin abanico
Patay na inin lawas co
Lawas co, Ay, Ay, madedesmayo
San bahas na demasiado

Lubi-Lubi

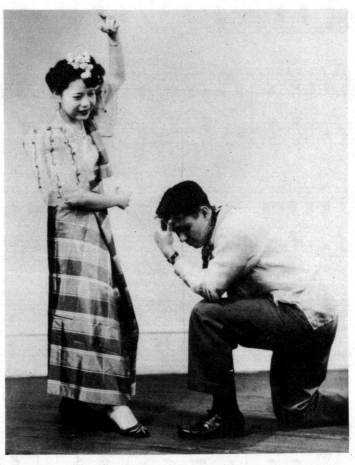

MARAMION, Figure VIII (b)
(see page 185)

Mag-Asik

This is a Tiruray dance for girls, performed in Nuro, Cotabato. According to the natives the word "mag-asik" means to sow seeds. A large kerchief or piece of bright colored cloth about a yard square is spread in the middle of the floor. The dancers go around the cloth with small, heavy steps but with graceful hand and arm movements. The dance consists of two parts which the natives call "komaligue" and "mag-asik." Three girls numbered No. 1, No. 2, and No. 3 perform this dance.

COSTUME. The dancers wear tight blouses with long tight sleeves and a peplum gathered at the waist. The blouse is made of shiny material in different colors. The favorite colors of the Tiruray girls are bright red, yellow, blue, orange, purple, and black. A "patadiong," ankle length, is worn as a skirt. A necklace made of gold, beads, or old silver coins is worn around the neck and reaches down to the waist. The rich wear metal belts about six inches wide. A "sarong" hangs on the left (or right) shoulder. (See illustration.) Only the lower lip is painted.

MUSIC is divided into two parts: A and B. It is played continuously as many times as necessary.

COUNT *one, two* to a measure.

FORMATION. The cloth is spread on the floor or stage. The three dancers enter one by one, moving around the cloth as indicated in the direction given below.

Steps Used:

I. Heavy small steps going forward, with four or more steps to a measure. Both feet are flat on the floor.

II. Small close steps right or left. Take four steps to one side (to change direction, feet are not closed on fourth step). Take one close step for every count.

III. Stand in place with the weight of the body on the left foot. The knees are slightly bent and the R foot stamps four or more times to a measure. The body sways slightly to right and left following the arm and hand movements.

INTRODUCTION

Music Introduction.

Dancers enter from backstage or from a corner. (No. 1 is followed in line by No. 2 and No. 3.)

NOTE: Music plays continuously because the number of steps taken in one figure cannot be estimated in this dance. Everything depends upon the individual dancer.

I

Girl No. 1 enters doing Step I with the following hand movements.

The right (or left) hand is in continuous motion, going slowly up and down in this manner: When the hand goes up the fingers are pointed downward, stiffly and close together. The elbow is bent and is raised as the hand is raised. The hand moves upward (parallel to and close to the body), palm facing the body. When the hand goes down the wrist is flexed, the fingers point upward, palm facing out, and the elbow is lowered. The hand moves close to the body. The movement of the right hand is changed every four counts, four counts going up and four counts going down. The left (or right) hand holds the "sarong" down at the side with the second and third fingers pinching the cloth tightly.

Girl No. 2 follows three feet behind No. 1.

Girl No. 3 follows three feet behind No. 2.

The three dancers circle the cloth counterclockwise using Step I, maintaining a distance of three feet from each other. See diagram A.

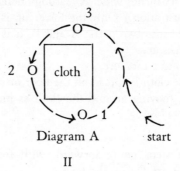

Diagram A   start

II

Girls stand around cloth facing in, dancing Step III. Repeat same hand movements as in figure I.

III

Do Step I once going clockwise. Repeat counterclockwise. Hold hands about two inches over shoulders with palms down, fingers close together. Fingers are moved up and down from the wrist imitating the flying movements of birds, elbows close to the body. (See illustration.)

Dancers finish on one line in rear of cloth, facing audience. (See diagram B.)

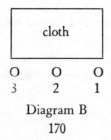

Diagram B

MAG–ASIK, Figure III

IV

Do step II. Bend arms forward (hands horizontal on chest) with palms down, right hand on top of the left, fingers stiffly together. Lower and raise the hands slowly. (As the left hand goes down the right goes up and vice versa.) Do this four times.

NOTE: The hands are raised to shoulder level and lowered to four inches below the waist.

V

Do Step II eight times to the right and left alternately.

Starting position: arms parallel to each other at left side, wrists flexed upward, fingers stiffly together, palms down, elbows straight and stiff.

From the starting position move arms to the right side, keeping arms parallel to each other. At end of fourth step, fingers must be hyper-extended and the wrists bent downward jerkily. (Palms always down.)

Move arms eight times to sideward right and left. Arms and feet move with each change of direction.

171

VI

With No. 1 leading, all do Step I going around cloth twice counter-clockwise. Hands on hips with the little finger sticking out and waggling. Dancers finish standing around cloth with left shoulder toward center. (See diagram below.) .

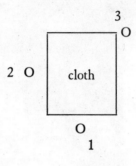

VII

Do Step III. Hold "sarong" with second and third fingers of right (left) hand. Move hands alternately as in figure I. (As right hand moves up left hand goes down.)

(a) With No. 1 leading, do Step I going around cloth. No. 3 stoops down as if picking up cloth but does not. She continues off stage. No. 2 does same.

(b) No. 1 picks up the cloth by two upper corners and holds it between thumb and second finger. The three remaining fingers are separated and hyperextended. (Uses both hands.)

Does Step I going forward, holding cloth in front of body, elbows straight. Shakes cloth in time to music.

(c) Does Step II four times to right and left sides. Moves cloth to right and left sides simultaneously with movements of the feet. Elbows remain rigid. Gives strong shake of cloth at end of each fourth close step.

(d) Faces audience. Does Step III. Holds cloth in one corner with right hand. Left hand hangs stiffly at side with fingers and elbow straight, palm down. Moves right hand up and down as in figure I four times.

EXIT

Does Step I. Turns around once before going out. Holds cloth with right hand in front at chest level. When she is turned away from the audience, she looks back over her right shoulder. Just before going off stage she puts cloth over left shoulder.

Mag-Asik

TIRURAY

A. BUENAVENTURA

173

Mananguete

(Tubâ Gatherer)

"Mananguete" is a Visayan occupational dance, found in Kolambugan, Lanao, among the settlers from the Visayan islands. It depicts in pantomime all the stages of "tubâ" (liquid taken from the coconut bud) gathering. Sharpening the scythe ("sangot" in Visayan), cleaning the bamboo containers ("sugong" in Visayan), climbing coconut trees, getting tubâ, pounding, squeezing and straining the sap of the mangrove bark ("tañgal"), mixing of "tubâ," and tasting are portrayed.

Equipment used:

For Boys	For Girls
(1) Bamboo tube container	(1) Basket
(2) Scythe	(2) Wine Glass
(3) Cleaner	(3) Pounder
	(4) Mangrove Bark

Costume. The girls are dressed for work in "patadiong," "chambra" or "kimono" and a short skirt (mascota). A piece of cloth or a large neckerchief covers the head. The boys wear colored trousers (red, brown, or navy blue) and shirts. The trousers and the sleeves are rolled and all are barefoot.

Music is divided into three parts: A, B, C.

Count *one, two, three* to a measure.

Formation. Boys stand in two parallel lines facing the audience. Girls do not enter until figure III. From one to any number of pairs may take part in this dance.

Audience

X   X

X   X

X   X

INTRODUCTION

Music Introduction.

The boys get ready for entrance by placing the coconut husk cleaner inside the bamboo container, and hanging it over the right shoulder. They hold the scythe with the R hand. .... 8 M.

ENTRANCE

Music A.

Starting with the R, boys enter in two parallel lines executing waltz steps forward to their proper places. They take distances of about six feet from each other, by executing waltz steps R and L in place. .... 32 M.

I

Music B.

Boys put down the bamboo container a little towards their right side, and assume a semi-kneeling position facing the audience (see illustration).

(a) Do in pantomime the motion of sharpening the scythe. Hold the handle with the right hand and the blade of the scythe with the left hand. Push the scythe forward (ct. 1) with two circular motions clockwise (cts. 2, 3). .... 1 M.

(b) Repeat (a) fifteen times more. .... 16 M.

(c) In pantomime, go through the motion of testing the edge

176

MANANGUETE, Figure I Sharpening

177

of the blade with the finger nail or a hair. At the first trial shake
the head signifying that the blade is not sharp. .... 4 M.

(d) Go through the sharpening motion again as in (a)
four times. .... 4 M.

(e) Try the blade again. Pull one hair and cut it with the
scythe. Nod the head signifying that it is sharp. .... 6 M.

(f) Stand up and put the scythe at the right side of the waist
(in the belt). .... 2 M.

II

Music C.

Boys' Part:

(a) Hold the bamboo container bottom down with the L
hand, and the coconut husk cleaner with the R hand. Insert the
cleaner and go through the motion of cleaning in time to the
music. Clean the sides and the bottom. .... 16 M.

Take out the husk cleaner.

(b) Raise the bamboo container obliquely right with the bottom up and examine (2 M.). Shake the head as if to say "no" (2 M.). 4 M.

(c) Go through the motion of cleaning again, moving the
cleaner up and down in time to the music. .... 2 M.

(d) Take out the husk cleaner and beat it against the container twice (second and third beats of measures 7 and 8) to shake
off the dirt. .... 2 M.

(e) Repeat (b) raising it to the left side. Finish it with a nod
of the head as if saying "yes." .... 4 M.

(f) Hang the bamboo container over right shoulder (2 M.).
Place the husk cleaner at the left side of the waist (in the belt)
(2 M.). .... 4 M.

III

Music A.

Boys' Part:

(a) Go through the motions of climbing a coconut tree. .... 16 M.

Girls' Part:

(a) Starting with the R foot, take sixteen waltz steps forward
to places, inside boys' lines. (See diagram p. 180.) Girls carry a
basket on their heads containing "tañgal" bark, a small wine glass,
and a pounder. Hold the basket with the R (or L) hand. .... 16 M.

MANANGUETE, Figure IV (d) Pouring

```
X O                    O X

X O                    O X

X O                    O X
```

Boys' Part:

(b) Go through the motion of tapping the bud with the scythe, then of tying the bamboo container to the bud to hold it in place. .... 8 M.

(c) Go through the motion of going down the tree. Hang the bamboo container at the back of the right shoulder. .... 8 M.

Girls' Part:

(b) Sit down and go through the motion of pounding the "tañgal" bark in time to the music. Pound on the second and third beats of each measure. .... 8 M.

(c) Pounding the "tañgal" on the first beat of each measure. 8 M.

IV

Music B.

Partners face each other. The boys are in half-kneel-on-right position and the girls in kneeling position. (See illustration.) The boys place the bamboo container in front of them.

Girls' Part:

(a) Go through the motion of squeezing the sap of the "tañgal" into the bamboo container. Wring the pounded "tañgal" bark four times, on the first beat of measures 1–4. .... 4 M.

(b) Put down the squeezed bark and take more from the basket. Repeat (a). .... 4 M.

(c) Watch the boy as he stirs the mixture. .... 8 M.

Boys' Part:

(a) Watch the girls as they squeeze the sap. .... 8 M.

(b) With the handle of the husk cleaner go through the motion of stirring and mixing the "tubâ" and "tañgal" sap. ...... 8 M.

Girls' and Boys' Part:

(d) The girls hold the glass while the boys pour the "tubâ" mixture into the glass. .... 4 M.

(e) Girls go through the motion of drinking the "tubâ." Boys watch. .... 4 M.

(f) Repeat (d). .... 4 M.

(g) The girls offer the "tubâ" and the boys drink it. Partners nod to each other as if saying "it is good." .... 4 M.

Music C.

Place utensils on the floor. All stand in front of the equipment facing audience.

    (a) Partners join inside hands. Execute four step-swing steps sideward R and L. Free hands of boys on waist and girls holding skirts. . . . . 4 M.

    (b) Drop hands. Take four waltz steps clockwise around the equipment, starting with the R foot, arms in lateral position moving sideward R and L. . . . . 4 M.

    (c) Repeat (b) going counterclockwise. . . . . 4 M.

    (d) Join inside hands again and repeat (a). . . . . 4 M.

    (e) Partners face each other. Execute seven sway balance steps R and L, arms in lateral position, R and L high alternately. 14 M.

Music—For Finale.

    (f) Take a three-step turn left in place and bow to partner or audience. . . . . 2 M.

Mananguete

VISAYAN

A. BUENAVENTURA

183

Maramion

This is a courtship dance popular in the islands of Cebu and Bohol. "Maramion" means fragrant or beautiful. This dance is usually sung by the performers or by the spectators

It is a courtship story in pantomime.

COSTUME. Girls are dressed in Visayan folk costume in "patadiong," camisa, soft neckerchief over one shoulder, and zapatilla or "chinelas." Boys are dressed in "barong tagalog" with white trousers.

MUSIC is divided into two parts: A, B.

COUNT *one, two, three* to a measure.

FORMATION. Dancers stand in two parallel lines with the partners facing each other about six feet apart. Girls stand at their partners' right when facing the audience. From one to any number of pairs may take part.

I

Music A.

    (a) Raise the hands to waist level, elbows close to the waist and palms facing downward (cts. 1, 2, 3). .... 1 M.

    (b) Turn the hands outward putting the palms up. Partners look at each other. .... 1 M.

    (c) One sway balance step with a point to the right. Arms in fourth position, R arm high. .... 2 M.

    (d) Repeat (a) and (b). .... 2 M.

    (e) One sway balance step with a point to the left. Arms in fourth position, L arm high. .... 2 M.

    (f) Repeat all (a, b, c, d, e). .... 8 M.

II

Music B.

    (a) Partners take two waltz steps forward (R, L) to meet at the center, girls holding skirts, boys' hands on waist. .... 2 M.

    (b) One waltz step sideward R and L. Hands as in (a). .... 2 M.

    (c) One waltz step sideward R and L. Shake hands and bow to each other. .... 2 M.

    (d) Partners take two waltz steps forward (R, L) exchanging places. Pass by right shoulders. Hands as in (a). .... 2 M.

    (e) Repeat all, finishing in proper places. .... 8 M.

III

Music A.

    Repeat figure I. .... 16 M.

Music B.

(a) Repeat (a) of figure II. .... 2 M.

(b) One waltz step sideward R and L. The boy holds the right hand of his partner with his right and places it over his heart. 2 M.

(c) One waltz step sideward R and L. The boy points to heaven with his left forefinger, as if saying "Heaven is my witness, I love you so . . .," his right hand still holding the girl's right hand. The girl shakes her head as if saying "No, no, I do not love you" and withdraws her right hand quickly. .... 2 M.

(d) Repeat (d) of figure II. .... 2 M.

(e) Repeat all (a, b, c, d), finishing in proper places. .... 8 M.

V

Music A.

Repeat figure I. .... 16 M.

VI

Music B.

(a) Repeat (a) of figure II. .... 2 M.

(b) The boy kneels on right knee. He takes the R hand of the girl and attempts to kiss it (4 M.).

The girl takes four waltz steps sideward R and L. She does not let him kiss her hand and prevents him from doing so by pushing against his forehead with her left hand. .... 4 M.

(c) The boy stands and both repeat (d) of figure II. .... 2 M.

(d) Repeat all (a, b, c), finishing in proper places. .... 8 M.

VII

Music A.

Repeat figure I. .... 16 M.

VIII

Music B. Play slowly at the last two measures in the repetition.

(a) Repeat (a) of figure II. .... 2 M.

(b) The boy kneels on the right knee. He places his left elbow on the left knee and supports his forehead in a very much. depressed attitude. The girl looks at the boy in a more sympathetic manner. She executes one waltz step sideward R and L. .... 2 M.

(c) She pities the boy and takes both of his hands to help him up. They bow and smile. .... 2 M.

(d) Repeat (d) of figure II. .... 2 M.

(e) Repeat all (a, b, c, d), finishing at proper places with a bow to partner. .... 8 M.

NOTE: Repetitions of figure II may be omitted. The music plays continuously, A and B alternating.

Maramion

Cebu and Behol

186

Mazurka

(Ballroom)

This was one of the most popular ballroom dances during the Spanish regime. It is lively and interesting.

There are many figures used in this dance and each locality has its own way of arranging the sequence. The figures or steps given below are the most common.

FORMATION: Partners hold as in the ordinary dancing position. The stretched arms remain straight, swinging up and down, following the movements of the body.

COSTUME: Girls wear the old-style costume, boys the "barong tagalog" with black trousers.

MUSIC is divided into three parts: A, B and C.

COUNT *one, two, three* to a measure.

NOTE: Girls start with the R and boys with the L foot.

I

Music A.

    (a) Slide R (L) foot obliquely forward (cts. 1, 2), close R (L) to L (R) foot without putting weight on it (ct. 3). . . . .   1 M.

    (b) Three steps in place or going around in place R, L, R (L, R, L) (cts. 1, 2, 3). . . . .   1 M.

    (c) Repeat (a) and (b) L and R (R and L) alternately, seven times. . . . .   14 M.

    (d) Repeat all. . . . .   16 M.

II

Music B.

    (a) Two mazurka steps R (L).   2 M.

    (b) Cut L (R) foot with R (L) laterally (cts. 1, 2), step L (R) in place (ct. 3). . . . .   1 M.

    (c) Step R (L) foot close to L (R) (cts. 1, 2, 3). . . . .   1 M.

    (d) Repeat (a, b, and c), three times. . . . .   12 M.

    (e) Repeat all. . . . .   16 M.

III

Music A.

    (a) Slide R (L) foot obliquely forward (cts. 1, 2), close R (L) to L (R) foot putting the weight on it (ct. 3). . . . .   1 M.

    (b) Repeat (a) starting with the L (R) foot (cts. 1, 2, 3). . .   1 M.

(c) Six steps in place or moving around starting R (starting L) foot (cts. 1–6). .... 2 M.

(d) Repeat (a, b, c), three times. .... 12 M.

(e) Repeat all. .... 16 M.

IV

Music C.

(a) Three mazurka steps R moving clockwise (L counterclockwise). .... 3 M.

(b) Three steps in place or moving around R, L, R (L, R, L) (cts. 1, 2, 3). .... 1 M.

(c) Repeat (a and b) three times L and R alternately. ..... 12 M.

(d) Repeat all. .... 16 M.

NOTE: The figures may be repeated in any order, as many times as desired, going in any direction.

MARAMION, FIGURE VI (b)

(see page 185)

Mazurka

MINDORO

From collection of
San Agustin Family

A I-III

189

Pagtatahip

(Winnowing)

"Pagtatahip" is an occupational dance, usually performed after the "Pounding Rice" dance. Generally, boys do the pounding and girls do the winnowing.

Winnowing is the process of separating the husks from the grain after the "palay" has been pounded. The beauty of this dance depends upon the graceful and skillful movements of throwing the pounded "palay" into the air and catching them again with accuracy.

Like the planting and pounding dances this is also done to the accompaniment of songs and musical instruments.

COSTUME. The girls wear short skirts and "tapis." For the blouse they may use "chambra" with long sleeves or "camisa" with the sleeves rolled up. A piece of cloth or large kerchief is tied around the head. Each dancer is provided with a shallow basket ("bila-o") and three or four handfuls of pounded "palay."

MUSIC is divided into two parts: A and B.

COUNT *one, two, three* to a measure.

FORMATION. Dancers stand in two lines eight feet apart. From eight to sixteen girls may take part in this dance. A mat may be spread in the center of the floor for the cleaned rice.

O   O

O   O

O   O

O   O

INTRODUCTION

Music Introduction. Play as many times as necessary.

As the introduction is played the girls get four or five handfuls of pounded "palay" from the mortars and put them in their baskets. They form two lines, carrying their baskets at the right side of the waist. .... 4, 8, 12 or 16 M.

I

Music A.

Starting with the R foot, dancers execute sixteen waltz steps forward to proper places. Free hand (left hand) holding the skirt. .. 16 M.

192

Music Interlude.

Dancers face each other holding their respective baskets with both hands, ready for winnowing. .... 4 м.

II

Music B.

(a) Rotate the basket clockwise three times (cts. 1, 2, 3), and pause (cts. 1, 2, 3). .... 2 м.

(b) Repeat (a) seven times more. .... 14 м.

III

Music B.

(a) Shake the basket so that the grains are thrown upward (cts. 1, 2, 3). Catch them again as they fall (cts. 1, 2, 3). .... 2 м.

(b) Repeat (a) seven times more. .... 14 м.

NOTE: When shaking the basket the front side is tilted up. These movements may be faster, that is, taking two movements in one measure.

IV

Music B.

(a) Rotate the basket twice clockwise (cts. 1, 2) and shake once upward (ct. 3). Catch the grain (cts. 1, 2, 3). .... 2 м.

(b) Repeat (a) three times more. .... 6 м.

(c) Hold the basket with the left hand, pick out the husks and small particles of dirt with the right hand (cts. 1, 2, 3). Throw them away (cts. 1, 2, 3). .... 2 м.

(d) Repeat (c) three times more. .... 6 м.

V

Music A.

Dancers hold baskets with the right hand at the right side of the waist.

(a) Starting with the right foot, all waltz forward, forming a circle around the mat (see diagram below). .... 8 м.

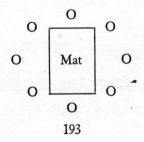

193

(b) All empty the baskets by letting the grain fall slowly on the mat. .... 8 M.

Music Interlude.

All walk backward to proper places in the circle. .... 4 M.

VI

Music B.

Dancers hold the basket in front with the left hand at the brim.

(a) Waltz R forward, hitting the bottom of the basket forward with the right hand as if emptying it (cts. 1, 2, 3). .... 1 M.

(b) Waltz L backward, swinging right hand backward (cts. 1, 2, 3). .... 1 M.

(c) Repeat (a) and (b) seven times more. .... 14 M.

VII

Music B.

(a) Place the basket on the head, balancing it with the left hand. Place R hand on waist.

Execute four sway-balance steps with a brush, R and L alternately. .... 8 M.

(b) Turn right about (face out) and repeat (a). .... 8 M.

Music Finale. Play as many times as necessary.

In two lines, dancers waltz forward to go out, holding the empty basket at the brim with the right hand, left hand swinging backward and forward .... 4, 8, 12 or 16 M.

PAGTATAHIP, Figure V

Pagtatahip

NATIONAL

Music by
A. Buenaventura

B II-III-IV-VI

Palay Dance

"Palay" literally means either the plant or the grain from which rice is obtained. Husked rice is the staple food of the Oriental people.

This dance has an interesting story. The first figure depicts the graceful swaying of the palay plants in the breeze. Other lovely figures portray the cutting, harvesting, and threshing of palay.

It can be danced on any occasion but is most appropriate as an after-harvest celebration. The "Planting Rice" dance may be performed as an introduction.

This dance was arranged for the "Agricultural Pageant" which the University of the Philippines presented in 1929 at the Philippine Carnival Auditorium.

Costume. Dancers are dressed in peasant work costumes. They are barefoot and carry stalks of "palay" in both hands.

Formation. Partners stand opposite each other about eight feet apart, girls standing at their partners' right when facing the audience.

Audience

X O   X O

X O   X O

X O   X O

Music is divided into four parts: A, B, C and D.

Count *one, two, three* to a measure.

Entrance. Use "Planting Rice" music. Dancers enter with gay walking steps.

I

Music A.

Dancers face the audience.

Execute sixteen waltz steps sideward R and L. Hold arms in fifth position, swaying sideward R and L. .... 16 M.

II

Music B.

Partners face each other.

(a) Take two close steps sideward right (cts. 1–6). Hands in fifth position swaying sideward right (cts. 1–2), sway to sideward left (ct. 3). Sway arms sideward right (cts. 1, 2, 3). .... 2 M.

197

(b) Take two close steps sideward left. Arm movements as in above, starting from sideward left. . . . . 2 M.

(c) Four waltz steps forward R and backward L. Arms swinging forward-upward (cts. 1, 2, 3) and downward-backward (cts. 1, 2, 3). . . . . 4 M.

(d) Repeat all (a, b, and c). . . . . 8 M.

III

Music A.

Eight sway-balance steps with a point, R and L. R arm in fifth position and L hand on waist when going to the right, reversing the hand positions when going to the left. . . . . 16 M.

IV

Music C.

Partners face the audience.

(a) "Sarok" (1 M.) and pivot turn with point to the right (3 M.). Cross the hands down in front in "sarok" and have the R arm up and L hand on waist in the pivot turn with point. Turn the wrist of the R hand at every measure. . . . . 4 M.

(b) Repeat (a) to the left. Reverse the hand positions. . . . . . 4 M.

(c) Repeat (a and b). . . . . 8 M.

V

Music A (slower).

Partners face the audience.

(a) Starting with the inside foot take three steps sideward to partner's place (cts. 1, 2, 3). Girls pass in front of their partners. Girls sway arms parallel sideward right, boys sideward left (cts. 1, 2, 3). . . . . 1 M.

(b) Point sideward with inside foot. Sway arms to opposite side (girls' sideward left and boys' sideward right). (cts. 1, 2, 3). 1 M.

(c) Girls move the arms in a double-arm-circle counterclockwise, boys move the arms clockwise (cts. 1–6). The inside foot remains pointing for six counts. . . . . 2 M.

(d) Repeat (a and b) going back to places. Girls pass in front of their partners. Arms in opposite direction. . . . . 2 M.

(e) Repeat (c), reversing the directions of the arms. . . . . 2 M.

(f) Repeat all (a, b, c, d, and e). . . . . 8 M.

198

Music D.

Partners face each other.

(a) *Boys:* Take four (small) waltz steps backward, starting with the R foot. Arms in lateral position moving sideward R and L.

Girls: Take four (big) waltz steps forward, starting with the R foot. They follow their partners, arms as in above. Finish with partners standing near each other. . . . . 4 M.

(b) Boys' hands down shaking "palay" stalks three times (cts. 1, 2), pause (ct. 3). Girls shake "palay" stalks overhead in the same manner. . . . . 1 M.

(c) Repeat (b) three times more reversing hand positions every measure. . . . . 3 M.

(d) Girls turn right about. Partners execute mincing steps sideward right, R foot in front (cts. 1–5). Point L in front (ct. 6). Hands on waists. . . . . 2 M.

(e) Repeat (d) going sideward left, L foot in front. . . . . 2 M.

(f) Three quick stamps in place (R, L, R) (cts. 1, 2) pause (ct. 3). Hands on waist. . . . . 1 M.

(g) Repeat (f) (L, R, L). . . . . 1 M.

(h) Take four steps forward going to proper places, starting with the R foot (cts. 1, 2, 3, 4). Hands on waists.

The girls upon reaching their proper places, turn right about. Partners bow to each other. Arms in second position (cts. 5–6). . . . 2 M.

(i) Repeat all (a, b, c, d, e, f, g, h). This time boys move forward and girls backward. Reverse the arm positions in (b) and (c). Boys face right about in (d). Boys turn right about in (h) in place. . . . . 16 M.

VII

Music A.

Partners face the audience and join inside hands.

(a) Take eight step-swing steps forward, R and L alternately. Place free hands on waists. . . . . 8 M.

(b) Turn inward to face about and repeat (a). . . . . 8 M.

Saludo:

Three step turn right in place and bow either to partner or to audience. . . . . 2 M.

EXIT:

Use the same music as in the entrance. Walk gaily, starting with the R foot.

Palay Dance

NATIONAL

Music by
J. HERNANDEZ

For saludo — *slowly*

Play music in this order:

I - A
II - B
III - A
IV - C
V - A
VI - D
VII - A
Saludo

Pandang-Pandang

This is a very popular wedding dance in the province of Antique. It is performed by the bride and the groom only during the wedding feast. While the newlyweds are dancing, parents, relatives, and friends throw money and give gifts to them. Usually the parents and relatives of the bride sit on one side and those of the groom sit opposite. They watch each other closely and each faction tries to outdo the other in generosity. They pile their gifts and money on their respective sides.

According to legend there was once a newly married couple who danced this traditional wedding dance. In the course of the dance a gecko (lizard) got into the trousers of the groom without the spectators noticing it. In his attempt to drive the gecko away he hopped, moved about, and hit his thighs and buttocks in time to the music so that nobody would notice what he was trying to do. He did not even stop dancing. The spectators, thinking him a very animated and enthusiastic dancer, and his dance beautiful and extraordinary, clapped their hands to cheer him on. From that time on the dance became popular and spread throughout the province.

COSTUME. The dancers will appear more natural if they wear the old style wedding dress. If such dresses cannot be secured the girl may be dressed in any old-style dress (Maria Clara, paloma, serpentina). The boy wears "barong tagalog" with black trousers.

MUSIC is divided into two parts: A and B.

COUNT *one, two, three* to a measure.

FORMATION. Partners stand opposite each other four feet apart. When facing the audience, girl should be at partner's right. Only one pair should dance but if desired any number may take part.

I

Music A.

(a) Step R foot forward toward partner (ct. 1), close L to R foot in first position (cts. 2, 3). . . . . 1 M.

(b) Shake hands (cts. 1, 2, 3). The head is bent forward. The girl gives her second and third fingers only (an old custom of shaking hands) and she looks down shyly. . . . . 1 M.

(c) Step L foot backward (ct. 1), close the R to the L foot in first position (cts. 2, 3). Bow to each other, the girl still looking down (cts. 1, 2, 3). Hands hanging loosely at the sides. . . . . 2 M.

(d) Take four sway-balance steps, R and L. Arms in fourth position, right and left arm high alternately. 8 M.

(e) Execute a waltz-turn right in place (take two waltz steps). Girl holding skirt, boy's hands on waist. . . . . 2 M.

203

(f) Repeat (a) and (b). Step backward to proper place after shaking hands. .... 2 M.

(g) Repeat all (a, b, c, d, e, and f). .... 16 M.

II

Music B.

Boy's Part:

(a) Step R foot forward (ct. 1), bring the left knee up in front, clap hands under the left knee on the second and third beats, and hop on the R foot on the third count (cts. 2, 3). The trunk is bent slightly forward and the knee raised high to make clapping easier. .... 1 M.

(b) Repeat (a) seven times more, turning clockwise in place. Clap hands under the right and left leg alternately. The boy looks at the girl as he turns around. .... 7 M.

Girl's Part:

(a) Starting with R foot, take eight waltz steps forward moving clockwise around the boy. Clap hands at the second and third beats of every measure. Move the hands sideward right and left and the head turns to the right and left. .... 8 M.

Boy and Girl:

Repeat all, reversing direction. Finish in proper places. .... 8 M.

III

Music A. (Play once only.)

(a) Execute a slide-step turn right in place (six measures). Right arm high in fifth position doing a "kumintang" every measure, left hand on waist. .... 6 M.

(b) Starting with the R foot, take two waltz steps forward to partner's place passing by right shoulders, arms in lateral position at waist level, moving sideward right and left. Finish facing partner. .... 2 M.

(c) Repeat all (a and b) finishing in proper places. .... 8 M.

IV

Music B.

Boy's Part:

(a) Repeat the step-hop as in figure II. This time he hits his buttocks and thighs with the palms of his hands in the second and third beats of every measure. .... 16 M.

204

Girl's Part:

(a) The girl repeats the same movements as in figure II. ... 16 M. Finish the dance with a bow to the audience.

NOTE: The boy becomes more and more enthusiastic as the music progresses. The dance may be repeated many times. At actual wedding celebrations many repetitions mean more money and presents for the performers.

The money and gifts are collected by the groom and given to the bride. A shy couple or poor dancers receive little because people do not enjoy giving to them.

Pandang-Pandang

ANTIQUE

Notation by
A. BUENAVENTURA

A 1-3 (Play once)

PANDANG-PANDANG, Figure II (a)
(see page 204)

Pandango

(Ilocano)

This "Fandango" or "Pandango" is very popular. Although it is danced in many different versions, lively motion is always present.

Each locality has its own characteristic movements. It may be danced with the use of a hat, "salakot," glass of wine, handkerchiefs, or with the hands empty.

The dancers are free in their movements and may go in any direction. Even the steps and figures are not definite; everything depends upon the skill and ability of the dancers. The "pandango" described below was found in Camiling, Tarlac.

COSTUME. The girl wears "balintawak" style, the boy "barong tagalog" with colored trousers and a "buri" or "balangot" hat. Both dancers are barefoot.

MUSIC. One part only, repeated six times.

COUNT *one, two, three* to a measure.

FORMATION. This is a single couple dance but may be performed by several couples. Partners stand at one side or corner of the room. Girl stands at partner's right.

INTRODUCTION

Music Introduction.

Partners join inside hands. Boy leads girl to the center of the room or stage. Girl turns counterclockwise under the arch of their joined hands and both bow to the audience. .... 2 M.

I

Girl's Part:

(a) The girl stands at the middle of the room, tapping her R foot on the first and third beats of every measure. She holds her skirt, raising the right side a little to show the R foot. .... 24 M.

(b) Pause. .... 1 M.

Boy's Part:

(a) The boy holds the hat with the right hand, left hand on waist. He dances around the girl counterclockwise by taking two waltz steps forward (R, L) (cts. 1, 2, 3, 1, 2, 3) and a waltz-turn right (cts. 1, 2, 3, 1, 2, 3). The right hand is swayed sideward right and left on the first two measures, the hat held with two hands (right hand holding the top and the left hand the brim of the hat) turning it down and up while doing the waltz-turn. .... 4 M.

(b) Repeat (a) five times more. The boy turns around the girl once or twice, finishing at the left side about four feet from her at the end of the twenty-fourth measure. .... 20 M.

(c) Puts on the hat. .... 1 M.

II

Girl's Part:

(a) The girl executes two close steps forward (R, L) and a waltz-turn right. Finish the turn facing in any direction. Hands holding the skirt. .... 4 M.

(b) Repeat (a) five times more. Finish each turn facing in different directions. On the last turn face audience. .... 20 M.

(c) Pause. .... 1 M.

Boy's Part:

(a) Execute twelve R and L sway-balance steps with a brush, arms in fourth position, R and L arms high alternately. As he executes the sway-balance steps he moves little by little around the girl either clockwise or counter-clockwise. Touch the hat smartly with the right hand every four measures. .... 24 M.

(b) Take off the hat and put it on the head of the girl. .... 1 M.

III

Girl's Part:

(a) Take two waltz steps forward (R, L) and a waltz-turn right, arms in lateral position moving sideward right and left. 4 M.

(b) Repeat (a) five times more, going in any direction as if avoiding the boy. .... 20 M.

(c) Take off the hat. .... 1 M.

Boy's Part:

(a) Boy executes the same movements as the girl, following her wherever she goes. .... 24 M.

(b) Pause. .... 1 M.

IV

Boy's Part:

(a) The boy stands at the middle and taps his R foot at the first and third beats of each measure, hands on waist. He follows the movements of the girl with his eyes. .... 24 M.

(b) Pause. .... 1 M.

Girl's Part:

    (a) Repeat the steps of the boy in figure I. She tries to put the hat on the boy's head as she goes around him but does not actually do so. .... 24 M.

    (b) Puts the hat on her own head. .... 1 M.

V

Girl's Part:

    (a) Tries to get away from the boy by taking two waltz steps forward (R, L) and a waltz-turn right, arms in lateral position moving sideward right and left. Finishes in the middle of the room at the end of the sixteenth measure. .... 16 M.

    (b) Executes pivot turn right with a point, right arm in fifth position doing a "kumintang," left hand on waist or holding the skirt. .... 4 M.

    (c) Repeats (b) to the left. Reverses the arm position. ...... 4 M.

    (d) Puts the hat on the floor upside down between them .... 1 M.

Boy's Part:

    (a) The boy follows the girl as she passes, executing the same steps as the girl. Finishes standing at the left side of the girl about four feet from her at the end of the sixteenth measure. .... 16 M.

    (b) Claps hands in time to the music (every first and third beats) as the girl executes the pivot turn with a point. .... 8 M.

    (c) Pause. .... 1 M.

VI

Partners dance around the hat counterclockwise by taking the following steps:

    (a) Tap R foot close to L in first position (ct. 1, pause, ct. 2), tap R in fourth in front (ct. 3), arms in fourth position, hands doing a "kumintang." .... 1 M.

    (b) Repeat (a). .... 1 M.

    (c) Execute a waltz-turn right covering about one-sixth of an imaginary circle around the hat (two waltz steps). Arms in lateral position at shoulder level, moving sideward right and left. 2 M.

    (d) Repeat all (a, b, c) five times more finishing in proper places. .... 20 M.

    (e) Pause. .... 1 M.

VII

Music is played faster in (b).

Girl's Part:

    (a) Clap hands on the first and third beats of every measure. 8 M.

Boy's Part:

(a) Cross the L foot in rear of R and bend the trunk forward-downward slowly until the head reaches the hat on the floor. The arms are raised sideward at shoulder level, moving up and down with flying motions to maintain balance. The head should pick up the hat unaided. .... 8 M.

NOTE: Play as much music as necessary. It may take more than eight measures to pick up the hat. Much depends upon the agility of the individual dancer.

(b) As soon as the boy succeeds in getting the hat on he pursues the girl. She evades him by executing the following steps in a faster tempo:

The waltz steps and waltz-turn alternately going in any direction. Sometimes they are face to face or back to back after each turn. The boy follows the girl closely. .... 16 M.

(c) Finish facing the audience with the girl standing at the right of the boy. Join inside hands. The girl turns counterclockwise under the arch of their arms and both bow to audience. .... 2 M.

Pandango

ILOCANO

Pandango

(Visayan)

The "pandango" (derived from the Spanish "fandango") is so popular that it is found in many places in the Philippines. There are many versions of this dance, and even within one locality, dancers have different ways of performing it. It has gay and sprightly figures. It may be danced at any social gathering and is usually accompanied by clapping.

The "pandango" described below is from the province of Leyte. In some places, the musicians do not stop playing until four or five couples have danced, one after the other. When one couple tires another takes its place, until there are no more who want to dance. The musicians play faster and faster after each repetition until the dancers are exhausted.

COSTUME. Girl wears "patadiong" and boy "barong tagalog" with white or red trousers.

MUSIC (one part of sixteen measures) will be found in *Philippine Folk Dances and Games* by Reyes-Ramos, page 19.

COUNT *one, two, three* to a measure.

FORMATION. Partners face each other about six feet apart. Girl stands at boy's right when facing the audience. Only one couple dances.

NOTE: It is not advisable for too many to dance at the same time because the couples go in all directions.

I

The boy holds a hat in his right hand and waltzes around looking for a partner. He approaches his choice executing waltz steps, and puts the hat on her head. This is an invitation for the girl to dance with him. .... 16 M.

II

The girl signifies her intention to dance by standing up and going to the center of the floor with the hat still on her head. The boy dances around her. He executes waltz and waltz-turn steps right alternately. He finishes at the left side of the girl. In the meantime the girl executes waltz steps sideward right and left, arms in lateral position moving sideward right and left. .... 16 M.

III

Partners face each other about six feet apart.

(a) Take two sway-balance steps with a brush (R, L), arms in fourth position, right and left arm high alternately. .... 4 M.

(b) Take one waltz-turn right (use four waltz steps) starting with the R foot. Girl holds arms in fifth position, moving sideward right and left. The boy places his hands on waist. ......: 4 M.

(c) Repeat (a) and (b) starting with the L foot. Reverse the arm positions in (a). Turn left in (b). .... 8 M.

IV

The music is played a little faster.

(a) Starting with the R foot, take two waltz steps forward to meet at center, arms in lateral position moving sideward right and left. Finish in back-to-back position. .... 2 M.

(b) Take one waltz step sideward right and one left. Arms as in (a). .... 2 M.

(c) Turn right about to face each other. Repeat (b). .... 2 M.

(d) Starting with the R foot, take two waltz steps backward to proper places. Hands as in (a). .... 2 M.

(e) Repeat all (a, b, c, and d). .... 8 M.

V

Play the music faster.

(a) Jump in place with R foot across the L in front. Bend body slightly forward and cross hands in front with the right hand over the left (cts. 1, 2, 3). .... 1 M.

(b) Turn left about on the balls of the feet. Finish the turn with heels together, body erect and arms in second position (cts. 1, 2, 3). .... 1 M.

(c) Take one waltz step sideward right and one sideward left. Arms in lateral position moving sideward right and left. .... 2 M.

(d) Repeat all (a, b, and c) three times more. .... 12 M.

VI

Play the music much faster.

With the girl leading, partners execute waltz steps and waltz-turns alternately going in any direction. The boy simulates pursuit of the evasive girl.

NOTE: To end the dance the girl takes off the hat and both bow to the audience. The hat is given to a new boy who starts looking for a partner. The same dance may be repeated or variations introduced.

Pandango Sa Ilaw

"Pandango sa Ilaw" (dance with oil lamps), this version from Mindoro, is the most difficult of all the Pandangos. It is quite unusual and colorful. The female dancer gracefully and skillfully balances three lighted "ting-hoy" or oil lamps—one on her head and one on the back of each hand.

A few boys and girls may take part as townsfolk or onlookers. They clap their hands in time to the music, adding life and gaiety to the dance.

COSTUME. The girl is dressed in "balintawak," the boy in long red trousers and "barong tagalog."

MUSIC is divided into three parts: A, B, C.

COUNT *one, two, three* to a measure.

FORMATION. Partners stand about six feet apart facing the audience. The three lighted oil lamps are placed on the floor between them. The girl stands at partner's right. (See diagram below.) The oil lamps are of two sizes, the one to be placed on the head (No. 2) being larger than the two for the hands.

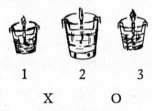

1   2   3

X   O

INTRODUCTION

Music Introduction.

    (a) Standing on the L foot, tap R in front (cts. 1, 2), tap once more (ct. 3). Place left hand on waist, R hand hanging loosely at the side. .... 1 M.

    (b) Repeat (a). .... 1 M.

    (c) Three-step turn right in place and bow to the audience. Place both hands on waist. .... 3 M.

I

Music A.

    Partners face right.

    (a) Take two waltz steps forward (R, L—2 M.), one waltz turn right (2 M.). Arms in lateral position moving sideward R and L with forearm turns. .... 4 M.

    (b) Repeat (a) three times more moving clockwise around the oil lamps. .... 12 M.

214

(c) Turn right about and repeat all (a and b) moving counterclockwise. The girl finishes with the lamps in front of her. .... 16 м.

II

Music B.

Girl's Part:

(a) Cross R foot in front of L and bend knee slightly (this position is held for thirty-two measures), arms bent forward at shoulder level. Move right (1 м.) and left elbows (1 м.) upward twice on cts. 1, 2 of each measure. The wrists are relaxed so that the hands dangle at every movement. .... 24 м.

(b) Place a lamp on the back of the right hand. .... 8 м.

Boy's Part:

(a) Repeat the movements of figure I going clockwise around the girl. Take the same arm movement of the girl in figure II (a). 24 м.

(b) Take lamp No. 1 and help the girl place it on the back of her right hand. .... 8 м.

III

Music C.

Cross-waltz step: With a spring, step R (L) forward across L (R) in front, raising the L (R) in rear at the same time (ct. 1), step L (R) in rear of R (L) (ct. 2), step R (L) in the same place (in front) (ct. 3).

(a) Starting with the R foot, take sixteen cross-waltz steps around the lamps clockwise. Boy's hands on waist, girl's free hand holding the skirt. .... 16 м.

(b) Turn right about and repeat (a) moving counterclockwise. Finish in proper places facing the audience. .... 16 м.

IV

Music A.

(a) Starting with the R foot, execute waltz steps (tiny steps) backward. The girl bends left arm upward and flutters the fingers in time to the music. Boy's hands are placed on the waist. (See illustration.) .... 8 м.

(b) Repeat (a) moving forward to original places. .... 8 м.

(c) Boy gets lamp No. 2. Partners repeat (a). Free hand of boy on the waist. .... 8 м.

(d) Boy puts the lamp on the head of the girl who stands still. .... 8 м.

215

Music B.

(a) Take one waltz step sideward R and L (2 M.), waltz-turn right (2 M.). Arms of boy and L arm of girl in lateral position at shoulder-level moving sideward R and L alternately, or L hand of girl holding the skirt. .... 2 M.

(b) Repeat (a) seven times more moving around the lamp clockwise. .... 14 M.

(c) The boy gets the third lamp and places it on the back of the left hand of the girl. The girl stands still while the boy is placing the lamp on her hand. .... 8 M.

(d) *Girl's Part:*

(1) Step R across L in front and bend right knee slightly. Raise L foot in rear at the same time (cts. 1, 2), step L in rear of R foot (ct. 3). Step R foot sideward (cts. 1, 2, 3). Hold lamps in front or obliquely forward at shoulder-level. .... 2 M.

(2) Repeat (1) three times more (L, R, L). .... 6 M.

Boy's Part:

(1) Continue waltzing around the girl counterclockwise. .... 8 M.

VI

Music C. Play once.

Girl's Part:

Stand with feet in third position, R foot in front, knees relaxed. Do the following hand movements, hands first at shoulder level in front:

(a) Raise R hand and lower L hand slowly. (Cts. 1–6.) ...... 2 M.

(b) Reverse the movements of the hands. .... 2 M.

(c) Cross the hands in front, R over the L hand. .... 2 M.

(d) Back to the starting position. .... 2 M.

(e) Repeat (a) and (b). .... 4 M.

(f) Lower both hands and bend the knees slightly. .... 2 M.

(g) Raise both hands and straighten the knees. .... 2 M.

Boy's Part:

(a) Repeat figure I, going clockwise around the girl. .... 16 M.

VII

Music C. Play once.

(a) Partners execute eight sway-balance steps with a point, R and L, moving counterclockwise little by little, arms in third position, R and L high alternately. .... 16 M.

Music C. Play once.

The boy takes the two lamps from the hands of the girl (one in each hand) leaving one on her head.

(a) Partners repeat the steps of figure I, going in any direction with the boy following the girl. .... 14 M.

(b) Three-step turn right in place and bow to the audience. 2 M.

Boy's Arm Movements:

(a) The boy moves the lamps one up and the other down (2 M.), crosses the hands in front, R over L (2 M.), L over R (2 M.), circling R hand clockwise and L counterclockwise (2 M.). 8 M.

(b) Repeats (a) up to 6 measures. .... 6 M.

(c) Hands at the sides while bowing. .... 2 M.

Girl's Arm Movements:

(a) Repeat the arm movements of figure I for 14 measures. 14 M.

(b) Takes the glass from her head with the R hand and opens the hands sideward while bowing. .... 2 M.

PANDANGO SA ILAW, Figure VI (a)

Pandango Sa Ilaw

MINDORO

Music by
A. BUENAVENTURA

218

B II–V

Paruparóng-Bukid

(Meadow Butterfly)

"Paruparóng-Bukid" is a very popular folk song. Little boys and girls love its easy, catchy melody and the story behind the song.

A flirtatious meadow butterfly goes fluttering about in the middle of the street, showing off her finery. She wears a one-yard tunic over a little petticoat, a skirt with an incredibly long train, and an ornamental comb. She primps before a mirror and seems pleased with her reflection. She walks coquettishly, swaying her hips.

The steps given below are arranged for small children. The dance must be accompanied by the song to give expression to the pantomimic movements of the dancers. It is danced by girls only.

CostUME. The dancers are dressed in "balintawak." The skirt must have a long train, sometimes tucked in at the waistband, a petticoat, and "tapis" (apron). A large comb is also worn.

Music * is divided into two parts: A and B.

Count *one, two, three* to a measure.

FORMATION. The dancers stand four feet apart in one line or in a semicircle facing the audience (see diagrams A and B). Any number of dancers may take part.

```
                              O               O

  O  O  O  O  O  O          O                 O
                                 O   O

          A                       B
```

I

Music A. Sing the first verse.

(a) Take one waltz step forward R (cts. 1, 2, 3) and backward L (cts. 1, 2, 3), hands on waist. .... 2 M.

(b) Starting with the R foot, take three steps forward (cts. 1, 2, 3). Close L to R foot and pause (cts. 1, 2, 3). Raise arms sideward and wave the hands as if flying. .... 2 M.

(c) Take one waltz step sideward R (cts. 1, 2, 3) and L (cts. 1, 2, 3), hands holding the "tapis." .... 2 M.

(d) Take four stamps in place (cts. 1, 2, 3, 4), pause (cts. 5, 6), waving the "tapis" to and fro with the R and L hands when stamping. .... 2 M.

(e) Holding the "tapis" with the R hand, raise it to show its length. .... 2 M.

* Words, music, and illustration for this dance will be found in *The Progressive Music Series, Philippine Edition*, Book One, page LX.

(f) With open palm of the R hand measure the left sleeve of the "camisa" when singing "sang dangkal ang mangas." ...... 2 M.

(g) Turn right about. Starting with the R foot take four waltz steps forward to proper places. Have the train of the skirt down while doing the waltz steps. Finish facing front and tuck up the train in the waist band. .... 4 M.

(h) Repeat all. .... 16 M.

II

Music B. Sing the second verse.

(a) Take three steps sideward right (R, L, R—cts. 1, 2, 3) and point L in front (cts. 1, 2, 3). Touch or point at the comb with the R hand, L hand holding the skirt. .... 2 M.

(b) Repeat (a) to the left.
Reverse the hand positions. .... 2 M.

(c) Point R in front (cts. 1, 2) close R to L (ct. 3), hands holding the skirt, raising it at the right side with the right hand to show the petticoat. .... 1 M.

(d) Repeat (c) three times more pointing and raising skirt. 3 M.

(e) Starting with the R foot, take three steps forward (cts. 1, 2, 3), hands holding skirt. .... 1 M.

(f) Close L to R foot (ct. 1), pause (cts. 2, 3). Imitate looking at self in a mirror (cts. 1, 2, 3), while singing "At mananalamin." 2 M.

(g) Starting with the R foot, take three steps backward (cts. 1, 2, 3). Place hands on waist. .... 1 M.

(h) Close L to R foot (ct. 1) and pause (cts. 2, 3). Hands on waists. .... 1 M.

(i) Move the hips four times sideward R and L while singing "kendeng-kendeng." Pause on the last measure. .... 3 M.

(j) Repeat all. .... 16 M.

NOTE: The dance may be repeated as many times as desired.

Pasakat

This is a French ballroom quadrille which was introduced in the Philippines by the Spaniards and by the Filipinos who returned from travels during the later part of the nineteenth century. Only people of high social standing danced this during the Spanish regime. It is an easy but stately and elegant dance.

It was originally known as "Pas de Quatre" or "Paso de Cuatro" but Filipinos later on corrupted the word to "Pasakat."

According to reports from the old people this dance was at one time (close of the nineteenth century) prohibited by religious leaders and pious parents because the waists and hands of the girls were held by the boys.

The dance described below was discovered in Sta. Rosa, Laguna.

Costume. Ladies wear the Maria Clara style. Gentlemen wear black trousers with white embroidered "barong tagalog" or long "barong tagalog" with a black jacket. (See illustration.)

Music is divided into six parts: Introduction, A, B, C, D, and E.

Note: The music for this dance was copied from an old manuscript, composer unknown.

Count *one, two, three, four* to a measure in 4/4 time and *one, and, two, and,* to a measure in 12/8 time.

Formation. Dancers stand in square formation. Each couple take a corner of the square, ladies stand at partners right always. (See diagram 1.) Only four pairs are in one square, but any number of squares may take part.

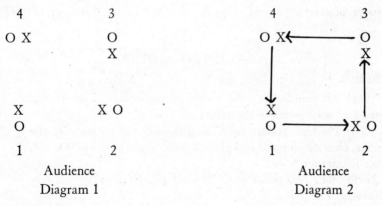

Diagram 1

Diagram 2

Audience

Steps Used:

"Pasakat" Step.

(a) Partners join inside hands, lady's free hand holding the skirt and gentleman's on waist.

223

Starting with the inside foot take one polka step forward. Swing the inside hands forward, looking at the outside foot (away from partner) at the end of the polka step (cts. 1, *and* 2, *and*). . . . . 1 M.

(b) With the outside foot, take one polka step forward. Swing the inside hands backward, partners look at each other. . . . . 1 M.

(c) Release the inside hands and hold as in the ordinary ballroom dance position. Turn around clockwise six steps in place or in any direction indicated (cts. 1, *and* 2 *and,* 1 *and*). Pause (ct. 2, *and*). . . . . 2 M.

ENTRANCE

Music Introduction.

Position: Ladies stand at partners' right, holding his right arm with her left hand (popularly known as "abrasete") or partners may join inside hands.

Starting with the R foot, partners walk majestically to proper places. (See diagram 1.) Take one step for every two counts. . . . . 7 M.

I

"PASAKAT" TO CORNERS

Music A. Play twice.

(a) Each couple execute one "pasakat" step to opposite corners. Pair 1 go to the corner of Pair 2, Pair 2 to Pair 3, Pair 3 to Pair 4, Pair 4 to Pair 1. (See diagram 2.) . . . . 4 M.

(b) Repeat (a) three times more. All couples traveling from corner to corner in a counterclockwise direction. All finish in their proper places. . . . . : . . . . 12 M.

II

LADIES FORM STAR

Music B.

(a) All couples face the center of the square. Execute one "pasakat" step going to the center. . . . . 4 M.

(b) Partners release hold. Ladies join right hands at the center. Gentlemen stand and place R hand at the back of the waist. (See illustration.)

Ladies take two polka steps forward (R, L) moving half-way clockwise. . . . . 2 M.

(c) Ladies stop in front of the opposite gentleman, lady 1 in front of gentleman 3, lady 2 in front of gentleman 4, lady 3 in front of gentleman 1, lady 4 in front of gentleman 2. Gentleman turn their new partners to their proper corners. (Pasacat step (c).) 2 M.

(d) Repeat (a) going to center again. . . . . 4 M.

224

PASAKAT, FIGURE II (b) LADIES FORM STAR

(e) Ladies repeat (b) finishing in front of partners. .... 2 M.

(f) With proper partners, gentlemen repeat (c) going to their proper places. .... 2 M.

III

LADIES EXCHANGE PLACES

Music C. Play twice.

(a) Pairs 1 and 2, 3 and 4 face each other. All execute "pasakat" step (a and b) to meet at the center. .... 2 M.
Gentlemen exchange ladies. Take new partners to proper places by doing "pasakat" step (c). .... 2 M.

(b) Gentlemen 4 and 1, 3 and 2 and their new partners face each other. Repeat (a). .... 4 M.

(c) Gentlemen 1 and 2, 3 and 4 and their new partners face each other. Repeat (a). .... 4 M.

(d) Repeat (b). All ladies finish in proper places with their own partners. .... 4 M.

NOTE: In this figure the ladies are traveling, the gentlemen always return to their proper places after taking a new partner.

IV

FORM SINGLE FILE

Music D. Play once.

(a) All take two "pasakat" steps to form in line with Pair 1. Pair 1 do the steps in place, Pair 4 move forward to be in line with Pair 1, Pair 3 must pass the corner of Pair 4 to be in line with Pairs 1 and 4, and Pair 2 must pass the corners of Pairs 3 and 4 to be in line with Pairs 1, 4, and 3. (See diagram 3 below.) All finish with right shoulders toward the audience, all ladies at the right side of their partners. (See diagram 4.) .... 8 M.

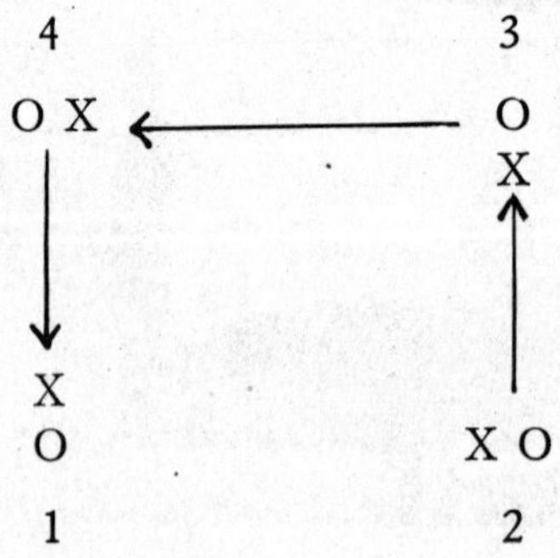

Diagram 3

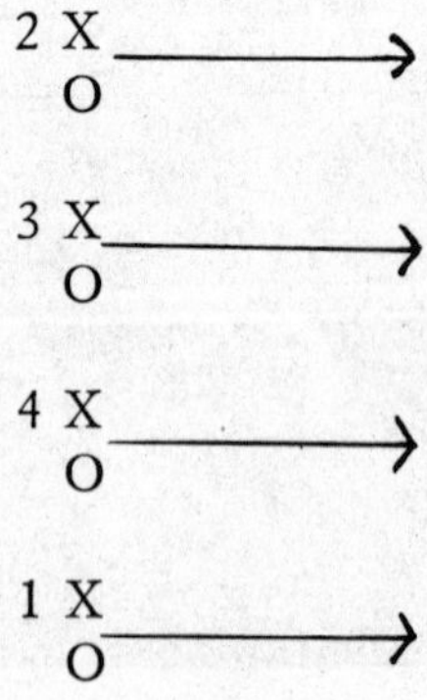

Diagram 4

226

PASAKAT, Figure V (a) See Saw

V

SEE SAW

Music D. Play twice.

(a) All take one "pasakat" step forward going to opposite side of the square (see diagram 5 and illustration). Finish the turn facing about with the lady at the right side. .... 4 M.

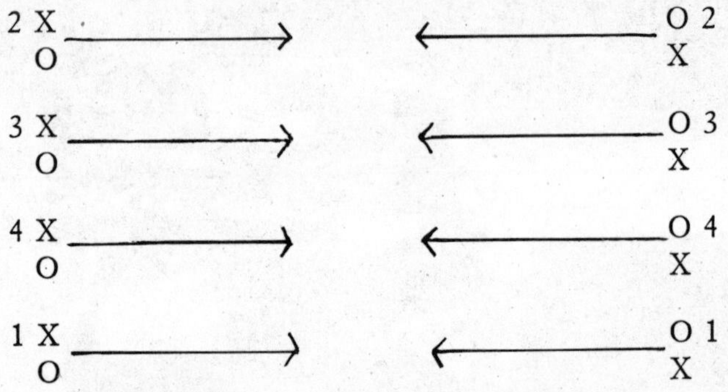

```
2 X  ·                                    O 2
  O  ───────────→        ←───────────     X

3 X                                       O 3
  O  ───────────→        ←───────────     X

4 X                                       O 4
  O  ───────────→        ←───────────     X

1 X                                       O 1
  O  ───────────→        ←───────────     X
```

Diagram 5   Diagram 6

(b) Repeat (a) going back to starting place (see diagram 6). Finish the turn facing about with the ladies at the right side. .... 4 M.
   (c) Repeat (a). .... 4 M.
   (d) Repeat (b). .... 4 M.

VI

Music D. Play once.

All execute two "pasakat" steps going back to square formation, Pair 1 do the steps in place and Pairs 4, 3, and 2 retrace their steps in figure IV. .... 8 M.

VII

"SALUDO"

Music E.

(a) All face the audience. All execute two "pasakat" steps. Pairs 1 and 2 do the steps in place. Pairs 4 and 3 moving forward in line with Pairs 1 and 2. All finish facing the audience. (See diagram 7.)

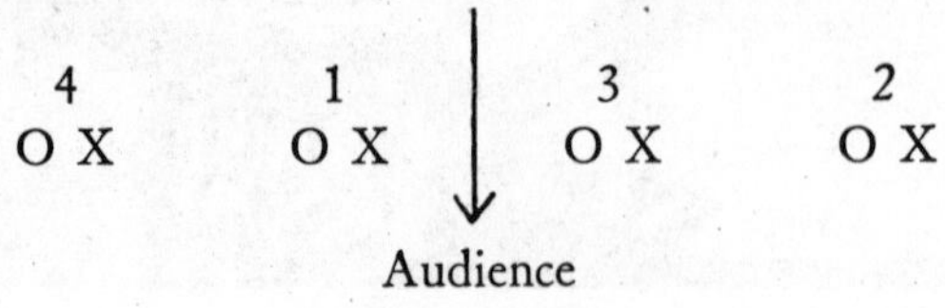

```
     4         1    │    3         2
   O X       O X    │  O X       O X
                    ↓
```

Audience

Diagram 7

228

Pair 4 stand at the extreme right of the dancers followed by Pairs 1, 3, and 2. . . . . 8 M.

(b) Partners join right hands overhead. Gentlemen stand in place with the left hands on waist. Ladies turn counterclockwise (1 M.) and clockwise (1 M.) under the arch of the raised arms, left hand holding skirts. . . . . 2 M.

(c) Partners turn around clockwise once using walking steps, right hands still joined. . . . . 1 M.

(d) All face the audience, ladies at the right of partners. Bow to the audience. . . . . 1 M.

EXIT

Music as in Entrance.

Partners turn about and gentlemen swing the ladies to their right side. Repeat the steps in Entrance. . . . . 7 M.

SUA–SUA, Figure I (b)
(see page 314)

Pasakat

D IV - V - VI

con 8va

Play D 4 times

233

Polkabal

This dance acquired its name from two well-known steps, "polka" and "valse" (waltz), corrupted into one word, "polkabal" or "porkabal," by the people of Atimonan, Tayabas, where it was found.

"Luksong Uak," "Ensayo," "Paseo," "Contra-gansa," "Punta y tacon," "Wagayway" and "Jardin" are some of the lively steps and figures included in this interesting discovery. In the original dance, the "Paseo" and "Ensayo" are danced at the intermissions making it rather long and monotonous. These two steps are used here as figures, not as interludes.

COSTUME. Girls may wear any old-style costume (Maria Clara, "serpentina," "siete cuchillos," etc.). Boys wear "barong tagalog," with black trousers.

MUSIC is divided into two parts: A and B. It is repeated four times and played in a regular 2/4 tempo.

COUNT *one, and, two and* or *one, two.*

FORMATION. Partners stand opposite each other four feet apart. Girls stand at partner's right when facing the audience. Two pairs make a set or form a square in this dance. From one to any number of sets may take part. (See diagram A.)

Audience

1 X	O 1	1 X	O 1	1 X	O 1
I		II		III	
2 X	O 2	2 X	O 2	2 X	O 2

Diagram A

INTRODUCTION

Music Introduction.

Partners face the audience.

Step R foot forward, point L in fourth in rear, left hand of girl holds skirt, right hand on waist. Boys have both hands on waist.   2 M.

I
LUKSONG UAK

Music A.

Partners face the center of the square.

Boys' Part:

(a) Step R foot toward the center of the square (ct. 1), hop on the same foot and raise the left foot in rear (ct. 2). Half turn

235

POLKABAL, Figure I (b) Luksong Uak

right by pivoting on the R foot and step L immediately toward the center (ct. 1), hop on the L and raise the R foot in rear (ct. 2). Hands on waist. . . . .   2 м.

(b) Half-turn right by pivoting on the L foot and immediately step R toward the center (ct. 1). Dancers are now at the center, facing center (diagrams B and C and illustration). Take three hops on the R foot, L foot raised in rear, arms in third position, L arm high. . . . .   2 м.

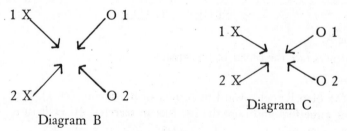

Diagram B

Diagram C

(c) Step L outward from the center (ct. 1) hop on the same foot and raise R foot in rear (ct. 2). Half-turn left by pivoting on the L foot. Immediately step R outward going to proper places (ct. 1), hop on the same foot and raise the L in rear (ct. 2). Hands on waist. . . . . 2 M.

(d) Step L foot backward (in place if already there) (ct. 1), raise R foot in front and *scissors kick* (bring R foot swiftly down and raise the L simultaneously) (ct. 2). (See diagram D.) . . . . . . 1 M.

Diagram D

(e) Cross-turn right, that is, cross the L in front of R foot (ct. 1), make a full turn right by pivoting on the balls of the feet (ct. 2). . . . . 1 M.

Girls' Part:

Girls do the same, starting with the opposite foot (L foot) and turning the opposite way. In (a) and (c) girls hold skirts. . . . . 8 M.

(f) Boys and girls repeat all movements. . . . . 8 M.

II

"PASEO AT ENSAYO"

Music B.

Partners face the audience.

"Paseo":

(a) Place the inside heel sideward, bend the body in, arms in fourth position, outside arm high on count 1. Feet together, trunk erect, arms down at the sides on count 2. . . . . 1 M.

(b) Each set casts off with pair 1 leading. Take five change steps forward, starting with the outside foot. Finish in proper places (see diagram E), arms hanging loosely at the sides moving gracefully forward and backward as the change steps are executed. . . . . 5 M.

NOTE: Boys' hands on waist and girls holding skirts if a large group participates.

237

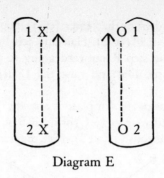

Diagram E

(c) Girls raise L foot, boys R, and scissors kick as in figure I (d). .... 1 M.

(d) Cross-turn (girls turn left and boys turn right) as in figure I (e). .... 1 M.

"Ensayo":

(a) Take six step-swing steps sideward (L and R alternately for the girls, and R and L alternately for the boys). Arms are in lateral position at shoulder level moving in opposite direction with the feet. .... 6 M.

(b) Repeat scissors kick and cross turn as in (c) and (d) above. .... 2 M.

III

"PUNTA Y TACON"

Music A.

Partners face audience.

(a) Place the heel of the inside foot sideward and bend the body in (ct. 1). Hop on the outside foot and raise the inside foot in rear of the outside foot at the same time (ct. 2). Girls hold skirts, boys' hands on waist. .... 1 M.

(b) Step sideward with the inside foot raising the toe of outside foot (heel remains on the floor), bend the body toward the outside (ct. 1). Hop on the inside foot and raise the outside foot in rear of the inside foot (ct. 2). Hands as in (a). .... 1 M.

(c) Repeat (b) starting with the outside foot.

(d) Take three-step turn (right for the boys and left for the girls) to partner's place. Girls pass in front of partner. Hands as in (a). .... 1 M.

(e) Repeat all (a, b, c, d) three times more, always starting with the inside foot in (a). Finish in proper places. .... 12 M.

IV

"CONTRA–GANSA"

Music B.

Partners face audience.

(a) Leap outward starting with the outside foot (ct. 1). Step the inside foot across the outside foot in front (ct. *and*), and quickly step the outside foot to place (ct. 2, *and*). .... 1 M.

(b) Repeat (a) two times more, starting with the inside and outside foot alternately. .... 2 M.

(c) Take three-step turn to partner's place as in figure III (d). 1 M.

(d) Repeat all (a, b, c) three times more, finishing in proper places. .... 12 M.

Throughout this figure, girls hold skirts, boys have hands on waists.

V

"WAGAYWAY"

Music A.

Partners face audience.

(a) Place the heel of the inside foot sideward and bend the body in the same direction, arms in third position, outside arm high (ct. 1), position (ct. 2). .... 1 M.

(b) Repeat (a) with the outside heel placed sideward outside. Reverse the position of the arms. .... 1 M.

(c) Pivot-turn with both feet flat on the floor. (Boys turn right and girls left.) Right arm of boys and left of girls in fifth position, the other hand on waist (cts. 1, *and*, 2, *and*, 1, *and*, 2, *and*). .... 2 M.

NOTE: In executing the pivot-turn the leading foot steps on count 1 and the rear foot slides to close on count *and*, until the turn is completed.

(d) Repeat all (a, b, c) three times more, starting with the outside, inside, and outside foot alternately. Reverse the position of the arms for every corresponding change of direction in turning. 12 M.

NOTE: If starting with the outside foot, the pivot-turn is outward and if with the inside foot, the turn is inward.

VI

"CONTRA–GANSA DOBLE"

Music B.

Partners face each other.

239

A. Pair 1 join hands crosswise with right hands over the left. Execute the following steps moving sideward away from the audience.

(a) *Boys' Part:*

Jump with the L foot over the R in front (ct. 1), hop on R and raise the L foot sideward (ct. *and*), step the L in rear of R foot (ct. 2), step R foot sideward (ct. *and*). . . . . 1 M.

(b) Repeat (a) five times more moving sideward away from the audience at every jump. Finish in Pair 2's place. (See diagram F.) . . . . 5 M.

Girls' Part:

Girls do the same, starting with the R foot across the left in front. 5 M.

(c) Partners drop hands, separate and do the scissors kick and cross-turn as in figure I (d) and (e) respectively to finish in Pair 2's place. . . . . 2 M.

Pair 2.

While Pair 1 are doing their steps, Pair 2 execute the following steps simultaneously.

(a) Repeat the "Ensayo" as in figure II (a) moving toward the audience. . . . . 6 M.

(b) Repeat the scissors kick and turn as in figure I (d) and (e). Finish in Pair 1's place. (See diagram F.) . . . . 2 M.

1

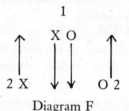

Diagram F

B. (a) Pair 2 join hands with arms crossed and repeat the movements of Pair 1 above. (See diagram G.)

Pair 1 repeats the movements of Pair 2 above, doing the "Ensayo" moving to their proper places. . . . . 8 M.

2

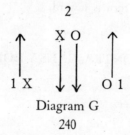

Diagram G

240

POLKABAL; Figure VII (a) Corrida

VII
"CORRIDA"

Music A.

Partners face audience.

(a) Raise the inside foot sideward and quickly step sideward (ct. 1), take three more tiny steps or shuffling steps, moving sideward toward partner's place (cts. *and, 2, and*), outside arm raised in fifth position and inside arm bent in front at shoulder level. (See illustration.) . . . . 1 M.

(b) Repeat (a) once more finishing in partner's place. Girls pass in front of partners. . . . . 1 M.

(c) Pivot-turn as in figure V(c). Boys turn right, right arm high in fifth position, left hand on waist. Girls turn left, left arm high in fifth position, right hand on waist. . . . . 2 M.

(d) Repeat (a, b, c) going back to proper places. Reverse the pivot-turn and the arm positions in (c). . . . . 4 M.

(e) Repeat all (a, b, c, d). . . . . 8 M.

VIII
"JARDIN"

Music B.

Partners meet at center forming a single line facing the audience. Girls stand in front of partners. Join hands, boy's right with the girl's right, and his left with her left.

(a) Raise left arm high, right arm down at the sides. Bend the body to the right. Execute a pivot-turn to the right. . . . . 4 M.

(b) Reverse the arm positions and bend the body to the left. Execute a pivot-turn to the left. . . . . 4 M.

(c) Repeat all (a, b). . . . . 8 M.

"SALUDO"

Music Finale.

Partners join right hands. Girls turn clockwise under the arch of arms (three-step turn in place). . . . . 1 M.

Release hands. Girls step L sideward, a little to the left of partners (ct. 1). Partners bend body to the right, arms in third position, L arm high. Look at partner (ct. 2). 1 M.

Polkabal

Play 4 times

Polka Sala

(Ballroom)

This is an old ballroom dance found in Calapan, Mindoro. During the Spanish regime the polka was very common and was sometimes combined with other ballroom dance steps like the "polka mazurka" and the "polka-valse." Its simple and interesting figures make it an enjoyable experience.

COSTUME. Girls may wear any old-style costume and boys "barong tagalog" with black trousers.

MUSIC is divided into three parts: A, B, and C.

COUNT *one, and, two,* and, to a measure.

FORMATION. Partners hold as in ordinary ballroom dance position. The extended arms remain straight in the old style position. Partners may go in any direction but formations may be arranged if desired. From one to any number of pairs may take part.

I

Music A.

Partners execute polka steps going in any direction. .... 16 M.

II

Music B.

Partners release polka positions and join inside hands, the girl at the right side of the boy. Free hand of the girl holds the skirt, boy's free hand on waist.

(a) Starting with the outside foot, partners take one polka step forward (cts. 1, *and,* 2, *and*). .... 1 M.

(b) Place the heel of the inside foot forward (cts. 1, *and*), touch toe backward (cts. 2, *and*). .... 1 M.

(c) Release the hold and turn about (girl turns left and boy right about). Join inside hands after turning. Repeat (a and b). 2 M.

(d) Release the hold and turn about (girl turns right and boy left about). Join inside hands after turning. Repeat (a and b). .... 2 M.

(e) Repeat (c) and (d) alternately, five times more going in any direction. .... 10 M.

Free hand of the girl holds skirt, boy's on waist.

III

Music A.

Partners release. The boy stands behind the girl, both facing the same direction. Join both hands and extend them to the sides (the girl's right in the boy's right and her left in his left).

(a) Lower the right hands and bend the trunk slightly to the right. Point R foot sideward right (cts. 1, *and*), point it close to the L foot (cts. 2, *and*). . . . . 1 M.

(b) Take one polka step sideward right (cts. 1, *and*, 2, *and*). 1 M.

(c) Reverse the position of the arms and bend to the left. Repeat (a) and (b) starting with the L foot. . . . . 2 M.

(d) Repeat all (a, b, and c) three times more. . . . . 12 M.

IV

Music C.

Dancers have the same position as in figure III.

(a) Take four galop steps sideward right. Left arm high and right down. . . . . 2 M.

(b) Take four galop steps sideward left. Reverse the arm positions. . . . . 2 M.

(c) Repeat (a) and (b) three times more, going in any direction. . . . . 12 M.

NOTE: The whole dance may be repeated as many times as desired.

245

Polka Sala

(Demonstration)

For mass demonstration.

This dance, for large groups, should be performed outdoors. The steps and costumes are the same as those in the Polka Sala. The participants are arranged in equal numbers in parallel lines. (See diagram.) Girl stands at the right side.

Audience

1 X O	1 X O	1 X O	1 X O
2 X O	2 X O	2 X O	2 X O
1 X O	1 X O	1 X O	1 X O
2 X O	2 X O	2 X O	2 X O
1 X O	1 X O	1 X O	1 X O
2 X O	2 X O	2 X O	2 X O
1 X O	1 X O	1 X O	1 X O
2 X O	2 X O	2 X O	2 X O

I

POLKA FORWARD

Music A.

(a) Partners join inside hands. Starting with the outside foot, take eight polka steps forward. Swing the inside hands backward and forward alternately at the same time looking at and away from partner alternately. Free hand of girl holds skirt, boy's on waist. .... 8 M.

(b) Drop inside hands. Turn about (girl turns right and boy left) and join inside hands. Free hands as in (a). Repeat (a), starting with the inside foot. Swing the inside hands forward and backward. .... 8 M.

II

POLKA, HEEL AND TOE

Music B.

Drop inside hands. Turn about (girl turns left and boy right) and join the inside hands. Free hand as in I (a) throughout this figure.

(a) Starting with the outside foot, partners take one polka step forward. .... 1 M.

247

(b) Place the heel of the inside foot forward (cts. 1, *and*), touch toe backward of the same foot (cts. 2, *and*). Look at partner on count 2, *and*. .... 1 M.

(c) Drop hands and turn about (girl turns left and boy right). Join inside hands and repeat (a) and (b). .... 2 M.

(d) Drop hands and turn about (girl turns right and boy left). Join inside hands and repeat (a) and (b). .... 2 M.

(e) Repeat (c). .... 2 M.

(f) Repeat all (a, b, c, d, e). .... 8 M.

III
POINT, CLOSE, POLKA STEP

Music A.

Take the same position as in figure III of the ballroom Polka Sala.

Repeat figure III of the same dance. .... 16 M.

IV
GALOP RIGHT AND LEFT

Music B.

Take the same position as in figure III.

(a) Take four galop steps sideward right. .... 2 M.

(b) Take four galop steps sideward left. .... 2 M.

(c) Repeat all (a and b) three times more. .... 12 M.

V
POLKA CLOCKWISE

Music A.

(a) Partners face each other and join right hands. Free hands as in figure I (a).

Take four polka steps clockwise, starting with the right foot. Finish in proper places. .... 4 M.

(b) Drop right hands and join left hands. Free hands as in (a). Starting with the right foot, take four polka steps counterclockwise. Finish in proper places. .... 4 M.

(c) Repeat all (a and b). .... 8 M.

VI
POLKA, HEEL AND TOE

Music B.

Repeat figure II. .... 16 M.

Music A.

    (a) Repeat figure III. .... 16 м.

All No. 1's start with the R foot and all No. 2's with the L foot.

VIII

RIGHT AND LEFT SQUARE

Music B.

    Repeat the steps of figure IV in the following manner:

    (a) Take four galop steps sideward right. .... 2 м.

    (b) Turn right and take four galop steps sideward right. .... 2 м.

    (c) Repeat (b) two times more. Finish facing front. (See diagram A.) .... 4 м.

    (d) Repeat all, going to the left and turning always to the left. See diagram B. .... 8 м.

    Partners join inside hands and bow on the last measure.

start   start

Diagram A   Diagram B

Purpuri

This dance is found in many parts of the Philippines under different names and in various versions. It is sometimes known as "La Jota Purpuri," "Papuri," "Puri-puri," and "Purpuri."

"Purpuri" is coined from Potpouri which means a medley or mixture. This is an Ilocano dance found in Camiling, Tarlac.

COSTUME. The dancers are dressed in typical Ilocano costume.

MUSIC is divided into five parts: A, B, C, D, and E.

COUNT *one, two, three* to a measure.

FORMATION. Partners face each other about six feet apart. When facing the audience, girl stands at partner's right. From one to any number of pairs may take part.

INTRODUCTION

Music Introduction.

Partners make a three-step turn in place and bow to each other. Girl holding skirt and boy's hands in second position when bowing. .... 2 M.

I

Music A.

(a) Execute seven sway-balance steps with a point, R and L, arms in fourth position, right and left arm high alternately. ...... 14 M.

(b) Take a three-step turn left to places, girl holding skirt, boy's hands on waist. .... 2 M.

(c) Repeat all (a and b), starting with the left foot. Reverse the arm positions in (a). Turn to the right in (b). .... 16 M.

II

Music B.

(a) Take one sway-balance with a point to right, arms in fourth position, R arm high. .... 2 M.

(b) Take a two-step turn left to place (cts. 1, 2), point L foot in rear of R and bend the knees slightly (ct. 3). Pause (cts. 1, 2, 3). Girl holds skirt and boy places his hands on waist while turning on counts 1, 2, and when pointing the L foot in rear of R foot, the left hand is in reverse "T" position doing a "kumintang," the right hand on waist. Hands are down at the sides during the pause. .... 2 M.

(c) Repeat (a) and (b), starting with the L foot, reversing arm position in (a). Turn to right in (b), reverse arm movements.   4 M.

(d) Repeat all (a, b, c) three times more. . . . .   24 M.

III

Music C.

(a) Starting with the R foot, partners take four waltz steps to meet at center. On the fourth waltz, the girl turns right about, back toward her partner, arms in lateral position moving sideward right and left alternately. . . . .   4 M.

(b) Take four slide steps sideward right. Place left hand on waist, right hand doing a "kumintang" on every measure. . . . .   4 M.

(c) Repeat (b) going to sideward left. Reverse the hand positions. . . . .   4 M.

(d) Starting with the R foot, partners go back to proper places with four waltz steps. Boy moves backward and girl moves forward. On the fourth waltz step she turns right about to face her partner. Arms as in (a). . . . .   4 M.

(e) Repeat all (a, b, c, d), this time the boy turning about in (a) and (d) on the last measure. . . . .   16 M.

IV

Music A.

Repeat figure I. . . . .   32 M.

V

"PATAY"

Music B.

(a) Partners take two slide steps obliquely forward to center (R, L). Girl holding skirt, boy's hands on waist. At the end of the second slide step they are standing left shoulder to left shoulder.   2 M. ·

(b) Make a three-step turn right in place and finish in one line facing each other (cts. 1, 2, 3). The boy faces toward and the girl away from the audience. Point L foot across the R in rear and bend the knees slightly. The boy bows his head down into the crook of his left elbow, right hand holding the left to support the weight of his head. The girl touches the arm of the boy gently as if to console him (cts. 1, 2, 3). See diagram (a). . . . .   2 M.

(c) Repeat (a) and (b). Partners finish facing each other at the center, exchanging places. See diagram (b). . . . .   2 M.

(d) Repeat (a) and (b), this time they finish in one line facing each other, the girl toward and the boy away from the audience. See diagram (c). . . . .   4 M.

251

(e) Repeat (a) going to proper places. See diagram (d). ....   2 M.

(f) Make a three-step turn right, finish facing each other (cts. 1, 2, 3). Point L foot in rear of R and bend knees slightly. "Kumintang" with the right hand, left hand on waist. ....   2 M.

(g) Repeat all (a, b, c, d, e, f) this time the girl doing the "patay" movement and the boy consoling her. ....   16 M.

```
              O                        X
  X O         X          O X           O          X O
  start      (a)         (b)          (c)         (d)
```

VI

Music C.

(a) Starting with the L foot, the boy takes four waltz steps forward to the girl, while she does four waltz steps sideward, R and L. Arms in lateral position, the boy moves sideward L and R, the girl sideward R and L alternately. ....   4 M.

(b) Starting with the L foot, the boy takes four waltz steps backward to his proper place while the girl (starting R) does four waltz steps forward following the boy, arms as in (a). The trunk is bent forward, arms swaying from side to side. ....   4 M.

(c) Repeat (b), this time with the girl moving backward to her place and the boy following her. ....   4 M.

(d) Repeat (a) this time with the boy moving backward to his place. ....   4 M.

(e) Repeat all (a, b, c, d), with the girl moving forward first, the boy waltzing in place. Finish in proper places. ....   16 M.

"SALUDO"

Music Saludo.

Partners take a three-step turn right in place and bow to each other. The girl holds her skirt and boy's hands in second position when bowing. ....   3 M.

VII

Music D. Play slowly.

Girl holds her skirt, boy's hands on waist throughout this figure.

(a) Starting with the R foot, take two slide steps forward.   2 M.

(b) Starting with the R foot, take three steps forward (cts. 1, 2, 3), point L foot in fourth in front (cts. 1, 2, 3). ....   2 M.

(c) Repeat (a) and (b) once more going to partner's place. Pass by right shoulders. Finish facing partner. ....   4 M.

(d) Repeat all (a, b, and c) going to proper place. ....   8 M.

252

VIII

Music E.

Hands as in figure VII throughout this figure.

(a) Starting with the R foot, take three steps forward to meet partner at the center (cts. 1, 2, 3). .... 1 м.

(b) Take three quick stamps in place (L, R, L) (cts. 1, 2), pause (ct. 3). .... 1 м.

(c) Take three steps backward to places, starting with the R foot (cts. 1, 2, 3). Feet together and pause (cts. 1, 2, 3). .... 2 м.

(d) Repeat all (a, b, and c). .... 4 м.

(e) Repeat (a). .... 1 м.

(f) Join right hands overhead. Girl takes a three-step turn counterclockwise under the arch of the arms, bowing to partner or to the audience. .... 3 м.

PURPURI, Figure V

Purpuri

C III-VI

Saludo

poco rall.

255

D VII

256

Redoba

The "Redoba" is an old lively ballroom dance found in Mindoro. According to story, it was introduced in the Philippines around 1860 by the foreigners who came from the Old World. Originally spelled "Redowa," it was later changed to "Redoba," as pronounced by the natives.

COSTUME. Girls wear old-style costume, boys "barong tagalog" with black trousers.

COUNT *one, two, three* to a measure.

FORMATION. Dancers hold in old ballroom dance position, arms (right hand of the girl and the left of the boy) straight down and close to the body.

Dancers may go in any direction, or formations may be arranged to make staging more effective.

I

Music A.

Partners waltz (step, close, step) around in any direction. ...... 16 M.

II

Music B.

(a) Girl—Slides R foot sideward right (ct. 1), cuts R foot sideward with the L (ct. 2), cuts L with the R foot, raising the L in rear of R (ct. 3). .... 1 M.

Boy—Does the same, starting with the L foot. .... 1 M.

(b) Repeat (a) fifteen times alternating the feet, going in any direction. .... 15 M.

III

Music A.

Repeat I. .... 16 M.

IV

Music C.

"Tres en tres" or "tatlohan."

(a) Girl—Hops on the R foot three times (cts. 1, 2, 3), hops on the L three times (cts. 1, 2, 3). .... 2 M.

Boy—Does the same, starting with the L foot. .... 2 M.

(b) Girl—Cuts R and L feet sideward (laterally) alternately six times (cts. 1, 2, 3, 1, 2, 3). This may be done in place or turning. 2 M.

258

Boy—Does the same, starting with the L foot. .... 2 M.

(c) Partners repeat (a) and (b) four times going in any direction. .... 12 M.

NOTE: The whole dance may be repeated as many times as desired. The music is played in this order.

Redoba

MINDORO

Rigodon
(Rigaudon)

This dance was first introduced in the court of Louis XIII by a dancing master from Marseille named Rigaud.

Introduced in the Philippines, the "rigodon" has become the most popular of the quadrilles. It is usually performed at the beginning of formal dances, with government officials and people of high social standing in the community participating. The music is a lively 2/4 or 4/4 rhythm.

There are many versions of the "rigodon." The one described below is the most common and the simplest to perform.

COSTUME. Evening dress should be worn if the "rigodon" opens a formal dance, but any kind of Filipino costume may be used on other occasions.

MUSIC is divided into six parts: A, B, C, D, E, F.

COUNT *one, two* to a measure.

FORMATION. Partners stand side by side with the ladies always on the right side unless otherwise indicated. The dancers are arranged in a square formation. From four to any number of even pairs may take part (see diagram). Couples 1 and 2 are head pairs or "cabeceras," 3 and 4 are side pairs or "costados."

3

O X

1 X   O 2
  O   X

X O

4

NOTE: The definite number of steps to be taken will depend upon available space. Consequently the repetitions of the music cannot be stated. After a figure is finished the musicians are signaled by clapping or stamping.

The steps may be started with R or L foot, one step for each count.

I
LADIES MEET

Music A.

Head Pairs.

(a) Pairs 1 and 2 cross-over (going to opposite place).

(b) Cross-over again (going to proper places).

(c) Ladies 1 and 2 meet at center (followed at four paces by their partners), join right hands and swing around half-way. Drop right hands. Lady 1 joins left hand with left hand of Gentleman 2, and Lady 2 does the same with Gentleman 1. Swing half-way around.

(d) Gentlemen take own partners to opposite places. This means that Pair 1 will be in the place of Pair 2 and vice-versa.

(e) Cross-over (going to proper places).

Side Pairs.

Pairs 3 and 4 repeat all.

II
"ZETA"
(Letter Z)

Music B.

Head Pairs.

Lady 1 and Gentleman 2 dance first.

(a) Face right. Starting with the R foot, take three steps forward (R, L, R) and close L to R.

(b) Starting with the L foot, take three steps backward (L, R, L) and close R to L.

(c) Face each other and advance forward to opposite place, passing by right sides.

(d) Face right and repeat (a) and (b).

(e) Face each other and go to proper places, passing by left shoulders. About three-fourths of the way they stop, turn and bow to each other, then walk backward to proper places.

(f) Lady 2 and Gentleman 1 repeat all.

Side Pairs.

(a) Lady 3 and Gentleman 4 repeat all.

(b) Lady 4 and Gentleman 3 repeat all.

III
"CASAMIENTO"
(Wedding)

Music C.

Head Pairs.

(a) Lady 1 and Gentleman 2 meet to the center, join R hands and swing a full turn around clockwise. Finish standing sideways still with R hands joined. Lady 2 and Gentleman 1 advance forward and join left hands with own partners. (See diagram.)

262

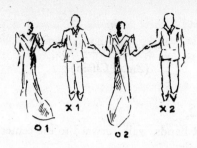

Ladies stand in one line side by side facing the Gentlemen who are also in one line side by side facing them.

(b) Swing the joined hands three times from side to side.

(c) Drop hands. Partners go to opposite place with inside hands joined.

(d) Cross-over, going to proper places.

Lady 2 and Gentleman 1 repeat all.

Side Pairs.

(a) Lady 3 and Gentleman 4 repeat all.

(b) Lady 4 and Gentleman 3 repeat all.

IV

"HATID" OR "VISITA"

(Visit)

Music D.

Head Pairs.

(a) Pair 1 join inside hands. Advance forward and stop in front of Pair 2. Pairs 1 and 2 bow to each other.

(b) Pair 1 drop hands. Gentleman 1 crosses hands in front, palms up. He receives the left hand of his partner with his left and the right hand of Lady 2 with his right. Then he walks backward towards his proper place leading the two ladies who walk forward with him. Gentleman 2 walks behind the two ladies following them.

(c) About three-fourths of the way they release hands and the gentlemen take their own partners to opposite places.

(d) Cross-over, going to proper places.

(e) Pair 2 starts first and repeats all.

Side Pairs.

(a) Pair 3 starts first and repeats all.

(b) Pair 4 starts first and repeats all.

Note: Sometimes the "hatid" or "visita" is done in this manner. Gentleman of Pair 1 upon reaching Pair 2's place, gives his partner to Gentleman 2. Gentleman 2 crosses his hands and walks forward with the two ladies.

V

"CADENILLA"
(Small Chain)

Music E.

(a) *Pairs 1 and 2.*

Each couple join R hands, walk forward to the center or one pair may approach the other pair.

Partners swing once clockwise.

(b) Couples drop hands and join left hands with the left of the opposites, that is Lady 1 joins left hand with left of Gentleman 2 and Lady 2 with Gentleman 1. Swing once counterclockwise with the new partner.

(c) Finish as in the diagram, facing in.

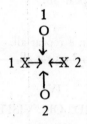

(d) Gentleman 1 crosses hands in front and receives his partner's right hand with his right and the left hand of the opposite lady with his left. Both ladies are facing him. He walks backward to his proper place with the two ladies walking forward. Gentleman 2 follows them.

(e) Upon reaching Pair 1's place Gentleman 1 releases the hands of the ladies. Gentleman 2 then crosses his hands in front and receives the ladies in the same manner, his right hand with the right hand of his partner and his left with the left hand of the opposite lady. Gentleman 2 walks backward to his proper place with the two ladies. Gentleman 1 remains in his place.

(f) Lady 1 goes back to her proper place. Gentleman 1 and Lady 2 execute the do-si-do movement. They bow to each other before returning to their proper places.

(g) Repeat all with Gentleman 2 taking the ladies first to his place. Do-si-do is done by Gentleman 2 and Lady 1 this time.

Side Pairs.

(h) Repeat all with Gentleman 3 taking the ladies first to his place. Do-si-do by Gentleman 3 and Lady 4.

(i) Repeat all with Gentleman 4 taking the ladies first to his place. Do-si-do by Gentleman 4 and Lady 3.

VI

"CAMBIO PAREJA"

(Change Partners)

Music F.

Head Pairs.

(a) Pairs 1 and 2 meet at the center and exchange partners. Gentlemen receive opposite ladies' left hands with their left.

(b) Gentlemen walk backward to proper places with the new partners who walk forward with them. Place the new partner at the left side.

Side Pairs.

(c) Pairs 3 and 4 do the same.

All.

(d) All gentlemen step in front of the new partner and bow to each other.

(e) Gentlemen then go to the lady at their left. Join both hands with the new partner and swing once clockwise. Gentlemen place their partners at their right side after the turn.

(f) Repeat all (a, b, c, d, e). The head pairs always changing partners first, then the side pairs. These movements are repeated as many times as necessary until the partners meet at their proper places.

NOTE: If many pairs are taking part this figure may be omitted.

VII

"CADENA"

(Grand Chain)

Music F.

Execute the "Grand Chain" movement as described in the foregoing explanations.

VIII

"SALUDO"

(Bow)

Music F.

Ladies take the right arm of their partners ("Abrasete").

Head Pairs meet to center and bow to their opposites. Walk backward to places.

Side pairs do the same.

NOTE: Sometimes at the end of the Rigodon an old-time waltz is danced to open the ballroom dancing.

Rigodon

TRADITIONAL BALLROOM
SQUARE DANCE

Notation by
T. LAMUG

270

Play Nº 6-7 as many times as desired.

Rogelia

This is a courtship dance from the province of La Union. "Rogelia" is the name of a girl whom a boy loves. Alternate singing by the boys and girls is a unique feature.

The original song is long and difficult for the non-Ilocano speaking dancers to remember, hence some parts have been omitted. Four selected verses retain the meaning of the story. The words are sung with Music D.

Boys

Ta issem mo ñga apag bettac
Aling-liñgay daguitoy matac
Isudat pudno a mangted ragsac
Mamarusing pudno ñga ayat.

Girls

No dayta ayat ñga ibag bagam
Ditoy pusoc, awan, qt saan,
Ta ammoc a pacabasolan
Cada Tatang ken ni Nanang.

Boys

Ala cadin saranayennac
Dita asim ñga aw-awagac
Ta matayac la iti cunac
Dagus ñgarud, a batakennac.

Girls

Ay Manong ket baybay-am
Dayta ayat ñga ibagbagam
Ta diac cayat a matulawan
Ti dayaw co kina-balasang.

COSTUME. The girls may be dressed in typical Ilocano checkered (black and white) skirt. A white "camisa" with white soft "pañuelo" hangs over one shoulder. The boys wear the "barong tagalog" of Ilocano material and black or white trousers.

MUSIC is divided into seven parts: A, B, C, D, E, F, and G.

COUNT *one, two, three* to a measure.

FORMATION. Partners stand opposite each other about six feet apart. When facing the audience, girl stands at partner's right. Two couples make a set. From one to any number of sets may take part. (See diagram A.)

```
      1 X           O 1

      2 X           O 2
```
Diagram A

INTRODUCTION

Music Introduction.

Take a three-step turn right in place and bow to partner. Girls holding skirts, boys' hands are in second position when bowing. .... 2 M.

I

SWAY BALANCE WITH A RAISE

Music A.

(a) Take eight sway-balance steps with a raise, R and L. Arms in fourth position, right and left arm high alternately. Execute a "kumintang" on the last two counts of two measures. 16 M.

II

RIGHT AND LEFT SQUARES

Music B.

Dance to the right in the square.

(a) Take one close (or waltz) step sideward right (cts. 1, 2, 3) and one sideward left (cts. 1, 2, 3). .... 2 M.
Girls holding skirts and boys' hands on waist throughout this figure.

(b) Execute a waltz-turn right moving to the place of the next dancer to the right, that is, Boy No. 1 goes to the place of boy 2, boy 2 to girl 2, and girl 2 to girl 1, and girl 1 to boy 1. Finish turn facing the opposite dancer. .... 2 M.

(c) Repeat (a) and (b) three times moving counterclockwise. (See diagram B.) Finish in proper places. .... 12 M.

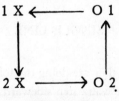

Diagram B

(d) Dancers to the left in the square. Repeat all starting with the left foot and turning to the left. Move in a clockwise direction.   16 M.

III

STAR RIGHT AND LEFT

Music C.

Dancers face right, the girls facing toward and the boys away from the audience.

(a) Starting with the inside foot, take two slide steps to the center. Girls holding skirts, boys' hands on waist. . . . .   2 M.

(b) Starting with the outside foot, take two slide steps away from the center. Hands as in (a). . . . .   2 M.

(c) Repeat (a). . . . .   2 M.

(d) Dancers of each set face the center of the square. Draw R foot backward and bow to opposites. Arms are opened in second position in bowing. . . . .   2 M.

(e) Join right hands at the center to form a star. Starting with the right foot take three steps forward (cts. 1, 2, 3) and point L in front (cts. 1, 2, 3). Move in a clockwise direction. Free hand of the girls holding skirts, boys' free hands on waist.   2 M.

(f) Repeat (a) two times more starting L and R foot alternately. (See diagram C.) . . . .   4 M.

Diagram C

(g) Starting with the L foot, take three steps backward to proper places (cts. 1, 2, 3), close feet together and pause (cts. 1, 2, 3). Hands as in (a). . . . .   2 M.

(h) All face left. Repeat all. Join the left hands as in (e) and move in a counterclockwise direction. Finish facing partner.   8 M.

IV

SINGLE LINE

Music D. Play four times.

Boys sing Verse I while they are doing the following steps:

(a) Partners take one waltz step sideward right (cts. 1, 2, 3) and one sideward left. . . . .   2 M.

Arms in lateral position moving sideward right and left throughout this figure.

(b) Take a three-step turn right (or a waltz-turn right) moving obliquely forward right to form a single line at the center. Partners finish the turn facing each other. .... 2 M.

(c) Repeat (a) and (b) finishing the turn in partner's place. 4 M.

Girls sing Verse II.

(d) Repeat (a) and (b) two times more finishing in proper places. .... 8 M.

Boys sing Verse III.

(e) Repeat (a, b, and c), starting with the left foot and turning left. Move the arms sideward to the left first. .... 8 M.

Girls sing Verse IV.

(f) Repeat (e) finishing in proper places. .... 8 M.

V

PARTNERS CLOCKWISE

Music E.

Dancers face right as in figure III.

(a) Point the outside foot sideward. Girls hold arms in reverse "T" position executing a "kumintang," boys' right arms in reverse "T" executing a "kumintang" and left on waist. Look at the pointing foot. Close the feet together on the last count of the second measure. .... 2 M.

(b) Starting with the inside foot, take two close (or slide) steps to the center. Arms as in (a) "kumintang" on each measure. 2 M.

(c) Partners face each other and join right hands. Starting with the right foot, take three waltz steps forward moving clockwise. Free hand of girls holding the skirts, boys' on waist. .... 3 M.

(d) Take one waltz step going back to proper places. Finish facing partner. .... 1 M.

(e) Partners face left. Repeat all, turning counterclockwise in (c). .... 8 M.

VI

KNEELING

Music F.

(a) Raise R foot in fifth in front and immediately step forward (cts. 1, 2), close the L to R in first position (ct. 3). Girls holding skirts, boys' hands on waist. .... 1 M.

275

(b) Step L foot forward (ct. 1) and kneel on the right knee (cts. 2, 3). Partners are in one line by each other's right shoulder. 1 M.

(c) Stand and take two waltz steps forward (R, L) to partner's place. Hands as in (a). Finish facing partner. . . . . 2 M.

(d) Repeat (a) and (b) going to proper places. . . . . 4 M.

(e) Repeat all (a, b, c and d). Finish facing partner. . . . . 8 M.

VII
STEP, CLOSE, STEP BACK AND POINT

Music G.

(a) Step R foot in fourth in front (ct. 1), step L close to R in first position (ct. 2), step R foot in fourth in rear (ct. 3). Point L foot in fourth in front (cts. 1, 2, 3). Arms in fourth position, right arm high. . . . . 2 M.

(b) Repeat (a) three times more in place L and R. Arms as in (a) left and right arms high alternately. . . . . 6 M.

(c) Repeat (a) and (b) moving little by little forward going to partner's place. Pass by each other's right shoulder. The fourth time should be done turning right about to face partner. . . . . 8 M.

(d) Repeat all (a, b, and c) finishing in proper places. . . . . 16 M.

VIII
"PANDACA"

Music F.

Dancers of each set face the center of their respective square.

(a) Draw R foot backward and bow to the opposite, swing arms sideward to second position (cts. 1, 2, 3), close the feet together and all join hands forming a single circle facing the center (cts. 1, 2, 3). . . . . 2 M.

(b) Pair 1 steps forward to pass under the arch of the arms of Pair 2 on measure 3. . . . . 1 M.

(c) Pair 1 drop inside hands as soon as they have passed the arch of arms of Pair 2 and have turned around the backs of Pair 2. Girl 1 turns around girl 2, and boy 1 around boy 2. The outside hands of Pair 1 are still joined with those of Pair 2 (measure 4). . . . . 1 M.

(d) Pair 1 join their free hands again as soon as they have gone around the backs of Pair 2. . . . . 1 M.

(e) Pair 2 turn their back to Pair 1. They go backward under the arch of the arms of Pair 1. All hands are still joined. . . . . 1 M.

(f) Pair 1 go under the arch of Pair 2's arms (1 M.) and then turn under their respective arms. All are now in their proper

ROGELIA, FIGURE VIII (g)

places after the turn. The hands are joined until the end of this
figure. . . . . 2 M.

    (g) Repeat all, with Pair 2 going under the arch of the arms
first. (See illustration.) . . . . 8 M.

    (h) Repeat all, with girls going under first. . . . . 8 M.

    (i) Repeat all, with boys going under first. Finish with a
bow to partner. . . . . 8 M.

NOTE: Play the last measure slowly for bowing.

Rogelia

LA UNION

Notation by
A. BUENAVENTURA

1. *Boys* Ta is-sem mo ñga a-pag bet-tac A-ling-li-
2. *Girls* ayat ñga i-bag ba-gam Di-toy pu-
3. *Boys* din sa-ra-na-yen-nac Di-ta a-
4. *Girls* nong ket_ bay-bay-am Day-ta a-

Play 4 times

ñgay da-gui-toy ma-tac I-su-dat pud-no a mang-tedrag-
soc, a-wan, qt sa-an, Ta am-moc a pa-ca-ba-so-
sim ñga aw-a-wa-gac Ta ma-ta-yac la i-ti cu-
yat ñga i-bag-ba-gam Ta diac ca-yat a ma-tu-la-

280

sac Ma-ma-ru-sing pud-no ñga a - yat. 2. No day-ta
lan Ca-da Ta-tang ken— ni Na-nang. 3. A-la ca-
nac Da-gus ñga-rud, a ba-ta-ken.-nac. 4. - Ay Ma-
wan Ti da-yaw co kin-a -ba-la-   sang.

F 6-8
Lively

slowly for finale

G 7 Lively

282

Sakuting

The "Sakuting" is a folk dance of the Ilocanos and of the non-Christian people in the mountain provinces. The dance described here was found in Abra among the Christian Filipinos.

At Christmas time, it is customary in the Ilocos regions to dance this in front of homes and in the town "plaza." Groups of boys and young men go to the lowlands to perform from house to house. They receive from spectators, gifts or "aguinaldos" of money, drinks, fruit, or typical Filipino delicacies especially prepared for the Christmas season.

NOTE: This may be danced by both boys and girls, or, as in the original, by boys alone.

COSTUME. Girls wear "balintawak" style with "siesgo" skirt (no train). The boys wear red trousers and "barong tagalog" made of coarse, cheap material. Each dancer holds two sticks (one in each hand) with which to produce rhythmic sounds, timed with his steps. The stick is about one and one-half feet long and tapers at the end like a candle. It is held at the big end.

MUSIC is divided into ten parts: Entrance, A, B, C, D, E, F, G, H, and I.

COUNT *one two* or *one, and, two* to a measure of 2/4 time, and *one, two, three* to a measure of 3/4 time.

FORMATION. Partners stand opposite each other about four feet apart. They are placed according to height, with the smallest couple in front. Four couples make a set or group. From one to any number of sets may take part. (See diagram A. Note staggered formation of partners.)

Audience

1 X   O 1

2 O   Group   X 2

3 X   I   O 3

4 O   X 4

1 X   O 1

2 O   Group   X 2

3 X   II   O 3

4 O   X 4

Diagram A

283

ENTRANCE

Music Entrance.

Starting with the R foot, dancers march forward to proper places with Pair 1 leading. Hold the right hand in front with the right elbow bent upward and the left hand placed at the back of the waist. Take one step for each count.

Then countermarch outward and inward. As soon as dancers are in proper places mark time and face partners until the music ends. (See diagram B.) .... 16 M.

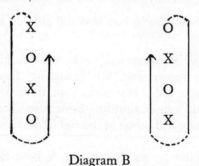

Diagram B

I

WEAVING IN AND OUT

Music A.

Pair 1 weaves in and out of pairs 2, 3, and 4 (see diagram C).

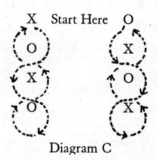

Diagram C

Pair 1 executes the following steps in weaving in and out of the other dancers:

Leap forward with the R foot (ct. 1), close L to the R foot (ct. *and*), step right forward (ct. 2). This is like a change step

284

except for the leap on the first count. Do this step for thirty measures and continue in place as soon as original position is reached.

Pairs 2, 3, and 4 do the following step in place: Cut L foot backward with the R (ct. 1), step L in place (ct. *and*), step R close to the L in first position. Do this for thirty measures.

Sticks are hit together in this manner: Hit the sticks together in front with R over L (ct. 1), hit together again L over R (ct. *and*), and R over L (ct. 2). Repeat alternating L over R and R over L. 32 M.

II
BASIC STEP

Music B.

    (a) Dancers bend downward and strike sticks on the floor (ct. 1), raise trunk up and strike sticks once in front (waist level) with R over L (ct. 2), and L over R (ct. 3). .... 1 M.

    Repeat the same. .... 1 M.

    (b) Take one waltz step sideward right. Strike own sticks together three times at sideward right (R over L ct. 1, L over R ct. 2, R over L ct. 3). .... 1 M.

    Repeat same to the left. Start with the stick L over R. .... 1 M.

    (c) With a spring, step R foot obliquely forward right and place the L heel in front at the same time. Partners should be in one line by left shoulders. This is done on count one, at the same time striking partner's left stick with own left (ct. 1), strike own sticks together twice (R over L, then L over R) (cts. 2, 3). .... 1 M.

    (d) With a spring, step L foot obliquely forward left and quickly close the R with the left foot. This brings the partners in a back-to-back position. At the same time, they hit each other's sticks (the right stick of the girl with the left of the boy, and the left of the girl with the right of the boy). The boy's knuckles are in front and the girl's behind (ct. 1), hit own sticks together twice (R over L, L over R) (cts. 2, 3). .... 1 M.

    (e) With a spring, step R foot backward and place L heel in front. This brings the partners side by side again as in (c). Hit sticks as in (c). .... 1 M.

    (f) Take one waltz step backward left to proper places. Hit own sticks together three times (R over L, L over R, R over L). ... 1 M.

    (g) Repeat the same, this time starting with the L foot and standing by right shoulders in (c). .... 8 M.

    (h) Repeat all (a, b, c, d, e, f, g). .... 16 M.

UNDER LEG

Music C.

(a) Starting with the R foot, take two waltz steps obliquely forward right so that partners stand in one line by left shoulders at the end of the second waltz step. Strike own sticks together three times to a measure. . . . . 2 M.

(b) Raise the R leg in front and strike own sticks together once under the raised leg (ct. 1), lower the leg and strike own sticks together twice (R over L, L over R) (cts. 2, 3). . . . . 1 M.

(c) Strike L stick once with the L of partner (ct. 1), own sticks together twice as above (cts. 2, 3). . . . . 1 M.

(d) Raise the L leg in front and strike own sticks together once under the raised leg (ct. 1), lower the leg and strike own sticks together twice as in (b). . . . . 1 M.

(e) Repeat (c). . . . . 1 M.

(f) Repeat (a) moving backward to places. . . . . 1 M.

(g) Repeat the same (a, b, c, d, e, f), this time partners stand by right shoulders. Strike sticks under L leg first in (b) and R stick with R stick of partner in (c). . . . . 8 M.

(h) Repeat all (a, b, c, d, e, f, g). . . . . 16 M.

IV

SILENT

Music D.

(a) Repeat II (a). Take two small steps forward (R, L) on counts 2, 3 so that partners are nearer each other at the end of the second measure. . . . . 2 M.

(b) Hold own sticks together with the right and left parallel to each other. Execute one waltz step sideward right. Swing own sticks together from the right side and strike partner's sticks together (ct. 1), strike own sticks together twice (R over L, L over R) (cts. 2, 3). . . . . 1 M.

Take one waltz step sideward left. Swing own sticks from the left side and strike partner's sticks together (ct. 1), strike own sticks together twice as above (cts. 2, 3). . . . . 1 M.

(c) With a spring, step the R foot obliquely forward right, placing the L heel in front at the same time. Partners are in one line standing by left shoulders. Bend trunk slightly forward and open arms at the sides without striking sticks (silent) (ct. 1), strike own sticks togther twice, trunk erect (cts. 2, 3). . . . . 1 M.

(d) Repeat II (d). . . . . 1 M.

(e) Repeat (c) of this figure stepping R foot backward. ...... 1 M.

(f) Repeat II (f). .... 1 M.

(g) Repeat the same (a, b, c, d, e, f), this time starting with the L foot, and standing by right shoulders. .... 8 M.

(h) Repeat all (a, b, c, d, e, f, g). .... 16 M.

V
RIGHT AND LEFT STICKS

Music E.

(a) Repeat III (a). .... 2 M.

(b) Take a waltz-turn right moving obliquely forward (2 waltz steps), partners finish facing each other in a single line. Strike own sticks together three times to a measure while doing the turn. .... 2 M.

(c) Strike R sticks once with partner's R (ct. 1), strike own sticks together twice as above (cts. 2, 3). .... 1 M.

Strike L stick once with partner's L (ct. 1), strike own sticks together twice (cts. 2, 3). .... 1 M.

(d) Take two waltz steps forward (R, L) to partner's place. Strike own sticks together three times to a measure. Finish facing partner. .... 2 M.

(e) Repeat the same (a, b, c, d) this time striking L stick with partner's L first and so on. Finish in proper places in (d). .... 8 M.

(f) Repeat all (a, b, c, d, e). .... 16 M.

VI
COMBAT

Music F.

Pairs 1 and 2 form a square and all face the center of the square. Pairs 3 and 4 do the same.

A. *Girls with Girls. Girls' Parts:*

(a) Girls of each set take two change steps forward to center of the square. (See diagram D.)

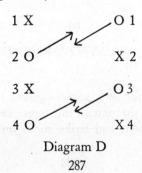

Diagram D

287

Girls stand with the right shoulder turned to opposite girl. Strike own sticks together three times to a measure (cts. 1, *and,* 2). .... 2 M.

(b) Strike R stick once with opposite girl's R (ct. 1), strike own stick together twice (cts. *and,* 2). .... 1 M.

Repeat same once more. .... 1 M.

(c) Turn the left shoulder toward the opposite girl. Repeat (b), striking with the L stick of the opposite girl (ct. 1), strike own sticks together twice (ct. *and,* 2). .... 1 M.

Repeat once more. .... 1 M.

NOTE: The girls execute change steps in place R and L alternately as they hit each other's sticks.

(d) Take two change steps backward (R, L) to proper places. Strike sticks as in (a).

Boys' Part.

(a) They execute change steps in place R and L alternately, hitting their own sticks together three times to a measure (ct. 1, *and* 2), while the girls dance in the center. .... 8 M.

B. *Boys with Boys.*

(a) *Boys' Part:*

Boys of each square repeat the girls' movements in part A above. .... 8 M.

Girls' Part:

Girls of each square repeat the boys' movements in part A above. .... 8 M.

C. *Neighbors Together.*

(a) Neighbors face, girl 1 and boy 2, boy 1 and girl 2, girl 3 and boy 4, boy 3 and girl 4.

They repeat the girls' movements in Part A. .... 8 M.

D. *Partners Together.*

(a) Partners face each other and repeat the girls' movements in Part A. .... 8 M.

VII

FLOOR, WAIST, OVERHEAD, BACK

Music G.

All face partners. Strike own sticks together three times to a measure (cts. 1, *and,* 2) throughout this figure except in (a).

(a) Bend trunk down and strike sticks on the floor three times (cts. 1, *and,* 2).

(When this is done outdoors, strike own sticks together three times near the ground to produce sounds.) .... 1 M.

(b) Raise trunk and strike own sticks together three times waist high in front. .... 1 M.

(c) Raise sticks overhead and repeat the same. .... 1 M.

(d) Place hands behind the waist and repeat the same. ...... 1 M.

(e) Repeat (a, b, c, d) three times more. .... 12 M.

(f) Face right about, away from partner, and repeat all. .... 16 M.

VIII

CIRCLE FORMATION

Music H.

Feet Movements:

(a) Face left. Starting with the R foot, take sixteen waltz steps clockwise (the two groups may be combined if desired). .... 16 M.

(b) Turn right about and repeat (a) counterclockwise. ...... 16 M.

Rhythm of Sticks:

(a) Strike own sticks together three times at the right side (R over L, L over R, R over L). .... 1 M.

(b) Repeat (a) to the left side. .... 1 M.

(c) Strike own sticks together four times to the right side (cts. 1, *and,* 2, 3). .... 1 M.

(d) Repeat (c) to the left side. ...:...................... 1 M.

(e) Repeat all, seven times more. .... 28 M.

NOTE: The sticks are struck in exact rhythm with the feet movements.

IX

LYRE

Music I.

All girls stand to form a circle, holding their two sticks horizontally and parallel to each other. The right stick is at the level of the head, the left at the level of the chest. (See illustration.)

Boy 1 stands in front of girl 1, boy 2 in front of girl 3, boy 4 in front of girl 4, boy 3 in front of girl 2. All boys are inside the circle. (See diagram E.)

(a) In the above position boys hit the girls' sticks as if playing a lyre with both hands (R hand up and L low). The girls hold their sticks firmly. The boys follow the notes of the melody (seven sounds). The right and the left sticks hit together at the same time. (See illustration.) .... 1 M.

SAKUTING, FIGURE IX (a)

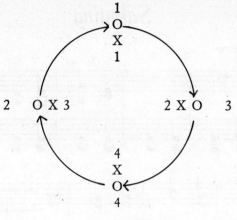

Diagram E

(b) Girls take three-step turn right in place. The sticks are not changed.

Boys take a three-step turn right moving to the next girl right (clockwise). .... 1 M.

(c) Repeat all (a, b) until the boys are back again to their original places. .... 6 M.

NOTE: If desired the boys may go around twice.

EXIT

Continuing the same music, all go to their original places and exit by executing waltz steps starting with the R foot. Hit own sticks three times to a measure at the R and L side alternately. Pair 1 casts off and leads the group.

NOTE: When hitting own sticks together it is always R over L, and L over R alternately.

Sakuting

F. Santiago

Entrance
Lively

Play 4 times

I IX

Repeat last part for exit

Salakot

The "Salakot" is a wide-brimmed hat. It protects the Filipinos from the sun's heat and from the rains. In this dance the "salakot" is used to enhance dance figures and hand movements.

It is best danced by girls only, but may be performed by both boys and girls.

The dance steps were arranged for Play Day, 1935, University of the Philippines.

COSTUME. Girls are dressed in "balintawak" and "bakya" (wooden shoes). If boys are taking part, they are dressed in "barong tagalog," with long red trousers and "bakya."

MUSIC is divided into three parts: A, B, C.

COUNT *one, two* or *one, and, two* to a measure of 2/4 time and *one, two, three* in 3/4 time.

FORMATION. Partners stand in front of each other eight feet apart. When facing the audience the girls stand at the boys' right. Any number of pairs may take part.

Audience

X   O

X   O

X   O

ENTRANCE

Music A.

Dancers enter in two columns holding the outer brim of the "salakot" with the R hand (top down), the inner brim resting against the waist. Free hand on the waist or holding the skirt.

(a) Step R foot forward (ct. 1), step L forward (ct. 2), three stamps in place (R, L, R) (cts. 1 and 2). . . . . 2 M.

(b) Repeat (a) six times to proper places. . . . . 12 M.

(c) Three-step turn right in place and bow to partner or to audience. Put on the "salakot" after bowing. 2 M.

I

Music B.

(a) ("Sarok")—Point R foot across L in front. Cross the hands in front and bend the body slightly forward (cts. 1, 2, 3). 1 M.

299

SALAKOT DANCE, Figure II

(b) Point R foot sideward. Open the arms sideward in second position, body erect (cts. 1, 2, 3) .... 1 M.

(c) Sway balance with a point to the right. Arms in fourth position, R arm high. .... 2 M.

(d) Repeat (a), (b), and (c), starting with the L foot. Reverse the arm positions in (c). .... 4 M.

(e) Starting with the R foot, partners take eight waltz steps clockwise. (See diagram 1.) Arms in lateral position shoulder-level moving sideward R and L. Finish in proper places. .... 8 M.

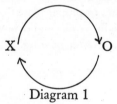

Diagram 1

(f) Repeat all (a, b, c, d, e). .... 16 M.

300

SALAKOT DANCE, Figure III

II

Music C.

All face the audience. Take off the "salakot" and hold it with two hands at the brim (R hand on top and L hand at the left side). (See the illustration.)

    (a) Step R foot sideward (ct. 1), brush L forward (ct. 2), hop on R in place (ct. 3). Swing the "salakot" to the right side. ...... 1 m.

    (b) Three stamps in place. (R, L, R) (cts. 1, 2, 3). The "salakot" remains at the right side. .... 1 m.

    (c) Step R foot across L in front (ct. 1), brush L forward (ct. 2), hop on R in place (ct. 3). Swing the "salakot" to the left side. The L hand is now on top and R down. .... 1 m.

    (d) Repeat (b). The "salakot" still at the left side. .... 1 m.

    (e) Waltz sideward, R and L. Swing the "salakot" to sideward, right and left. .... 2 m.

    (f) Waltz-turn right in place (use two waltz steps). Turn the "salakot" down-up-and-around. .... 2 m.

    (g) Repeat all (a, b, c, d, e, f) three times more. .... 24 m.

III

Music B.

Face partner. Hold the "salakot" on the right side with the R hand, its top toward the partner, L hand is at the side in second position.

(a) Point R foot obliquely forward right (cts. 1, 2), point R close to L foot (ct. 3). Turn the "salakot" so that the top is down on counts 1, 2 and in front toward the partner on count 3. Bend the body slightly forward in the direction the foot is pointing. (See illustration.) .... 1 M.

(b) Repeat (a) three times more. .... 3 M.

(c) Repeat all (a and b), pointing with the L foot. R hand still holding the "salakot." Repeat the same hand movements. .... 4 M.

(d) Starting with the R foot, partners take four waltz steps forward, passing by right shoulders. Hold the "salakot" with two hands (top of "salakot" in). Move it sideward R and L. ...... 4 M.

(e) Repeat (d) moving back to proper places. .... 4 M.

(f) Repeat all (a, b, c, d, e). .... 16 M.

IV

Music C.

All face the audience. Put the "salakot" down in front of the dancer. (See diagram 2.)

Diagram 2

(a) Point R foot obliquely forward (cts. 1, 2), point R close to L foot (ct. 3). Girls holding skirts, boys' hands on waist. ...... 1 M.

(b) Repeat (a) once more. .... 1 M.

(c) Waltz-turn right obliquely forward (use two waltz steps) covering one side of an imaginary square around the "salakot." Hands as above. .... 2 M.

(d) Repeat (a) and (b) three times more finishing at proper places. .... 12 M.

NOTE: Always finish facing the "salakot" after each "turn."

(e) Repeat the same movements as above, pointing with the L foot and waltz-turn to L. (See diagram 3.)

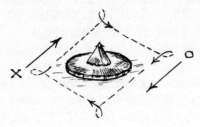

Diagram 3

V

Music B.

All face the audience.

(a) Four double sway-balance steps R and L, girls holding the skirts, boys' hands on waist. . . . .   16 м.

(b) Repeat (a). Arms in fourth position, R and L arm high alternately. . . . .   16 м.

VI

Music C.

Partners face away from each other.

(a) Starting with the R foot, take four waltz steps forward. Arms in lateral position moving sideward R and L. . . . .   4 м.

(b) Repeat (a) moving backward to proper places. Arms as above. . . . .   4 м.

(c) Turn right about to face partner. Repeat (a) going to partner's place. Pass by right shoulders. Arms as above. . . . .   4 м.

(d) Repeat (b) passing by right shoulders. . . . .   4 м.

All face the audience.

(e) "Sarok" with R foot across L (cts. 1, 2), point R close to L foot (ct. 3). Cross the hands in front on counts 1, 2, and raise R arm in fifth position, place L hand on waist on count 3. . . . .   1 м.

(f) Pivot-turn with a point to the right three times to complete one full turn. L hand on the waist. R arm in fifth amplified on counts 1, 2 bringing it back to fifth position on count 3. . . . . . .   3 м.

(g) Repeat (e) and (f), starting with the L foot. Pivot-turn with a point to the left. Reverse the arm positions. . . . .   4 м.

VII

Music A.

All face the audience. Take the "salakot" and hold it with both hands, the R hand on top and the L hand below, the top of the "salakot" toward the audience. (See illustration.)

(a) Circle the "salakot" in a vertical plane clockwise at the right side three times (cts. 1, 2, 1), pause (cts. 2)................ 2 M.

(b) Circle it counterclockwise three times at the left side. .... 2 M.

(c) Hold the "salakot" in front of the waist with the top up. Raise it up and down three times (cts. 1, 2, 3), pause (ct. 2) .... 2 M.

(d) Repeat (c) once more............................... 2 M.

(e) Repeat all (a, b, c, d)............................... 8 M.

At the last count of the sixteenth measure put the "salakot" on the head instead of pausing. .... 16 M.

EXIT

Music A.

Tilt the "salakot" a little bit to the right side and hold it with the R hand. Free hand of girls holding skirts, boys' free hand on waist.

Starting with the R foot, execute change steps forward, bending the head slightly to the right and left. Dancers go out in two lines.

SALAKOT, Figure IV
(see page 302)

Salakot

C II-IV-VI

Sayaw Kasiyahan

(Dance of Contentment)

A good harvest is an occasion for feasting, singing, and dancing. The Filipinos are traditionally fond of merrymaking, hence the "Dance of Contentment" symbolizes or depicts our country folk in the proper mood for a general celebration.

COSTUME. Girls wear "balintawak" and boys "barong tagalog" with white trousers.

MUSIC is divided into four parts: A, B, C,.and D.

COUNT *one, two, three* to a measure.

FORMATION. Partners stand opposite each other about eight feet apart. Girl stands at partner's right when facing the audience. Dancers are grouped together in sets of two pairs. From one to any number of sets may take part. See diagram below.

$$\left\{\begin{matrix} X & O \\ X & O \end{matrix}\right. \qquad\qquad \left\{\begin{matrix} X & O \\ X & O \end{matrix}\right.$$

INTRODUCTION

Music Introduction.

Boys face the audience, girls' back to audience. Stand in this position while the music is being played, ready for figure I. ...... 12 M.

I

Music A.

(a) Take one waltz step sideward right and one sideward left. Arms in fifth position moving sideward right and left. .... 2 M.

(b) Turn right about and repeat (a). .... 2 M.

(c) Turn left to face partner. Take two steps backward (R, L). Take one step for every measure, girls holding skirts, boys' hands on waist. .... 2 M.

(d) Step R foot close to L. Bring hands close to chest (elbow down, close to the waist). .... 1 M.

(e) Open hands sideward in second position and bow to partner. .... 1 M.

(f) Repeat all (a, b, c, d, and e). .... 8 M.

II

Music B.

Partners face each other.

(a) Execute four "papuri" steps, R and L, girls holding skirts, boys' hands on waist. . . . . 16 M.

III

Music C.

(a) Place R heel in front (cts. 1, 2), step R close to L foot (ct. 3). Right forearm bent upward and right hand "kumintang" counterclockwise, L hand on waist. . . . . 1 M.

(b) Repeat (a) with the L foot and "kumintang" left hand clockwise, right hand on waist. . . . . 1 M.

(c) Repeat (a) and (b). . . . . 2 M.

(d) Turn right about and repeat (a, b, c). . . . . 4 M.

(e) Turn right about and repeat all (a, b, c, and d). Finish facing the partner. . . . . 8 M.

IV

Music D.

(a) Starting with the R foot, partners take three small steps forward (cts. 1, 2, 3). Stamp L foot close to R (cts. 1, 2, 3), girls holding skirts and boys' hands on waist. . . . . 2 M.

(b) Repeat (a) once more starting with the L foot. Partners finish standing in front of each other about two feet apart. . . . . . . 2 M.

(c) Point R foot in intermediate in front (cts. 1, 2), and step R close to L (ct. 3). Bend body slightly to the right and hold hands as in (a). . . . . 1 M.

(d) Repeat (c) once more. Hands as in (a). . . . . 1 M.

(e) Repeat (c) and (d), starting with the L foot. Bend body to the left. Hands as in (a). . . . . 2 M.

(f) Starting with the R foot, partners take four waltz steps going clockwise. Hands as in (a). Finish facing each other. . . . . . . 4 M.

(g) Starting with the R foot, take two waltz steps backward to proper place. Hands as in (a). . . . . 2 M.

(h) Repeat (d) and (e) of figure I. . . . . 2 M.

V

Music A.

Partners face the audience.

(a) Repeat figure I. Girls turn right and boys turn left to face partner in (c). . . . . 16 M.

Music B.

(a) Execute eight sway-balance steps with a brush, R and L, arms in fourth position, R and L arm high alternately. .... 16 м.

VII

Music C.

Girls and boys in set face each other.

(a) Repeat figure III (a, b, c). .... 4 м.
(b) Turn right about so that dancers of one set face the dancers of the other set. Repeat (a). .... 4 м.
(c) Repeat all (a and b). Finish facing partner. .... 8 м.

VIII

Music D.

Dancers of each set face the center of their own square. (See diagram below.)

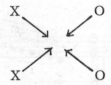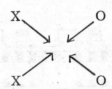

(a) Repeat figure IV (a and b) going obliquely forward to center of the square. (See diagram above.) .... 4 м.
(b) Repeat figure IV (c, d, and e). .... 4 м.
(c) Starting with the R foot, all the dancers in each set take four waltz steps going around clockwise, hands in lateral position moving sideward right and left. (See diagram below.) .... 4 м.

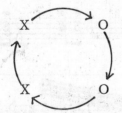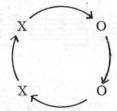

(d) Repeat figure IV (g) and (h). Finish with a bow to partner. .... 4 м.

NOTE: For entrance and exit use waltz steps and any part of the music, starting with the R foot, girls holding skirts, boys' hands on waist.

Sayaw Kasiyahan

J. HERNANDEZ

D IV-VIII

slowly for finale

Fine

312

Sua-Sua

This is a dance from Jolo, Sulu. Literally "Sua-Sua" means a small orange plant and is the name of a courtship dance and its accompanying song.

According to the Moros of the older generation, the movements in this dance have been modified and modernized. There is no doubt, however, that some parts are based on typically old Moro dances.

Dancers sing as they perform the dance. The natives often repeat the dance as many times as they like or until they are made to stop. The song goes this way:

Music A.

Sua-ko; Sua-ko, yampa tia num
Sua-ko; Sua-ko, yampa tia num
Ah-Mag dahon pa unom unom
Ah-Mag dahon pa unom unom

Music B.

Bang ma-ka tum-tum panon
Bang ma-ka tum-tum panon
Ah atay ko mag ka gomon
Ah atay ko mag ka gomon

Music C.

Kan ka pilaran, cambai sara-ran
Di ka dua han, di ka imanan
Ah mag pe-pin-tas, ha-la-man
Ah mag pe-pin-tas, da koman

Music D.

Kan kapilaran-iman

My little orange tree I had planted,
With its six lovely green leaves,
Reminds me of her
Thus causing my heart to beat.
That loveliest beauty among the many,
That pretty one I cannot change,
Walking hurriedly along the street
Hand in hand with me—
To that lovely beauty I lost my heart.

Literal translation of the song by Lt. Alpad Arasad.

COSTUME. The dancers are dressed in typical Joloano costume (see illustration), an open fan in each hand.

MUSIC is divided into four parts: A, B, C and D.

COUNT one, two to a measure.

FORMATION. This is danced by one couple but any number may take part. The dancers hold the open fans with the second and third fingers on one side towards the top, and the thumb, fourth, and little fingers

313

are under on the other side. Partners stand opposite each other about eight feet apart, the girl at the right side of her partner when facing the audience.

SUA-SUA STEP. Point R (or L) in fourth in front (ct. 1), slide forward with the toes of the same foot and put the weight on the whole sole of the foot at the end of the slide (ct. 2). The movement is repeated with the other foot. This step is used throughout the dance.

ARM MOVEMENTS. With an open fan held in each hand hold arms in second position or at shoulder level and turn the hands (from the wrists only) in a horizontal figure eight motion (see diagram below). It takes two counts to complete a figure eight motion.

For right hand   For left hand

INTRODUCTION

Music Introduction.

Partners walk to places, starting with the R foot. Take one step for every count. The fans are held down at the sides. .... 4 M.

I

Music A.

Partners face each other.

(a) Meet to center by taking four "sua-sua" steps, starting with the R foot. Arms as above moving continuously. .... 4 M.

(b) The girl continues moving forward by taking four "sua-sua" steps while the boy moves backward to his original position by taking four sua-sua steps backward. Both start with the R foot. Take the same arm movements. .... 4 M.

(c) Starting with the R foot, girl moves backward to her proper place by taking eight "sua-sua" steps. The boy takes the same steps moving forward, following closely. Arm movements are the same. .... 8 M.

II

Music B.

(a) Partners face each other and join both hands with the fans still open. Take four "sua-sua" steps clockwise, starting with the R foot. .... 4 M.

(b) Drop hands and both go to the center by taking four "sua-sua" steps, the boy moving backward and the girl forward. Do the same arm movements. .... 4 M.

(c) Join both hands again and take four "sua-sua" steps moving counterclockwise. .... 4 M.

(d) Take four "sua-sua" steps to boy's place. The boy moves backward, the girl forward, starting with the R foot, with the same arm movements. Partners finish standing side by side facing the direction of the original position of the girl. The girl stands at the right side of the boy.

III

Music C.

Partners join outside hands and raise them overhead, join the inside hands and hold them down at the back. The fans are still open.

(a) Starting with the outside foot, take four "sua-sua" steps to the center. Drop hands at the end of the fourth step. .... 4 M.

(b) Partners stand with their right shoulders near each other. Take four "sua-sua" steps moving clockwise. Do the same arm movements. .... 4 M.

(c) Turn about and repeat (b) counterclockwise. Finish with the girl standing at the right side, facing the original place of the boy. .... 4 M.

(d) Join outside and inside hands as above. Repeat (a) moving backward to girl's place. .... 4 M.

EXCHANGE PLACES

Music D.

(a) With "sua-sua" or plain walking steps, the girl goes to boy's original place, arms hanging loosely at the sides as she walks to the opposite side. The boy remains in the girl's place. .... 6 M.

WHOLE DANCE

Music A, B, C.

Repeat the whole dance (figures I, II, III). .... 48 M.

FINALE

Music D.

(a) Starting with the outside foot, partners make a three-step turn, by first turning under the arch of the front arms, then under the rear arms. .... 2 M.

(b) Boy kneels on right, hands down at the sides with the fans open. The girl stands in front of the boy. Right arm in reverse "T" and left hand down at the side. .... 4 M.

315

Sua-Sua

Notation by
A. Buenaventura

Jolo

C III

Exchange Places
D Finale

Surtido

Literally "surtido" means assortment. The dance is most interesting because it contains steps and figures found in the folk dances of many provinces. The "surtido" described here is a mixture of Visayan, Ilocano, Pampangan, Tagalog, and Bikol dance steps and music.

COSTUME. The girls may be dressed in "balintawak" style or "patadiong" and boys in "barong tagalog" with white trousers.

MUSIC is divided into eight parts: A, B, C, D, E, F, G, H.

COUNT *one, two, three* to a measure of 3/4 time and *one, and, two* or *one, two* to a measure of 2/4 time.

FORMATION. The girl stands at the right side of the boy. Two pairs standing opposite each other about eight feet apart make a set (see diagram below). From one to any number of sets may take part in this dance.

Audience

1(X   O)2
(   )
1(O   X)2

INTRODUCTION

Music Introduction.

Make a three-step turn right in place and bow to opposites, girls holding skirts, boys' hands on waist. .... 2 M.

I

Music A.

Girls hold skirts, boys' hands on waist throughout this figure.

(a) Partners take one waltz step forward R (cts. 1, 2, 3), point L foot in front (cts. 1, 2, 3). .... 2 M.

(b) Repeat (a) starting with the L foot, meeting the opposite pair at the center. (See diagram below.)

I X---→   ←---O 2

1 O ---→   ←---X 2

(c) Girls take two waltz steps obliquely forward left (R, L) while boys take two waltz steps obliquely forward right (R, L), letting the girls pass first. See diagram p. 319. .... 2 M.

318

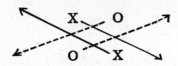

(d) Take two waltz steps to turn right about in place. At the end of the turn the two pairs are at places of the opposites, facing each other. .... 2 M.

(e) Repeat all (a, b, c, d) finishing in proper places. .... 8 M.

II

Music B.

(a) Take one waltz step forward R, girls holding skirts, boys' hands on waist. .... 1 M.

Turn right and take one waltz step sideward L. Hands as above. 1 M.

Turn left about by pivoting on the L foot and take one waltz step sideward R. Hands as above. .... 1 M.

Turn right about and take one waltz step sideward left. .... 1 M.

At the end of the fourth measure the partners are in one line with the opposites, girls standing inside facing the boys, and boys standing outside facing girls, girl 1 faces boy 2, and girl 2 faces boy 1. See diagram below:

X   1

O   2

O   1

X   2

(b) Take two slide steps sideward right. Arms in fourth position, R arm high. .... 2 M.

Take a waltz-turn right (two waltz steps) to return to the proper places, girls holding skirts and boys' hands on waist. ...... 2 M.

(c) Repeat all (a) and (b). .... 8 M.

III

Music C. Play three times. "Haplik."

A. *Girls' Part:* Face the center of the square, hold skirts throughout figure.

(a) Take two steps forward (R, L) to meet at center of the square. .... 1 M.

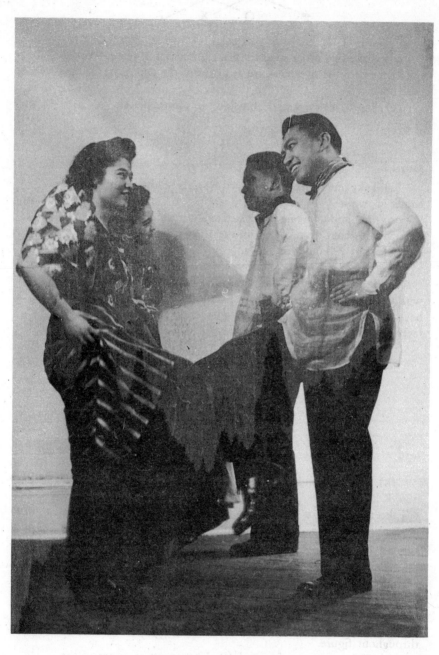

SURTIDO, Figure III (b)

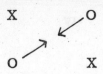

(b) Hop on the L foot, raise R knee in front, and swing the R foot inward (to left) (ct. 1), hop again on the L foot and swing the R foot outward (to right) (ct. 2). .... 1 M.

    (c) Three-step turn right in place (R, L, R). .... 1 M.

    (d) Repeat (b) hopping on the R foot and swinging the left foot. .... 1 M.

    (e) Three-step turn left in place (L, R, L). .... 1 M.

    (f) Repeat (b). .... 1 M.

    (g) Take two steps backward (R, L) to proper places. ...... 1 M.

    (h) Put R foot together with L. .... 1 M.

Boys' Part:

Stand in place and clap hands while girls dance in this manner:

    (a) Clap hands every beat of first two measures (four claps). 2 M.

    (b) Clap three times (cts. 1, *and*, 2). .... 1 M.

    (c) Clap twice (cts. 1, 2). .... 1 M.

    (d) Repeat (b). .... 1 M.

    (e) Repeat (c). .... 1 M.

    (f) Repeat (a). .... 2 M.

B. *Girls' Part:*

Clap hands in the same manner as the boys in (a). .... 8 M.

Boys' Part:

Boys do the same steps as the girls in (a).
Place hands on waist. .... 8 M.

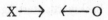

C. All dance, meeting the opposites at the center. Repeat the same steps as in (a), girls holding skirts, boys' hands on waist. 8 M.

IV

Music D. Play four times.

Partners face the opposites.

(a) Step R foot sideward (ct. 1), brush L forward (ct. 2) step
L foot close to R in first position (ct. 3). .... 1 M.

(b) Repeat (a) once more. .... 1 M.
R arm in fifth position, L arm bent forward at shoulder-level
for the first two measures.

(c) Take one waltz-turn right in place, girls holding skirts,
boys' hands on waist. ...., 2 M.

(d) Repeat (b) and (c) starting with L foot. Reverse the
arm positions. .... 4 M.

(e) Take four step-swing-hops forward passing the opposites
by the right shoulder. Hands as in (c). .... 4 M.

(f) Step R backward and point L in front (cts. 1, 2, 3), hands
as in (c) and body bent slightly forward. .... 1 M.

(g) Repeat (f) three times more (L, R, L) finishing in proper
places. Pass by right shoulder of opposites. .... 3 M.

(h) Repeat all (a, b, c, d, e, f, g). .... 16 M.

Music E. Play four times.

Partners face the opposites.

(a) Take one sway balance with a point to the right. Arms
in fourth position, R arm high. .... 2 M.

(b) Point L foot across the R in front (ct. 1), point L again in
intermediate in front (cts. 2, 3). Arms as in (a) doing a "kumintang" every three counts. .... 1 M.

(c) Repeat (b) once more. .... 1 M.

(d) Repeat all (a, b, c) starting with the L foot. Reverse the
arm positions. .... 4 M.

(e) Starting with the R foot, take three steps forward to meet
opposites at the center (cts. 1, 2, 3), point L in intermediate in
front (cts. 1, 2, 3), arms in fourth position R arm high. .... 2 M.

(f) Repeat (b) and (c). .... 2 M.

(g) Repeat (e) moving backward, starting with the L foot.
Reverse the arm positions. .... 2 M.

(h) Repeat (b) and (c). .... 2 M.

(i) Partners face each other and repeat all (a, b, c, d, e, f,
g, h). .... 16 M.

Music F.

Partners face opposites. Girls hold skirts, boys' hands on waist throughout this figure.

(a) Point R foot in front (ct. 1), step R close to L foot (cts. 2).   1 M.

(b) Repeat (a) with the L foot. ....   1 M.

(c) With the R foot leading, take four galop steps forward passing the opposites by right shoulders. ....   2 M.

(d) Starting with the L foot, repeat (a) and (b) in back-to-back position with opposites. ....   2 M.

(e) With the R foot leading, take four small galops backward passing by left shoulders of opposites. Finish in front of opposites (near each other). ....   2 M.

(f) Starting with the L foot, execute three stamps in place (L, R, L). ....:...............................   1 M.

(g) Hop on L and point R foot in front (ct. 1), hop on L again and raise R knee in front (toes pointed downward) (ct. 2).   1 M.

(h) Repeat (f) and (g) starting with the R foot. ....   2 M.

(i) Starting with the L foot, take four change steps backward to proper places. ....   4 M.

(j) Repeat all (a, b, c, d, e, f, g, h, i). ....   16 M.

VII

Music G.

(a) Starting with the outside foot, take one waltz sideward facing away from partners, arms at waist level in first position (ct. 1). Open arms in first position amplified, with a "kumintang" (cts. 2, 3). ....   1 M.

(b) Repeat (a) five times more, with the inside and outside foot. Move little by little forward to meet opposites at the center. Face toward and away from partner alternately. Do the same hand movements. ....   5 M.

(c) Starting with the outside foot, take four steps backward to proper places, girls holding skirts, boys' hands on waists (cts. 1, 2, 3, 1). Put feet together and pause (cts. 2, 3). ....   2 M.

(d) Repeat all (a, b, c). ....:...............   8 M.

Music H.

Partners face the opposites.

(a) Starting with the R foot, take four change steps forward to meet opposites at center, with the R arm bent upward doing the "kumintang," L hand on waist. Reverse the position of the arms, R and L, at every measure. ....   4 M.

(b) Starting with the R foot, take two heel and toe polka steps backward, girls hold skirts, boys' hands on waist. .... 4 м.

(c) Partners face each other and join right hands. Starting with the R foot, take four change steps clockwise, free hands of girls holding skirts, boys' hands on waist. .... 4 м.

(d) Drop the R hands and join L hands. Repeat (c) counterclockwise. .... 4 м.

(e) Starting with the R foot, dancers of each set take eight change steps forward making a big circle clockwise. "Kumintang" R and L hands alternately as in (a). .... 8 м.

(f) Repeat (e) moving counterclockwise. .... 8 м.
Finish with a bow to the audience.

SURTIDO, Figure VII (a)

324

Surtido

Tagala

"Tagala" is the name given to the women from the Tagalog regions.

CostUME. The girls are dressed in "balintawak" and the boys in "barong tagalog" with white trousers.

Music is divided into three parts: A, B, and C.

Count *one, two, three* to a measure.

Formation. Partners stand opposite each other about eight feet apart. The girls stand at their partners' right when facing the audience. From one to any number of pairs may take part in the dance.

INTRODUCTION

Music Introduction.

Take a three-step turn right in place and bow to partner, girls holding skirts, boys' hands on waist. .... 2 M.

I

Music A.

(a) Point R foot obliquely forward (cts. 1, 2), point R close to L (ct. 3). Arms are in amplified fifth position on counts 1, 2 and closed in fifth on count 3. .... 1 M.

(b) Repeat pointing with the R foot seven times more, 1/8 pivot turn each time on the L foot to complete turn. .... 7 M.

(c) Repeat (a) and (b) starting with the L foot and turning left. Arms as above. .... 8 M.

(d) Repeat all (a, b, c). .... 16 M.

II

Music B.

(a) Take three steps forward to meet the partner at the center (R, L, R) (cts. 1, 2, 3), girls holding skirts, boys' hands on waist. 1 M.

(b) Brush L foot forward. Arms in fourth position, R arm high (cts. 1, 2, 3). .... 1 M.

(c) Take three steps backward (L, R, L) (cts. 1, 2, 3). Same hand movements as in (a). .... 1 M.

(d) Brush R foot forward. Arms in fourth position, L arm high (cts. 1, 2, 3). .... 1 M.

(e) Repeat all (a, b, c, d) seven times more. .... 28 M.

330

III

Music C.

(a) Seven sway balance steps with a point, R and L, arms in fourth position, R and L arm high alternately. .... 14 M.

(b) Three-step turn left in place, girls holding skirts, boys' hands on waist. .... 2 M.

(c) Repeat (a), starting with the L foot. Arms as above (a). 14 M.

(d) Three-step turn right in place. Hands as above (b). ..... 2 M.

IV

Music A.

Partners face the audience.

(a) Repeat I (a) (b) and (c). .... 16 M.

Turn right about (back toward the audience).

(b) Repeat I (a) (b) and (c). .... 16 M.

At the end turn right about.

V

Music B.

Partners face the audience.

(a) Four double sway-balance steps, R and L, arms in fourth position, R and L arm high alternately. .... 16 M.

(b) Turn right about.

Repeat (a). .... 16 M.

VI

Music C.

Partners face each other.

(a) One waltz step forward R and backward L. R hand forward with the palm up on counts 1, 2, 3, bringing it close to the chest on counts 4, 5, 6. Place L hand on the waist. .... 2 M.

(b) Three-step turn right in place, girls holding skirts, boys' hands on waist. .... 2 M.

(c) Repeat (a) and (b) starting with the L foot and turning left. Reverse the arm positions. .... 4 M.

(d) One waltz sideward R and L, arms in lateral position moving sideward R and L. .... 2 M.

(e) Repeat (b). .... 2 M.

(f) Repeat (d), starting with the L foot, arms in lateral position moving sideward L and R. .... 2 M.

(g) Three-step turn left in place, arms as in (b). .... 2 M.

(h) Repeat all (a, b, c, d, e, f, g). Finish with a bow to partner or to audience. .... 16 M.

Tagala

Ti Liday

This is an Ilocano dance from Camiling, Tarlac. It was formerly known as "Contrabandista" but was changed to "Ti Liday" (sorrow) at the suggestion of Sen. Camilo Osias, because of the movements in this dance which express sorrow.

COSTUME. The dancers are dressed in Ilocano costume. (See illustration.)

MUSIC is divided into five parts: A, B, C, D, E.

COUNT *one, two, three* in a measure.

FORMATION. Partners stand opposite each other about six feet apart. When facing the audience the girls stand at the boys' right. From one to any number of pairs may take part.

Audience

X   O

X   O

X   O

I

Music A.

(a) Make a three-step turn right in place. Girls holding skirts, boys' hands on waist (cts. 1, 2, 3). . . . . 1 M.

(b) Cross L foot in rear of R and bend the knees slightly, girls' L hand holding the skirts, boys' L hand on waist, R arms of both bent upward. "Kumintang" the hand counterclockwise (cts. 1, 2, 3). . . . . 1 M.

(c) Repeat (a) and (b) starting with the L foot and turning to the left. Reverse the hand positions in (b). . . . . 2 M.

(d) Point R foot in front (cts. 1, 2), close R to L (ct. 3). Girls hold skirts, boys' hands on waist. . . . . 1 M.

(e) Repeat (d) five times more L and R alternately. . . . . 5 M.

(f) Do-si-do. Starting with the R foot, partners take three steps forward passing by right shoulders and three steps backward passing by left shoulders. Hands as in (d). . . . . 2 M.

(g) Step R foot close to L (cts. 1, 2, 3), hands as in (d). . . . . 1. M.

(h) Repeat (b). . . . . 1 M.

(i) Repeat (d), starting with the L foot, four times. . . . . 4 M.

(j) Repeat all (a, b, c, d, e, f, g, h, i). . . . . 18 M.

335

INTERLUDE

Music Interlude.

Pause. .... 2 M.

II

Music B.

This figure is called "patay" by the Ilocanos.

(a) Partners take two close steps obliquely forward right to center, girls holding skirts, boys' hands on waist (see diagram A).   2 M.

(b) Make a three-step turn right in place, finishing in a single line with the partners facing each other (cts. 1, 2, 3) (see diagram B). Hands as above. .... 1 M.

A   B

(c) Repeat the feet movements of figure I (b). Girls bend the head downward and support the forehead in the crook of their right arms as if crying, the left hand holding the R hand (fingers), supporting the weight of the head. The boys touch their partner's forearm lightly as if consoling her. .... 1 M.

(d) Pause and stand erect. .... 1 M.

(e) Repeat (a, b, c), finishing as in diagram C facing each other. .... 4 M.

C   D

(f) Pause and stand erect. .... 1 M.

(g) Repeat (a, b, c), finishing as in diagram D facing each other. .... 4 M.

(h) Pause and stand erect. .... 1 M.

(i) Repeat (a, b, c) finishing in proper places. Omit the "patay" movement after the turn and instead "kumintang" with the R hand, L hand on waist. .... 4 M.

(j) Pause and stand erect. .... 1 M.

III

Music C.

Execute eight sway balance steps with a point, R and L, arms in fourth position, R and L high alternately. .... 16 M.

IV

Music D.

Pause. .... 1 M.

(a) Partners do the do-si-do as in I (f), both finish facing the audience. .... 2 M.

(b) Pause (cts. 1, 2), stamp R foot twice in place (ct. 3 of the 4th measure and ct. 1 of the 5th measure). Pause (cts. 2, 3 of the 5th measure). Clap once with the first stamp of the R foot. Open hands in second position on the second stamp. .... 2 M.

(c) Repeat (a) and (b). .... 4 M.

V

Music E.

(a) Starting with the R foot, take two waltz steps forward to form a single line at the center, girls standing in front of partners, arms in lateral position moving R and L sideward. .... 2 M.

(b) Take four waltz steps, sideward R and L, arms bent upward at the elbow, doing the "kumintang" R and L alternately at every measure. Girls look over the R and L shoulders at their partners. Boys look at their partners. .... 4 M.

(c) Take two waltz steps (R, L) forward going to partner's place. Hands as in (a). .... 2 M.

(d) Repeat all (a, b, c) going to proper place in (c). .... 8 M.

(e) Repeat (a) finishing in back-to-back position with the partner. .... 2 M.

(f) Repeat (b) and (c). .... 6 M.

(g) Repeat (e) and (f) finishing in proper places. .... 8 M.

FINALE

Music Finale.

Repeat figure I (a) and (b). .... 2 M.

After doing the "kumintang" with the R hand wave it twice more. .... 2 M.

Hold the position of the feet as above until the last beat of the last measure.

Ti Liday

340

Tinikling

This dance is a favorite in the Visayan Islands, especially in the province of Leyte.

The "Tikling" is a bird with long legs and a long neck. The "Tinikling" dance, therefore, imitates the movements of the "Tikling" birds as they walk between grass stems or run over tree branches. This spectacular dance is usually accompanied by a song.

The performers dance along the sides and between two bamboo poles, about nine feet long, which are placed horizontally on the ground. The poles are struck together in time to the music. Skill is demonstrated in dancing between the bamboos, and in keeping the feet from being caught when the poles are struck together. There is much fun, however, when the bamboo players catch the feet of the dancers.

Two bamboo players sit opposite each other on the ground holding the ends of the bamboo poles (sometimes long pestles). Two pieces of board or bamboo, about thirty inches long and two inches thick, are placed under the poles, about one foot from the ends (see diagram 1).

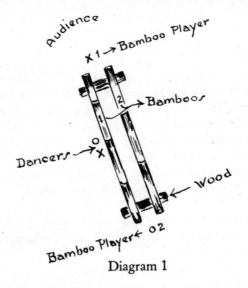

Diagram 1

COSTUME. Girls wear "balintawak" or "patadiong." Boys wear "barong tagalog" and long red trousers with one leg rolled up. They dance barefoot.

FORMATION. Dancers stand at the left side of the bamboo poles, girl in front, facing the audience. (See diagram 1.)

MUSIC is divided into two parts: A and B.

COUNT *one, two, three* to a measure.

BAMBOO RHYTHMS (abbreviation is B. R.).

341

B. R. I. Strike bamboo poles together once by sliding them against the boards or lifting them an inch or so (ct. 1), open the bamboos about a foot apart and strike them twice against the boards (cts. 2, 3). This is repeated as many times as necessary in regular rhythm:

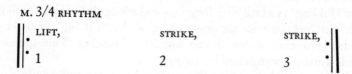

M. 3/4 RHYTHM

LIFT,	STRIKE,	STRIKE,
1	2	3

B. R. II. Strike bamboos once as above (ct. 1), open bamboos a foot apart and strike them three times against the boards (cts. 2, 3) with R, L, R hands of bamboo player number 1 and with L, R, L hands of number 2. The whole measure is played like this:

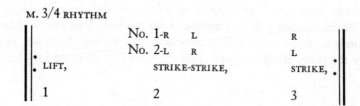

M. 3/4 RHYTHM

No. 1-R L   R
No. 2-L R   L

LIFT,	STRIKE-STRIKE,	STRIKE,
1	2	3

Tinikling Steps:

Tinikling Step Right—Hop on L foot outside (at the left side) the bamboos (ct. 1), hop on R between the bamboo poles (ct. 2), then hop on the L foot on the same spot (ct. 3) and raise R. (That is, when the bamboos are struck together on count *one*, the hop is done outside and when they are far apart the two hops are done between or inside on counts *two, three*). Bend R arm upward about head level and "kumintang" the hand counterclockwise, girl's L hand holding the skirt and boy's on waist. . . . . 1 M.

Tinikling Step Left—Hop on R foot outside (at the right side) the bamboo poles (ct. 1), hop on L between the poles (ct. 2) and hop on R on the same spot (ct. 3). Reverse hand positions. . . . . . . 1 M.

INTRODUCTION

Music Introduction.

(a) Starting with the R foot, dancers take four waltz steps forward going to proper places (see diagram 1), the girl holding the skirt, the boy's hands on the waist. . . . . 4 M.

Bamboo Rhythm—silent for (1 M.).

Strike bamboo poles together once at every first beat of the second, third and fourth measures (2-4 M.). 4 M.

(b) Dancers stand at the left side of the poles on the L foot. Tap with R foot twice between the poles on counts two and three of measure 5 (c). Repeat (b) three times more (6–8 m.). .... 4 m.

B. R. I. Play four times (4 m.). .... 4 m.

I

TINIKLING STEP

Music A (B. R. I).

(a) Take seven "tinikling" steps R and L alternately. Hand positions as described above. The first hop on count one of measure one may be omitted. .... 7 m.

(b) Step R foot outside pole No. 2 (ct. 1), hop twice on the L foot between, turning right about (cts. 2, 3). Girl holds skirt, boy's hands on waist. .... 1 m.

(c) Take seven "tinikling" steps L and R alternately. Hands as above. .... 7 m.

(d) *Girl* hops on L foot outside pole No. 2 (ct. 1), hops on R twice between the poles, going backward near bamboo player No. 1 (cts. 2, 3). Hands as above in 8 m.

Boy hops on L foot outside pole No. 1 (ct. 1), turns right about by hopping twice on the R foot between the poles going near bamboo player No. 2 (cts. 2, 3). Hands as in 8 m. .... 1 m.

They finish facing each other.

II

CLOCKWISE AND COUNTERCLOCKWISE

Music A (B. R. I).

(a) Girl stands at the left side of pole No. 2 and boy at the left side of pole No. 1. (See diagram 2.) Starting with the L foot, take four steps forward outside the poles (cts. 1, 2, 3, 4); turn right about and hop on L (ct. 5) and R foot (ct. 6) between the poles. Girl holds skirt, boy's hands on waist. .... 2 m.

(b) Repeat (a) three times more, going clockwise. On the eighth measure hop on L twice between the poles (cts. 5, 6). ...... 6 m.

(c) Repeat all (a, b, c), starting with the R foot on the other side of the poles (boy at right side of pole No. 2, and girl of pole No. 1). Reverse direction. .... 7 m.

NOTE: This time the figure is started by hopping on the R (ct. 1) and L foot (ct. 2) between the poles.

(d) *Girl* takes three steps forward about two feet away from pole No. 2. .... 1 m.

Boy takes three steps forward about two feet away from pole No. 1. Finish facing each other. (See diagram 3.) .... 1 m.

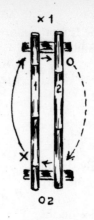

Diagram 2

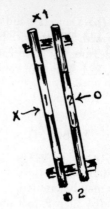

Diagram 3

III

KURADANG STEP

Music B (B. R. II).

(a) Take eight "kuradang" steps R and L alternately. Arms in fourth position, R and L high alternately. .... 16 м.

At the last measure the boy jumps over to the left side of his partner facing the same direction. (See diagram 4.)

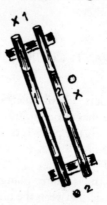

Diagram 4

IV

TINIKLING STEPS SIDEWAYS

Music B (B. R. I). Open the poles wider to accommodate the feet of the dancers.

Partners join inside hands. Free hand of the girl holding the skirt, and boy's free hand on his waist. (See illustration.)

344

(a) Hop on L foot outside the poles (ct. 1), hop on R (ct. 2) and on L between the poles (ct. 3).

(b) Hop forward on R foot outside across pole No. 1 (ct. 1), hop on L (ct. 2), and R foot between the poles (ct. 3). .... 1 M.

(c) Repeat (a) and (b) five times alternately. .... 5 M.

(d) Hop on R twice, outside pole No. 1, turning right about. Release the hold of inside hands (cts. 1, 2). Hop on L close R foot in place (ct. 3). .... 1 M.

(e) Join inside hands. Repeat (a, b, and c). .... 7 M.

(f) Hop on R foot outside pole No. 2. Release the hold of inside hands (ct. 1), pause (ct. 2). .... 1 M.

V
FEET APART

Music A (B. R. I).

(a) Girl turns right and boy left (facing each other), jump with both feet apart outside the poles (No. 1 and No. 2), join both hands and swing them sideways (ct. 1), jump twice with feet together between the poles, swing hands down in front between them (cts. 2, 3). .... 1 M.

(b) Repeat (a) twice more. .... 2 M.

(c) Jump with feet apart outside the poles (ct. 1), release hands and jump twice between the poles turning right about (cts. 2, 3). Partners are in back-to-back position. .... 1 M.

(d) Repeat (a), (b) and (c) except hand movements. Girl holding skirt, boy's hands on waist. .... 4 M.

(e) Repeat all (a, b, c, and d) except on the sixteenth measure, the girl does not turn. The boy turns right about facing the audience. .... 8 M.

VI
CROSS–STEP

Music A (B. R. I).

(a) Hop on L foot across pole No. 2 and raise R foot in rear (ct. 1), hop on R twice between the poles (cts. 2, 3). Girl's right hand on waist and L holding skirt, boy's hands on waist. .... 1 M.

(b) Hop on L outside pole No. 1 and raise R foot in front (ct. 1), hop on R twice between the poles (cts. 2, 3). Hands as above. .... 1 M.

(c) Repeat (a) and (b) three times more. On the last two counts of the eighth measure hop on R foot twice turning right about. .... 6 M.

345

(d) Repeat seven times (a) and (b) alternately. . . . . 7 M.

(e) *Girl* hops on L outside pole No. 2 (ct. 1), hops on R twice between poles moving backward near bamboo player No. 1 (cts. 2, 3).

Boy hops on L outside pole No. 1 (ct. 1), hops on R foot between poles moving forward near bamboo player No. 2 (ct. 2), hop on R again and face right about (ct. 3). . . . . 1 M.

VII
DIAGONAL

Music B (B. R. I).

(a) Hop on L foot outside the poles (girl outside pole No. 2, boy pole No. 1) (ct. 1), hop on R diagonally forward to the center of the poles (ct. 2). (See diagram 5.) Hop on L on the same spot (ct. 3). Join R hands on counts 2, 3. . . . . 1 M.

Diagram 5   Diagram 6

(b) Hop on R foot diagonally backward across the other pole (girl across pole No. 1, boy No. 2). (See diagram 6.) Release the hold of R hands (ct. 1), hop on L (ct. 2) and R (ct. 3) between the poles as above. Join R hands on counts 2, 3. . . . . 1 M.

(c) Repeat five times (a) and (b) alternately. . . . . 5 M.

(d) Leap to exchange places. . . . . 1 M.

(e) Repeat (a), (b) and (c). . . . . 7 M.

(f) Boy leaps to the left side of pole No. 1 and girl at the right side of pole No. 2 near bamboo player No. 2. (See diagram 7.) 1 M.

· 346

TINIKLING, FIGURE VII STEP SIDEWAYS

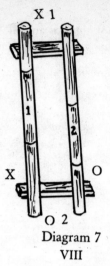

X 1

1

2

X   O

O 2

Diagram 7

VIII

WALTZ STEPS

Music B (B. R. II)—8 M.

(a) Starting with the R foot, take four waltz steps forward. Arms in lateral position moving sideward R and L alternately or inside hands joined. .... 4 M.

(b) Repeat (a) moving backward. .... 4 M.

(B. R. I)—8 M.

Girl dances in front of her partner.

(c) Hop on the outside foot once outside the poles (girl outside pole No. 2, boy pole No. 1) (ct. 1), hop on the inside foot twice between the poles (cts. 2, 3). Girl holds her skirt, boy's hands on waist. .... 1 M.

(d) Repeat (c) five times more moving forward little by little. 5 M.

(e) Boy jumps over to the left side of the girl and they join R hands. Girl makes a three-step turn left in place passing under the arch of arms (1 M.), and both bow to the audience (1 M.). ..... 2 M.

"TINIKLING"

Music A.

    1. An ini nga sayaw an ngaran "tinikling,"
       An binubuhat la an barobakingking;
       Kingking man han to-o, kingking man han wala;
       Lukso hin duruyog malaksi an kiwá.

Music B.

    2. An duhá nga kahoy guin i-iro intok
       Nga sinasabayan hin *bandok;*

348

Dida ha pag intok tigawas an ti-il
Kundi magduruyog nga waray sumikil.

Music A.

3. An ini nga sayaw guin titika dagmit
   Basi gud ma *tigui* an pagka ma-abtik
   An ti-il nga to-o sugad man an wala,
   Kong lagá matinko ilubon itawá.

Music B.

4. Na dugang an laksi kon ibinabalihas
   Dugang an pag pitig han lawas
   Baman kon dangaton san manga kakapoy
   Di ma babasulon bisan pa umukoy.

TINIKLING

1. This dance is called "tinikling,"
   All that is done is hop and hop.
   The right hops, the left hops.
   Jump together, the movement is fast.

2. The two pieces of wood are knocked together,
   Accompanied by hitting the ground with the feet.
   When the two pieces of wood are knocked together, the feet should
     be out
   But all must move together so that no one will be out of time.

3. The dance becomes faster
   So that one's lightness can be tested,
   The right leg, likewise the left
   If hit, should be endured and borne with laughter.

4. The speed increases when the change comes
   Together with the speed of the body
   Because when one is overcome by fatigue
   He will not be blamed for stopping.

Translated freely and literally by Mr. Prudencio Lim.

Tinikling

B III-IV-VII-VIII

DEFINITIONS OF DANCING TERMS

ARMS IN LATERAL POSITION—Both arms are at one side, either sideward right or left.

ARMS IN REVERSE "T"—Arms are side horizontal, elbows bent at right angles, forearms parallel to head, palms forward or facing inward.

BRUSH—With weight of the body on one foot, hit the floor with the ball of the foot after which the foot is lifted from the floor to any direction.

CLOCKWISE—Like the direction of the hands of a clock as they move.

COUNTERCLOCKWISE—The reverse direction of clockwise.

CROSSED ARMS—When partners are facing each other, the left hand of girl is joined to the left of boy and right hand to the right of partner as in ordinary hand shake position.

CROSS-OVER—When couples cross over, each pair proceeds in a straight line to the opposite place. The girls pass between the boys. Boys bow to each other when they meet in the middle or about one-third of the way, then proceed to the opposite place. Upon reaching the opposite place, partners turn about, girls stand at partners' right side. The vis-a-vis or the opposites do this movement.

CUT—To displace quickly one foot with the other, thus completely taking off the weight of the body from the displaced foot.

DOS-A-DOS (or DO-SI-DO) (back to back)—The vis-a-vis (opposites) both advance forward, pass each other's right side, step across to the right, move backwards without turning around and pass each other's left side to proper places.

FREE FOOT—The foot not bearing the weight of the body.

FREE HAND—The hand not placed anywhere or not doing anything.

GRAND CHAIN or GRAND RIGHT AND LEFT—Partners join inside or right hands facing each other. Boys all move counterclockwise and girls clockwise. Each boy in starting passes his partner on her right and drops her hand, joins left hand with the left of the next girl, who advances to meet him, and passes her on her left and drops hands, joins right hand with the next advancing girl, and so on. The girls do the same giving right and left hands to each succeeding boy. When partners meet for the first time they continue until they meet for the second time in their proper places. Then all turn about and reverse directions.

HOP—A spring from one foot to the same foot in place or in any direction. The other foot may be raised in any position (in front, in rear, sideward, or across).

INSIDE FOOT—The foot nearest one's partner, when partners stand side by side.

352

INSIDE HAND—The hand nearest one's partner, when partners stand side by side.

JUMP—A spring from one foot or both feet landing in any position of both feet (close, crossed, or open).

"KUMINTANG"—Moving the hand from the wrist either in a clockwise or counterclockwise direction.

LEAP—A spring from one foot landing on the other foot in any direction (forward, sideward, backward, or oblique).

OUTSIDE FOOT—The foot away from one's partner, when partners stand side by side.

OUTSIDE HAND—The hand away from one's partner, when partners stand side by side.

PLACE—To put the foot in a certain or desired position without putting weight on it. The sole of the foot rests flat on the floor.

POINT—Touch lightly with the toes of one foot, weight of the body on the other.

"SALUDO" or SALUTE—Partner to each other, to the audience, opposite dancers, or to the neighbor.

"SAROK"—Cross the right (or left) foot in front of the left (or right), bend the body slightly forward and cross the hands down in front with the right (or left) hand over the left (or right).

FOUR STAGES OF "SAROK"

SET—A dance formation like a quadrille or a unit composed of two or more pairs.

SLIDE—To glide the foot smoothly along the floor.

STAMP—Bring down the foot forcibly and noisily on the floor (like doing heavy steps).

STAR WITH RIGHT HAND—Four or more people advance to the center and join right hands and circle around clockwise using walking or change steps.

STAR WITH LEFT HAND—Same as "Star with Right Hand" only join left hands and turn counterclockwise.

STEP—To advance or recede by raising and moving one foot to another resting place. There is a complete transfer of weight from one foot to the other.

TAP—To rap slightly with the ball or tip of the toe, placing weight of the body on the other foot. There is no change or transfer of weight here.

FUNDAMENTAL DANCE STEPS

The dance steps listed below are the fundamental or basic steps most commonly used in Philippine folk dances. In some cases the names of the steps are the same as those found in foreign dances, but the manner of execution is entirely different. Some dance steps have no English equivalent names, so the native names are retained, such as "Kuradang," "Bacui," "Espunti," "Engaño," "Papuri," etc.

The steps are described as they are executed by our people.

"BACUI" STEP—Music: 3/4 time. Counts 1, 2, 3.

This step is found mostly in the Visayan dances. To right (4 measures).

("Sarok") Point R foot across the L in front, bend body forward and cross hands down in front with the right hand over the left hand (cts. 1, 2), step R foot in second position, raise trunk up and raise R arm to fifth position amplified, left hand on waist (ct. 3). Step the L foot across the R in rear, close the R arm to fifth position (cts. 1, 2), step R in second position and open R arm to fifth position amplified (ct. 3). Step L foot sideward right across the R in front, close R arm to fifth position (cts. 1, 2), step R in second position and open R arm to fifth position amplified (ct. 3). Step L close to R foot in first position, close R arm to fifth position (cts. 1, 2, 3). The left hand remains on waist for three measures.

To Left. (4 measures.)

Repeat the same movements, starting with the L foot, going sideward left. Reverse the position of the arms.

NOTE: This step may be done also this way: After the "sarok" and step sideward (cts. 1, 2, 3), the L foot may step across the R right *in front* instead of *in rear* on counts 1, 2. The rest of the movements are the same.

BLEKING STEP. Music: 2/4 time. Counts 1, 2.

(1) Place the R (or L) heel in fourth in front (ct. 1), step R (L) close to L (R) foot in first position (ct. 2), or

(2) Place the R (L) heel in fourth in front (ct. 1), with a jump, reverse the position of the feet (ct. 2), that is, placing the L (R) heel in front and the R (L) in position taking the weight of the body.

Music: 3/4 time. Counts 1, 2, 3.

(3) Place R (L) heel in fourth in front (cts. 1, 2), step R (L) close to L (R) foot in first position (ct. 3).

CHANGE STEP, TWO–STEP OR CATCH STEP.

Music: 2/4 time. Counts, 1, 2, or 1, *and* 2.

Step R (L) foot forward (fourth in front) (ct. 1), step L (R) close to R (L) foot in third in rear or in first position (ct. *and*), step R (L) foot quickly in fourth in front (ct. 2). This may be executed in any direction.

355

CLOSE OR FOLLOW STEP. Music: 2/4 time. Counts 1, 2.

(1) Step R (L) foot in fourth in front (ct. 1), close L (R) to R (L) foot in third in rear or in first position (ct. 2). This may be executed in any direction.

Music: 3/4 time. Counts 1, 2, 3.

(2) Step R (L) foot in fourth in front (cts. 1, 2), close L (R) to R (L) foot in third in rear or in first position (ct. 3). This may be executed in any direction.

(3) Step R (L) foot in fourth in front (ct. 1), close L (R) to R (L) foot in third or first position (cts. 2, 3). This may be executed to any direction.

NOTE: When this step is executed sideward, the same foot is leading always.

CROSS–STEP. Music: 3/4 time. Counts 1, 2, 3.

Step R (L) foot in second position (ct. 1), step or slide L (R) foot sideward right (left) across the R (L) in front (cts. 2, 3). Put the weight on the L (R) foot after the slide on the third count.

CROSS–WALTZ. Music: 3/4 time. Counts 1, 2, 3.

Step R (L) foot across the L (R) in front (ct. 1), step the L (R) in third position in rear of R (L) foot (ct. 2), step R (L) foot in fourth in front (ct. 3). Step on the ball of the rear foot on the second count.

CUT STEP. Music: 2/4 time. Counts 1, 2.

Raise R (L) foot in fourth in front in preparation. Cut the L (R) backward with the R (L) foot, thus displacing it at the same time taking the weight of the body (ct. 1). This may be done forward and backward, diagonally forward and backward, and sideward right and left. Take one cut for every count.

"ENGAÑO." Music: 3/4 time. Counts 1, 2, 3.

This step is found mostly in the Bicolano dances. It is similar to the sway-balance step.

(1) *"ENGAÑO" WITH A CLOSE.* (2 measures.)

To Right: Step R foot in second position (cts. 1, 2), step L across the R foot in front (ct. 3). Step R (L) foot in second position (ct. 1), close L to R foot in first position (cts. 2, 3). Do not put weight on the L when closing on counts 2, 3. Arms in third position, right arm high.

To Left: Start with the L foot, reverse the arm positions.

(2) *"ENGAÑO" WITH A WALTZ.*

To Right: Step R foot in second position (cts. 1, 2), step L across the R (L), foot in front (ct. 3). Step R foot in second position (ct. 1), step L close to R foot (ct. 2), step R in place (ct. 3) (waltz step in place). Arms in third position, right arm high.

To Left: Start with the L foot, reverse the arm positions.

NOTE: This is another way of holding the arms: Raise right (left) arm high in fifth position amplified and the left (right) bent in front at shoulder-level.

"ESPUNTI" STEP. Music: 3/4 time. Counts 1, 2, 3.

This step is found mostly in the Visayan dances.

(1) *To Left:* Starting position—feet in first position. Turn the left heel to sideward left without lifting the toes (pivoting or pushing on the ball of the L foot) and point R foot sideward right (ct. 1), lift the toe of the L foot and turn it to sideward left (pivoting or pushing on the heel of the L foot) at the

same time bringing the R foot to pointing position in fourth in front (cts. 2, 3). Repeat as many times as desired.

(2) *To Right:* Repeat (1) starting with the other foot moving to sideward right. Pivot on the R foot and point with the L foot.

NOTE: This may be done either moving right or left.

This step may be done also in the following manner: The first movement, that is, the pointing of the R foot sideward is done in two counts instead of one (cts. 1, 2), and the pointing in front in one count instead of two as described above (ct. 3).

GALOP STEP. Music: 2/4 time. Counts 1, 2.

Step R (L) foot in front and close immediately the L (R) foot with the R (L), thus displacing it and at the same time taking the weight of the body. It takes two galops in one measure. This is executed with one foot always leading and may be done in any direction.

GLIDE OR SLIDE STEP. Music: 2/4 time. Counts 1, 2.

(1) Glide or slide R (L) foot in second position (ct. 1), step or glide L (R) close to R (L) foot in first position (ct. 2). This may be executed in any direction.

Music: 3/4 time. Counts 1, 2, 3.

(2) Glide or slide R (L) foot in fourth in front (cts. 1, 2), step or glide L (R) close to R (L) foot in first or in third position in rear (ct. 3). This may be executed in any direction.

HOP–STEP. Music: 2/4 time. Counts 1, 2.

(1) This is done in the manner as the step-hop in the reverse order, that is, the hop is done on the first count and step on the second.

Music: 3/4 time. Counts 1, 2, 3.

(2) Hop on count 1, step on counts 2, 3.

"KURADANG" STEP. Music: 3/4 time. Counts 1, 2, 3 (2 м.).

Change step obliquely forward R (L) (cts. 1, 2), step L (R) across the R (L) in front (ct. 3); change step obliquely backward R (L) (cts. 1, 2), point L (R) in front (ct. 3).

MAZURKA STEP. Music: 3/4 mazurka time. Counts, 1, 2, 3.

Glide R (L) foot in second (ct. 1), cut R (L) sideward with the L (R) foot (ct. 2), hop on the L (R) foot and beat in rear or in front the R (L) foot close to the ankle of the L (R) foot (ct. 3). This step may be executed forward or going around also.

NOTE: It is most important that the cut be finished with an absolutely straight knee in order that the final action may bring out the bended knee position.

MINCING STEP. Music: 2/4 or 3/4 time. Counts 1, 2 in 2/4 time, and 1, 2, 3 in 3/4 time.

Starting Position: R (L) foot in fifth position in front, heels slightly raised. Execute tiny steps sideward right or left as many times as necessary. In 3/4 time take one step for every count, and in 2/4 time it may be two steps for every count.

In non-Christian dances the mincing step is usually done with both feet flat on the floor or the rear foot with slightly raised heel.

"PAPURI" STEP. Music: 3/4 time. Counts 1, 2, 3.

To Right: (4 measures).

(1) Step R foot in second position (cts. 1, 2), step the L sideward right across the R in front (ct. 3). Point R foot sideward left across the L in front (cts. 1, 2, 3) (2 м.).

(2) Repeat (1) once more putting the weight of the body on the R foot on the last three counts (2 м.).

To Left: (4 measures).

Repeat (1) and (2) starting with the L foot.

"PASO ESPAÑOL." Music: 3/4 time. Counts 1, 2, 3 (4 measures).

Take one waltz-balance forward right (left) (cts. 1, 2, 3).

Take one waltz-balance backward left (right) (cts. 1, 2, 3).

Step-brush-swing-hop forward with the R (L) foot (cts. 1, 2, 3), and with the L (R) (cts. 1, 2, 3).

POLKA STEP SERIES

(1) *PLAIN POLKA.* Music: 2/4 time. Counts 1, *and*, 2, *and* (1 measure). Step L (R) foot in fourth in front (ct. 1), step R (L) close to L (R) foot in third in rear (ct. *and*), step L (R) in fourth in front (ct. 2), pause (ct. *and*). Bend the body to the same direction of the step. This may be executed in any direction.

(2) *HOP POLKA.* Music: 2/4 time. Counts 1, *and*, 2, *and*.

It is a plain polka preceded by a hop before the first count of the music. The hop may be designated in the music by either a dotted or a grace note. Execute the step in the same manner as the plain polka.

Hop on L (R) foot, and step or slide R (L) forward (ct. 1), close L (R) in third in rear (ct. *and*), and step R (L) foot forward (ct. 2) and pause (ct. *and*). This may be executed in any direction.

(3) *GLIDE OR SLIDE POLKA.* Music: 2/4 time. Counts 1, *and*, 2, *and*, 1, *and*, 2, *and* (2 measures).

Take two glides forward and a plain polka. Slide L (R) foot in fourth in front (ct. 1), close R (L) to L (R) foot in third in rear (ct. *and*), glide R (L) foot in fourth in front (ct. 2), step L (R) close to R (L) foot in third in rear (ct. *and*). Take one plain polka forward starting with the L (R) foot (cts. 1, *and*, 2, *and*). This may be executed in any direction.

(4) *HEEL AND TOE POLKA.* Music: 2/4 time. Counts 1, *and*, 2, *and*, 1, *and*, 2, *and* (2 measures).

Place the L (R) heel in fourth in front (ct. 1, *and*), touch the L (R) toe in fourth in rear (ct. 2, *and*). Take one plain polka step forward. Starting with the L (R) foot (cts. 1, *and*, 2, *and*). This may be executed forward and backward only.

SCHOTTISCHE (NATIVE CHOTIS). Music: 4/4 time. Counts 1, 2, 3, 4.

Brush or slide R (L) obliquely forward or sideward (ct. 1), raise R (L) in fifth in front or rear (ct. 2), brush or slide R (L) again as in count 1 (ct. 3), raise up as in count 2 (ct. 4). Take three steps in place turning right (left) about (cts. 1, 2, 3), pause (ct. 4).

The turn may be a complete or half turn around either to right or left.

SLIDE STEP. The same as glide step.

SKIP STEP. Music: 2/4 time. Counts 1, 2.

The movements are the same as in step-hop. The only difference is that it is done in one count only, so that there are two skip steps in a measure of 2/4 time. This is executed in any direction.

SPANISH DRAW. Music: 3/4 time. Counts 1, 2, 3.

Step R (L) foot in second or in fourth in rear (ct. 1), draw or slide the L (R) foot slowly to R (L) in third in rear raising up the heels (ct. 2), and lower heels (ct. 3).

STEP–BRUSH–SWING–HOP. Music: 3/4 time. Counts 1, 2, 3.

Step R (L) foot in fourth in front (ct. 1), brush L (R) foot against the floor and raise it across the R (L) in front (ct. 2), hop on the R (L) (ct. 3). This may be executed in any direction.

STEP–HOP. Music: 2/4 time. Counts 1, 2.

(1) Step L (R) foot in fourth in front (ct. 1), hop on the same foot and raise the R (L) foot in front or in rear (ct. 2). This may be executed in any direction.

Music: 3/4 time. Cc   3.

(2) Step L (R) foot in fourth in front   .), hop on the same foot, and raise the R (L) foot in front or in rear   This may be executed in any direction.

STEP–SWING. Music: 2/4 time. Counts 1, 2.

(1) Step R (L) foot in second position (ct. 1), raise and swing the L (R) foot in fourth in front or across the R (L) in front (ct. 2). The toes of the raised foot are pointed downward and the knee is straight or slightly bent. This is done in any direction.

Music: 3/4 time. Counts 1, 2, 3.

(2) The movements are the same as above, but take two counts for stepping and one count for raising.

STEP–SWING–HOP. Music: 3/4 time. Counts 1, 2, 3.

Step R (L) foot in fourth in front (ct. 1), raise the L (R) knee in front (ct. 2), hop on R (L) foot swinging the L foot outward at the same time (ct. 3). This may be executed in any direction.

SWAY–BALANCE SERIES:

This is a peculiar, characteristic dance step of Filipino dances. The music is in 3/4 time. Counts 1, 2, *and,* 3 or 1, 2, 3.

A. (1) *SWAY BALANCE WITH A POINT* (2 м.).

To Right:

(a) Step R foot obliquely forward right (cts. 1, 2), step L across the R foot in front (ct. *and*), step R obliquely backward (ct. 3).

(b) Point L foot in fourth position in front (cts. 1, 2, 3). Hold arms in fourth position, R arm high. Execute a "Kumintang" with the right and left hands while pointing with the L foot on counts 1, 2, 3.

To Left:

Start with the L foot and reverse the arm positions.

(2) *SWAY BALANCE WITH A BRUSH* (2 м.).

To Right:

(a) Repeat the same movements as in (a) above (cts. 1, 2, *and,* 3).

(b) Brush L foot forward on the floor (ct. 1), let the L foot remain raised for counts 2, 3 (cts. 2, 3). Arms as above.

To Left:

Start with the L foot, reverse the arm positions.

(3) *SWAY BALANCE WITH A HOP* (2 м.).

To Right:

(a) Repeat the same movements as in (a) above (cts. 1, 2, *and,* 3).

(b) Raise the L foot across the R in front (cts. 1, 2), hop on the R foot (ct. 3). Arms as above.

To Left:

Start with the L foot, reverse the arm positions.

(4) *SWAY BALANCE WITH A RAISE* (2 м.).

To Right:

(a) Repeat the same movements as in (a) above (cts. 1, 2, *and,* 3).

(b) Raise the L knee in front with toes pointed downward. The body is slightly bent forward (ct. 1), and raised gradually upward to erect position (cts. 2, 3). The left arm is bent forward and is made to follow the movement of the body. The R arm is bent forward in level with the shoulder.

To Left:

Start with the L foot, reverse the arm positions.

Note: The Ilocano way has the body straight and the "kumintang" is done quicker on the last count only.

DOUBLE SWAY–BALANCE STEPS (4 м.).

To Right:

(a) Repeat the same movements as in sway balance with a point (a and b). Arms as above (2 м.).

(b) Step L sideward across the R foot in front (cts. 1, 2), step R sideward in second position (ct. 3) (1 м.).

(c) Point L foot in fourth in front (cts. 1, 2, 3) (1 м.). Girls holding their skirts, boys' hands at waist for the last two measures (b and c).

To Left:

Start with the L foot, reverse the arm positions.

The sway-balance series may also be done in the following manner. This was found fitted to some Filipino folk music and easier for small children and beginners to perform.

B. (1) *SWAY BALANCE WITH A POINT* (2 м.).

To Right:

(a) Step R foot obliquely forward right (cts. 1, 2), step L across the R foot in front (ct. 3).

(b) Step R obliquely backward (ct. 1), point L in fourth in front (cts. 2, 3). Execute a "kumintang" with the right and left hands while pointing with the L foot on counts 1, 2, 3 of the second measure.

To Left:

Start with the L foot and reverse the arm positions.

(2) *SWAY BALANCE WITH A BRUSH* (2 м.).

To Right:

(a) Repeat the same movements as in B (a) above (cts. 1, 2, 3).

(b) Step R obliquely backward (ct. 1), brush L foot forward (cts. 2, 3). Arms as above.

(3) *SWAY BALANCE WITH A HOP* (2 м.).

To Right:

(a) Repeat the same movements as in B (a) above (cts. 1, 2, 3).

(b) Step R obliquely backward (ct. 1), raise the L foot across the R in front (ct. 2), hop on the R foot (ct. 3). Arms as above.

(4) *SWAY BALANCE WITH A RAISE* (2 м.).

To Right:

(a) Repeat the same movements as in B (a) above (cts. 1, 2, 3).

(b) Step R obliquely backward (ct. 1), raise the L knee in front with toes pointed downward (cts. 2, 3). The body and arm movements are the same as above.

(5) *DOUBLE SWAY–BALANCE STEPS* (4 м.).

To Right:

(a) Repeat the same movements as in B (a) and (b) above (cts. 1, 2, 3, 1, 2, 3).

(b) Repeat the same movements as in A (b) and (c).

To Left:

Start with the L foot, reverse the arm positions.

TOUCH STEP. Music: 2/4 time. Counts 1, 2.

(1) Point R (L) foot in fourth in front (ct. 1), step R (L) close to L (R) in first position (ct. 2). This may be done in all positions.

(2) This may be taken in this manner also. Point R (L) foot in fourth in front (ct. 1), with a jump reverse the position of the feet, that is, pointing the L (R) in front and the R (L) in position taking the weight of the body. This is taking one count for every change of position of the feet.

Music: 3/4 time. Counts 1, 2, 3.

(3) Point R (L) foot in fourth in front (ct. 1), step R (L) close to L (R) in first position (cts. 2, 3).

(4) This may be done also by giving two counts in pointing and one count for closing the feet together.

TURNS

(1) *BRUSH–STEP–TURN.* Music: 3/4 time. Counts 1, 2, 3.

To Right:

(a) Step R foot in second position making a quarter turn at the same time (ct. 1), brush L forward (ct. 2), step L close to the R foot in first position (ct. 3) (1 м.).

(b) Repeat (a) three times more making a quarter turn every measure (3 м.). The turn is complete after the fourth step.

To Left:

Repeat all, starting with the L foot and turning around in place to the left.

(2) *CHANGE–STEP–TURN.* Music: 2/4 time. Counts 1, *and,* 2 or 1, 2.

(a) If a moderate turn is desired, execute two change steps (R, L or L, R) around in place, clockwise (to R) or counterclockwise (to L) (2 м.).

(b) If a fast turn is desired, execute only one change step to make a complete turn either to left or right (1 м.).

361

(c) If a slow turn is desired, execute four change steps around in place, either to right or left (4 м.).

(3) *CROSS–STEP–TURN OR PIROUETTE.* Music: 3/4 time. Counts 1, 2, 3.

Step R (L) foot in second position (ct. 1), cross the L (R) in front of the R (L), rise on toes of both feet and make a complete turn on the balls of the feet (ct. 2), lower heels and finish the turn with the R (L) foot in fifth position in front. Pause (cts. 1, 2, 3).

(4) *CROSS–TURN.* Music: 3/4 time. Counts 1, 2, 3.

Cross L (R) foot in front of R (L) (ct. 1), turn (or pivot) right (left) on the balls of the feet (ct. 2), lower heels down (ct. 3). Pause (cts. 1, 2, 3). Bend the knees slightly and swing the left (right) arm from second position and bend the body slightly to the left on count 1, swing the arm across the body in front to help proper balancing when turning on count 2, finish the turn with the body straight and feet together on count 3. The other hand may be on waist or holding the skirt or "barong tagalog."

(5) *PIVOT–TURN.* Music: 2/4 time. Counts 1, *and*, 2, *and*.

To Right: (2 м.).

(a) Step R foot in fourth in front (or a little close to fifth position) and bend the knee slightly (ct. 1), execute a quarter-turn right with a push on the ball of the L foot (heel of the L foot is raised), and raise the R foot slightly from the floor (ct. *and*). Repeat all once more (ct. 2, *and*).

(b) Repeat all (a) (cts. 1, *and*, 2, *and*). Finish at the starting position.

To Left: (2 м.).

Repeat (a) and (b) with the L foot in front making four quarter-turns to left always on the ball of the R foot.

(6) *PIVOT–TURN WITH A POINT.* Music: 3/4 time. Counts 1, 2, 3.

To right or clockwise: (4 м.).

Weight of the body on the L foot. Point R foot obliquely forward (cts. 1, 2), point R close to L foot in first position (ct. 3). Pivot on the L foot (heel) making a quarter turn right and at the same time pointing R foot obliquely right forward (cts. 1, 2), point R close to L foot in first position (ct. 3). Repeat twice more until a full turn is made. Finish facing to the front.

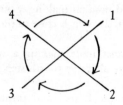

To left or counterclockwise: (4 м.).

Repeat the same movements pointing with the L foot and pivoting with the R.

NOTE: This step can be done in this manner—take one count for pointing in front and two counts for pointing close to the other foot.

The turn can be done also in eight points for eight measures. See the diagram.

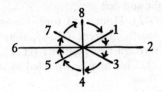

(7) *PIVOT–TURN WITH "SAROK" AND POINT.* Music: 3/4 time. Counts 1, 2, 3.

"Sarok" with R (L) foot across L (R) in front (cts. 1, 2), point R (L) foot close to L (R) in first position (ct. 3). Proceed as in pivot turn above (3 м.). This may be done also in eight measures.

(8) *SLIDE–TURN OR "PIANG–PIANG."* Music: 3/4 time. Counts 1, 2, 3.

To Right: (4 м.).

(a) Step R foot in second position making a quarter turn at the same time (ct. 1), slide the L foot forward (ct. 2), and slide it continuously close to the R in first position putting weight of the body on it at the end of the slide (ct. 3) (1 м.).

(b) Repeat (a) three times more, making a quarter turn every measure (3 м.). Use the ball or the toes only of the sliding foot.

To Left: (4 м.).

Repeat the same as above, starting with the L foot and turning around in place to the left.

(9) *THREE–STEP TURN.* Music: 3/4 time. Counts 1, 2, 3.

Step L (R) foot to second position (ct. 1), turn left (right) about and step R (L) to second (ct. 2), step backward across to the right with the L (R) foot, and complete turn to face front (ct. 3).

In teaching this to beginners have a point in fourth or in intermediate in front after executing the last turn (cts. 1, 2, 3). Do it with R and L foot pointing in front alternately.

(10) *THREE–STEP TURN IN PLACE.* Do all the above steps with the feet as close together as possible (in first position) (cts. 1, 2, 3). Finish with a bow and the feet are together (cts. 1, 2, 3).

(11) *WALTZ–TURN.* Music: 3/4 time. Counts 1, 2, 3.

(1) If a moderate turn is desired, take two waltz steps turning around either right or left in place.

(2) If a slow turn is desired, take four waltz steps to make a complete turn. Start with the R foot when turning right or clockwise and with the L foot in the reverse direction.

(3) If a fast turn is desired, take one waltz step to right or left to make a complete turn.

WALTZ–BALANCE. Music: 3/4 time. Counts 1, 2, 3.

Step R (L) in fourth or in intermediate in front (ct. 1), close L (R) foot to R (L) in first or third position in rear and raise heels (ct. 2), lower heels with the weight of the body on the R (L) foot. The knees are slightly bent before raising the heels. The body gently swayed in the opposite direction of the step. This may be executed forward, backward, obliquely forward and backward, sideward right and left.

WALTZ (BALLROOM). Music: 3/4 time. Counts 1, 2, 3.

Step L (R) foot in fourth in front (ct. 1), slide R (L) foot diagonally forward right (passing through first position) (ct. 2), step L (R) in third in rear of R (L) foot (ct. 3). This may be executed in all directions. The execution must be smoothly done.

WALTZ (NATIVE). Music: 3/4 time. Counts 1, 2, 3.

Step L (R) foot in fourth in front (ct. 1), step R (L) close to L (R) in first in third position in rear (ct. 2), step L (R) in fourth in front (ct. 3).

This may be executed in all directions. This is done like a change step in 3/4 time.

FUNDAMENTAL POSITIONS OF THE
FEET AND ARMS

Play the music (4/4) slowly. Count *one, two, three, four* to a measure in this particular exercise.

I. FEET

From first position point R (L) foot in second position......	ct. 1
Lower the heel down...	ct. 2
Point R (L) foot in fourth position in front.................	ct. 3
Bring R (L) foot close to L (R) foot in third position in front.	ct. 4
Point R (L) foot in fourth in front........................	ct. 5
Lower the heel down...	ct. 6
Slide R (L) foot to fifth position in front.................	ct. 7
Position (first position)...................................	ct. 8

To go to position slide the R (L) toe to fourth in front, to second and draw to first position, making a complete foot circle outward. The heel of the sliding foot sinks in coming to first position.

II. ARMS

From first position open the arms to second position.........	cts. 1, 2
Raise L (R) arm high to fifth position (to be in third position).	cts. 3, 4
Bend R (L) arm in front at waist level (to be in fourth position).	cts. 5, 6
Raise R (L) arm to fifth position.	ct. 7
Lower arms sideward-downward to position.	ct. 8

III. ARMS AND FEET TOGETHER

1. From first position point R (L) foot in second position (ct. 1), lower the heel down (ct. 2). From first position slowly open the arms to second position on counts 1, 2.............. cts. 1, 2

2. Point the R (L) foot in fourth in front (ct. 3). Bring the R (L) foot close to the L (R) foot in third position in front (ct. 4). Raise the L (R) arm high in fifth position (the other remains in second position) on counts 3, 4.................... cts. 3, 4

365

3. Point the R (L) foot in fourth in front (ct. 5), lower the R (L) heel down (ct. 6). Bend the R (L) arm in front at waist · level to be in fourth position on counts 5, 6.................... cts. 5, 6

4. Slide R (L) foot to fifth position in front (ct. 7) and bring it to first position as above (ct. 8). Raise R (L) arm to fifth position on count 7, then lower the arms sideward—downward to position on count 8.. cts. 7, 8

NOTE: If faster movement is desired, count one, two to a measure.

ALPHABETIC INDEX OF DANCES

CLASSIFIED INDEX

(a) *Outdoor Demonstration*

(NOTE: For outdoor performance use as many participants as possible.)

(b) *Stage or Indoor Programs*

(c) *Special Occasions*

(d) *Primary Grades*

(e) *Intermediate Grades*

(All in the above list and the following:)

(f) *High School and College*

(All of the above listed for the intermediate and the following:)

(g) *Old Ballroom Dances*

(h) *Song—Dances*

(i) *Regional Classification*

Bikol Dances (Southeastern Luzon)

Ilocano Dances (Northwestern and Central Luzon)

Tagalog Dances (Central Luzon)

Visayan Dances (Central Islands)

Non-Christian Dances (Mindanao and Sulu)

National Dances

50